CHRIS THERIEN

ROAD TO REDEMPTION

Chris Therien
with Wayne Fish

TRIUMPH
BOOKS

Library of Congress Cataloging-in-Publication Data available upon request.

This book is available in quantity at special discounts for your group or organization. For further information, contact:

Triumph Books LLC
814 North Franklin Street
Chicago, Illinois 60610
(312) 337-0747
www.triumphbooks.com

Printed in U.S.A.
ISBN: 978-1-62937-983-8
Design by Patricia Frey

Contents

Foreword

WHEN YOU'RE PUTTING on a hockey uniform alongside a guy several lockers away, day after day, year after year, you don't need to be a detective to recognize when something isn't right.

That player a few lockers down had the name "Therien" and the number "6" stitched on the back of his jersey. For a decade, he was one of the most likable, fun-loving, and talented competitors on the Philadelphia Flyers. His nickname is "Bundy" because he loved the father figure, Al Bundy, on the television show *Married with Children*, and that plays into his personality of not taking himself too seriously.

But as his playing days wound down and he transitioned into a career behind the microphone—first on radio, later television—one could sense there was something troubling going on away from the bright lights.

That is why I approached him one night a little more than 10 years ago on a train ride home from a game at the New York Rangers. In so many words, I warned him about the use of alcohol as to how it pertained to his job. Left unsaid but probably understood was the need for a lifestyle change.

It takes courage for one to look in the mirror and admit something has to be done, not only for his own sake but for the love and welfare of his family, friends, and the countless fans who look up to that person as a role model. Chris did exactly that.

And it requires emotional strength, both to make the decision to stop drinking and to seek out help from a professional organization to aid with recovery and rehabilitation. It's a humble man who acknowledges his flaws and is willing to do something about them.

Finally, a person must have mental fortitude to be willing to help others with a similar problem. The only people who can really assist those with an illness like this and say they understand what those people are going through are those who have walked in their shoes.

Believe me, Chris is not alone in his own personal battle. Over the years I've been aware of many others who faced similar adversity, some handling it better than others. The amount of pressure on your typical professional hockey player is nothing short of incredible and everyone has their own way of coping.

I got to know Chris quite well over the years, both as a player on the Flyers and later, when he was in broadcasting, as an assistant coach with the team. I watched how he paired with Éric Desjardins to form a No. 1 defensive unit in Philadelphia and dominate superstars such as Jaromír Jágr in head-to-head matchups.

It's no accident No. 6 wound up as the Flyers' all-time leader for games played by a defenseman. For his entire Flyers career, he never had a minus number after his name at the end of a season.

In the locker room, he kept everyone loose with his booming laugh and witty observations. That unfiltered personality made him so popular when he went on the air to analyze games. Fans were aware they were getting the straight stuff.

That is why I believe so many people are glad to see he's not only been clean and sober these past 11 years but also that now he's involved with an organization called Pennsylvania Recovery Center, which helps recovering alcohol abusers through a holistic approach.

The 1999–2000 Flyers team truly was a band of brothers, with veterans such as Keith Jones, Rick Tocchet, Keith Primeau, Bundy, and me forming a tight group that came within a game of the Stanley Cup Final.

We didn't win the championship that year, but I know one guy from that team is going all the way now to his own personal Cup with his life's work.

His name is Chris Therien.

—Craig Berube

CHAPTER 1

The Decision

ALTHOUGH IT HAPPENED more than 10 years ago, I remember the moment like it was yesterday.

Life-changing events have a way of staying fresh in your memory and this one will never fade from mine. Much of my adult life had been spent secretly battling a silent demon: one shared by millions of people, but each struggle unique in its own way.

It took an act as simple as cleaning an upstairs closet for me to come to grips with a harsh reality.

I was an alcoholic.

While rummaging through clothes and the like, I came upon a shoe with a water bottle jammed inside it. Only the bottle wasn't half-filled with water.

It was vodka.

I stared at the bottle for a moment, then gulped down its contents and threw the bottle in the trash.

There are two birthdates in my life: The first, December 14, 1971, when I officially entered this world and the second, February 7, 2011—the day of the infamous shoe incident—when I became the person I truly believe I was meant to be.

It took me decades to come to the reality I could be comfortable in my own skin without dulling my senses through various outside means.

We all make choices in life and I'm no exception. Some of my decisions were good; others—like acquiring and accepting an addiction to alcohol—were not.

Whether you become a professional athlete like I did or just someone who lives a so-called less glamorous existence, it's all pretty much the same when it comes to personal responsibility. We don't reside on an island. We have people who depend on us, people who we want to set a good example for, both in our public and private lives.

There was a long period in my adult years when I failed at that. It hurt to know I was letting myself down by not functioning at full capacity and even more painful that I was doing the same with the people I love.

As I alluded to earlier, just about every alcoholic can tell you the date he decided to give it all up. Mine was that day in early 2011 with an act as mundane as sorting out an upstairs closet.

MY FIRST STEP ON THE ROAD to redemption might have taken place on a train ride back from New York City where the Flyers had played the Rangers in a Sunday night game.

By this point in time, I was retired as a player and sharing the Flyers' radio broadcast booth with play-by-play man Tim Saunders.

Craig Berube, a Flyers assistant coach in those days, walked up the aisle to my seat on the train.

"Hey," he said, "can I talk to you for a second?"

Berube's stern expression told me this was something pretty serious.

"Sure," I said. I knew Craig had my best interests in mind and that he's not judgmental in a business that can have a lot of whispers and rumors.

Chief, as he is called affectionately by teammates and opponents alike, looked me straight in the eye. We'd been friends for a long time and we'd done our fair share of partying together during our days as teammates. But he realized my issues ran much deeper than just some late nights on the road. It was time for some straight talk.

"One of the coaches may have smelled booze on your breath over the past couple days," he said. Quietly, I admitted I had been drinking.

"Keep an eye out," Berube said, "because people are probably watching."

That was the same night my friend, Ben, picked me up upon returning to Philadelphia. It was snowing pretty hard as we set out for my home in New Jersey.

As we approached my town, I turned to him and instructed him to stop at the start of a dirt road near my house. I told him to pull over at a certain point on the dirt road, set the trip odometer back to zero.

The area was deserted. I had left a bottle of red wine hiding in the woods. As soon as the odometer hit about a quarter mile,

I told Ben to stop the vehicle. I got out with my dress shoes and dress pants on and trudged through eight inches of snow. Ben had no idea what I was doing. I reached in and grabbed a brand-new bottle of Carlo Rossi wine.

Cheap stuff, but it was going to get me through the night.

At that point, I hadn't really taken Chief's advice seriously or that the (assistant) coach who had probably detected the offending odor on me was Hall of Famer Joey Mullen, whom I love.

I remember getting back to the house about 12:30 AM and drinking that bottle of wine. In the next couple days, I talked to Chief again. I had dried out to a certain degree; I had tried to stop in 2006 when I was a complete mess. The difference leading up to the moment of truth was that I had medication that would help me with the withdrawal. That's why the times of sobriety in between relapses apparently lasted longer.

The medication had helped prevent me from suffering through the "shakes" and all the symptoms that alcohol withdrawal brought to me before. The pills and the meds that I had used before were working. But they were essentially a crutch. I was allowing myself a reason to keep drinking. But within myself, I did recognize it was still a major problem.

I knew that even though Craig had confronted me in a professional and very teammate-like manner, I already was aware this was the end of the line. I was tired and this time I was really tired of being like this and trying to chase the day—every single day—like this...of being a good father, husband, person, and a productive member of society.

With help from friends and colleagues who had been in the same dark place, I put myself in the AA (Alcoholics Anonymous) community.

I pledged to the Flyers, "You will never, ever hear about me drinking again because I never will."

Paul Holmgren, the Flyers general manager at the time, was really supportive. I'm truly grateful for that. That was the beginning of 11 years of continued sober broadcasting in good standing. It really got my feet under me. I became the great dad, the person I always wanted to be.

I started going to AA every day. We have a nice little community of guys who lean on each other. I realized the first time I decided to stay sober was when I chose to remain with the AA people. There were 120 meetings in 90 days.

Let's go back to February 7, 2011, for a moment.

When I found the aforementioned shoe in the closet and saw the water bottle with the vodka in it, I recognized instantly what it was before I opened it. I had hidden it there as every alcoholic seems to hide his liquor for whatever reason. It was an embarrassment. I saw it, took that bottle, and swigged that last one and a half ounces of vodka.

That was my farewell; that was the end. That was the last time I ever used alcohol. I bid it goodbye. I rinsed the bottle out and threw it in the trash can. The last day Chris Therien ever touched a sip of alcohol was February 7, 2011. That began the greatest 11-year journey of my adult life. And it was certainly the most meaningful because it wasn't just about me anymore. It was about my family and specifically my kids getting a dad that was all-in. All-in on being a parent, doing all the right things I had wanted to do.

There was nothing I wanted more in this world than to be a good dad. And I was sure not going to let these kids down. Nor my wife, Diana, who has done such a great job raising them.

My second chance at life was about to begin.

CHAPTER 2

Saturday Night Fever

DID I FIND HOCKEY, or did hockey find me?

Maybe it was a little bit of both.

It's safe to say being born in Ottawa, Ontario, Canada, had something to do with it.

And having two hockey-loving parents, Beth and Emile, certainly helped put me on course for a life journey on ice.

In his youth, my dad played hockey for St. Lawrence University in upstate New York and that undoubtedly provided a role model for my early years.

Ottawa has a history of great hockey players. More than a few have gotten out of the nation's capital and made careers for themselves.

Bill Clement and Guy Lafleur, just to name a couple. Larry Robinson was another, the great defenseman for Montreal. That was a team I always followed. As a kid I was programmed to be a Montreal Canadiens fan as early as I can remember. I had

Habs memorabilia all over the place. Half the city of Ottawa were Toronto Maple Leafs fans, but the eastern part of the city was Montreal Canadiens fans.

That's just kind of how it worked out. I was a diehard Canadiens fan even as a young kid. When my parents had dinner parties, I was allowed to watch the first period of the Canadiens games on our black and white TV in my bedroom. Those games started at 8:00 PM. It was like a thrill tradition. Saturday night the whole country was watching the game—*Hockey Night in Canada*. It felt like everyone was getting tuned up to watch hockey.

Because I was young, six or seven years old, I got to watch on Saturday night for one hour, just the first period. Then I got up in the morning full of anticipation to see how my beloved Habs did.

Most of the time in the '70s they were very, very good. In those days, they won four straight Stanley Cups (1976–79). After the Flyers and Bruins had won, Montreal took over and it was a real dynasty. I was enamored with the Canadiens. They were my team. I bled rouge, blanc, et bleu. Oddly enough, I somehow also owned a Flyers shirt when I was kid. I don't recall how I got it but there's a childhood photo of me standing next to my sister, and I'm decked out in my Flyers shirt. Go figure.

As much as I loved the Habs as a kid, my feelings changed over time. I can tell you, having played against them, been in the building, and gotten to know members of the organization, I gained a different perspective on that franchise. The Montreal Canadiens pissed me off because, on one hand, they exuded arrogance and a superiority complex. On the other hand, they perpetually whined and played the victim when something didn't go their way. My hockey life began in earnest at about that age, when my dad took me to tryouts for the South Ottawa Warriors, which was a very prominent minor hockey team in Ottawa at the time.

It was then my earliest friendships and relationships began. It was also a period in my life when I realized I was about to see some of the biggest idiots in the history of mankind with the minor league parents in the late '70s and early '80s. They were completely out of touch with reality.

There were kids from that team who went on to have collegiate careers, though none of them went as far as I did. Jay Flowers played at Union College, which was NCAA Division II at the time. Russell Hammond started for Cornell. A fair share of guys did go on from those youth teams. It was these youth teams that shaped and formed my voyage in life.

I realized about that age I was not always socially compatible. I went against the grain many times. I was not a favorite or more celebrated player at that age. I will say this: Canadian kids were far nastier, meaner than any experience I had when I went on to prep school in the United States.

Canadian kids were punks and there were a lot of them. In retrospect, that period in my childhood in Canada was not that great.

This probably had something to do with my birth month. Yes, if you were born later in the year, you were already behind most of your class in terms of development. I was a December birthday. I was almost a year younger than half or three-quarters of the kids I played with. I think that maturity and physicality at a younger age played a huge factor. Quite frankly, a lot of kids born in the last three or four months of a year don't make it because of their age.

I know now the only thing that was going to beat age, or a late birthday, was size alone. If you look at guys in the NHL that were all late birthdays, most of them were big people. The ones who made it from October, November, and December were all bigger people. Guys like Keith Primeau, me…it's not written in stone but it's absolutely a factor. And it probably played into a lot of nastiness, a lot of the stuff I had to deal with. As a kid, I was always younger than everybody else in my grade and certainly in sports as well.

My best friends were Rod Foley, Chris Rheaume, and Bino Cesario. They still are. They were all a year older than me. They were the next age group up, but we all clicked. We've all been in each other's weddings. And if it weren't for those guys, I probably wouldn't have a lot to call home about.

I was a mischievous kid at times. I saw a lot as a kid, some things that still stay with me. I saw a kid kept after school for something that wasn't even important. I was kept late, too. The kid got beaten with a meter stick. He pissed his pants all over the floor. It was unbelievable to see that happen. I was sitting next to him and thinking to myself, *This is insane.*

My dad had come to pick me up at school. I was 20 minutes late coming out. He stormed up into the room to see what was going on because there had been rumors about this authority figure being a bully. And, in my eyes, she was.

The interesting thing about my dad: I was not allowed to play or partake in summer hockey. He felt that I needed a break. I played soccer a little bit when I was very young and then my second sport was baseball. I was a pretty good little player until I was about 12, 13 years old.

When I went to high school at St. Pius, baseball was still my second sport while I was playing hockey and then when I packed it in for the year, I started playing football. I was a starting offensive lineman.

My dad felt that maybe a different sport was good for me. I wasn't particularly the best student either. I was a hard worker, though. I was intelligent enough to meet the bare necessities in grade school to pass my classes. But when more focus or concentration was needed, I could do that, too.

Later, going to a prep school in the United States was my dad's idea. He looked at it from an academic standpoint. He had a real affinity for the United States education program because he attended St. Lawrence.

He was thinking of me, sort of "Let me get this kid out of here." Even though Ottawa was a hockey hotbed, I think he felt like I needed to get out of the area and get a change of scenery, which he thought would be good and important for me.

That's where his idea for prep school in the United States came in. I'm sure glad I didn't end up in Wilcox, Saskatchewan.

CHAPTER 3

Another Lake Placid Miracle

ANY AMERICAN HOCKEY FAN of a certain age remembers where he or she was the weekend of February 22–24, 1980. Most likely in front of a television set with millions of other like-minded USA citizens.

It was the "Miracle on Ice," the home country's memorable upset of the powerful Soviet Union team by a 4–3 score on Friday night and a rousing 4–2 win over Finland on Sunday for the XII Winter Olympic Games gold medal at Lake Placid.

Many sports experts consider it the No. 1 achievement of American athletics in the 20th century. Some believe it gave American hockey just the sort of boost it needed to compete with Canada and Europe. No doubt it certainly re-energized the town of Lake Placid, which had previously hosted the Games in 1932. But that first version of the Olympiad was held before the advent of television, so results were a fairly well-kept secret.

To this day, one can spot 1980 USA memorabilia in store fronts along the town's main thoroughfare. Images of captain and hero Mike Eruzione, goaltender Jim Craig, and coach Herb Brooks abound. It was into this still hockey-crazed environment that I arrived just seven years later to start my stay at Northwood Preparatory School.

I probably wasn't one hundred percent certain at that point that hockey was going to be my destiny for life, but Lake Placid and Northwood certainly had the right culture and atmosphere to foster that future decision. As it turned out, the opportunity to go to a prestigious school, regardless of the hockey side of it, was a godsend.

Northwood had everything a young student with college aspirations could hope for—small, almost individualized, classes (at times, one teacher for, say, five students), a flexible curriculum, personalized schedules—not to mention the beautiful Adirondack Mountains as a backdrop.

I really didn't know Northwood had started way back in 1905 as the Lake Placid School, founded by Yale University graduate John Hopkins, and later became Northwood Preparatory School in 1927.

But I did know of two recent graduates who turned out to be pretty good hockey players: Mike Richter (Class of 1985), a goaltender who became famous for his play at the University of Wisconsin and later as the backstop on the 1994 Stanley Cup champion New York Rangers; and Tony Granato (Class of 1983), a future star with the Rangers, Los Angeles Kings, and San Jose Sharks.

So, in May 1987, I made the decision to go Northwood. I was thinking, *Man, I'm never going to have to see these (Canada) people again!* I actually felt good about that. I thought to myself, *I'm really looking forward to this change.*

I knew I was going to miss my parents and I had a lot of good things to remember about Ottawa, too. It wasn't all bad. There were a lot of good kids, too. But it wasn't a great time for me. I certainly welcomed anything new that was going to happen to me in life. It wasn't just about hockey. I still didn't believe I was a real, good player. I'd been cut from two teams.

Did I mention I might have been a bit overweight?

I was excited about going to Northwood and didn't tell anybody. A couple friends asked, and I said, "Yeah, I'm going to another school next year." Nobody knew, nobody cared. There were a lot of high schools in Ottawa but what they didn't know was that I was headed south of the border.

Summer came, high school at St. Pius had ended, and I was so excited about what was to come. My grandparents were there on getaway day. It was a rainy Sunday morning. My mom, dad, and sister standing there for the picture—that image is still with me. I had a short haircut, appeared really raw, and kind of looked like I was three months short of my 16th birthday, which I was.

I showed up at Northwood with a bunch of other kids. It was a totally different experience for me. They had meetings every night, 7:00 PM sharp and there would be a team huddle with the whole school. Teachers would have comments, and everyone would listen.

The hockey coach, Tom Fleming, was one of the most instrumental people in my hockey career, at least in terms of working. I went down two months early and met Fleming as well as athletic director Steve Reed. Both men were extremely bright: Tom went to Dartmouth and was voted "athlete of the half century." Steve played at Colby College in Maine.

They gave us a tour and they had no idea who I was, no clue, and why would they? I had no accomplishments to hang my hat on. No accolades of any sort. They just knew there was this Canadian kid coming in. I wasn't big yet but I guess they figured if the kid was coming in from Canada, he could play hockey.

Tom and Steve introduced me to Brett Kurtz, who happened to be the best player on the team and, in Fleming's words, one of the best prep players in the country. I never understood exactly what he meant until the next year when 10 or 11 players on the team received NCAA Division I scholarships.

That is really remarkable. Northwood was, for all intents and purposes, the greatest United States powerhouse prep school that there ever was. Now, people can hang their hat on certain schools and say certain things. But when you talk about high school hockey in the United States, Northwood was at the top of the food chain for many, many years.

I actually repeated my sophomore year to get more American curriculum. Of course, we studied Canadian history, along with the metric system and the different mathematical formulas that the two countries have. In some ways, it was just an extra year to get another $9,500 out of my dad. With the exchange rate, I realized what a toll that had taken on him. It was a lot. We were not a well-to-do family; we were not rich. But he squeezed what he could to get me to Northwood. It was the best gamble he ever made in his life.

As mentioned, I was a gangly kid, my body was still growing. It was truly a fresh start. It was a lot of fun. We had Mountain Day in the fall. Classes were 7:00 AM until 12:00 PM most days. We were done at noon every single Friday and I loved that. I would go and hang out with my buddies, a lot of my hockey teammates. We played in softball leagues. I enjoyed almost every minute of it. It was a different experience.

I felt like I was reborn. I was making new friendships, meeting more mature kids, getting older, and getting out of those mean years. The only thing that wasn't presented to me was the hockey portion of it. There was uncertainty because when I went in the year before, a lot of the kids on the varsity were coming back.

The roster that year was loaded. Scott and Steve Morrow were mainstays, and both went on to compete for the University of New Hampshire. There was Kurtz, along with a talented player named Mike Doers and also Dave Tretowicz, who went on to play for Clarkson. Mike Lappin became a star for Boston University and later St. Lawrence.

You get the idea. Guys from Northwood weren't going to colleges that were just okay. They were going to colleges that were absolutely loaded for bear. Big-time schools, big-time programs.

I did not believe in myself at all at that point. That's where my dad's hopes had to come in, his vision. Maybe he had seen something in me from the ages of 8 to 12. Maybe he thought, *This kid has a future in the game.* I wasn't quite as optimistic.

Tryouts happened in October, and I did great in my testing. I think I was second in the three-mile run around Mirror Lake right next to the town of Lake Placid. I came in second in about 18 minutes. I was pretty proud of myself. Aerobic fitness is no guarantee for success in hockey, but it sure can't hurt.

When I arrived, there had been only one freshman who had ever played, a kid by the name of Kent Salfi. His father, Jim, had played with my father at St. Lawrence. Kent went on to play for Maine, where he won a national championship, which tells you how good he was.

I had to earn everything I got. I had gotten cut by teams; my father was even an assistant coach on one. What we had gone through—the shame, the embarrassment of that. You wonder who you are as a person. I was wondering who I was as a kid. So, one thing I did like at Northwood: you're like a band of brothers with those guys in there and you're not alone.

My freshman year I actually played soccer for Northwood. I wasn't too bad considering I wasn't a soccer player. We would take bus trips up and down the mountains to play community colleges.

I got my wings at Northwood. I became a man, a winner at Northwood. At the end of the day, I could identify with who I was because of this school. It set up a lot of who I was the rest of my life. The things that I had to fight through mentally, emotionally, and physically at a young age—maybe that came back to haunt me years later with my alcohol addiction. From then on, I never thought that there was ever a day in my life to rest. I felt like I owed my dad something for putting that money out.

It was very, very strange, that sentiment. But that was how I thought. My dad was putting this money out, we were not rich. I was going to make it work somehow, even if I didn't necessarily know how. But I felt like I owed my mom and dad something for what they had done for me. That was important to me. I'm an extremely loyal person when it comes to doing the right thing. If somebody does something for me, I want to return that favor. I want them to know that I care deeply for them and that I'm on their team.

Hockey tryouts came and there were probably 40 to 45 kids for both teams: varsity and JV. So, I go out and I'm thinking I'm still a young guy, but I hadn't been on the ice for a long time. I put on my skates for probably the first time in a year. I got on the ice and looked like Bambi for a few minutes. The coach probably already had an idea what his team was and I most likely would have been cut even if I happened to be Wayne Gretzky. They kind of did things by the book right there. They have to get their older kids exposed to college scouts.

After the second day of tryouts, a list was put on the board. I went straight to see what names were on the varsity list and mine wasn't. So, I started JV and I remember one of the hardest calls I had to make was to my dad, who was so eagerly awaiting the news. He knew all those big names with the varsity. For a former collegiate hockey player, he probably had more anxiety than I did.

I called him and said, "Dad, I didn't make varsity, but I did make JV." We had a demanding schedule ahead of us and he was really positive. He was like, "Okay, go work your ass off. Work hard, get better, improve." So that's exactly what I did. I had a really good start to the year, played a few games. I remember listening to U2 and their newest album, *Joshua Tree*. That was sort of the soundtrack in my head.

In the fall, there was one development that changed the team's trajectory and changed mine. We had to go to a place called the Burlington Free Academy in Burlington, Vermont. Northwood was such a powerhouse that BFA only wanted to play our JV team. They had a big star who was going to the University of Vermont, a top recruit by the name of Jim Larkin. He went on to be a teammate of John LeClair's at UVM.

All I heard was Jim Larkin this and Jim Larkin that. My dad was there to watch. He had been to a half-dozen or so games and I had been okay, pretty good. So BFA decides to match up Larkin, a right wing, against me and it was almost a foretelling of what was to come in my future play against one Jaromír Jágr. I was that good that night.

At this point, I'm still all of about 5-foot-10. The game starts, the first shift Larkin has the puck, comes down the right side. I leapt forward and hit this guy in the chest so hard, so effectively, that I knocked the wind out of him. So, when you talk about the rebirth, the coming out, this was that one moment where everyone's eyes opened and they said a collective "Holy bleep!" And then, "Who is this guy, what is he?" I had dropped a bomb on this kid and then dominated him—remember, one of the top recruits in the USA. He probably had never been over-whelmed like this in his life. He didn't get a point. We shut them out and if I were him with all those kids and playing against someone no one had ever heard of, I would have kept a low profile for a while.

I remember walking out of the building that night and I was pretty excited. I thought, *Wow, I've never done something like that.* I had never played that well, never moved the puck out of the zone that efficiently. It was like the man upstairs said, "Here you go kid, this is what it's like." As I was walking out of the building, there was a pay phone by the bus. Our coach was on it, talking to the varsity coaches. I heard him say, "You better get this kid up there now, because I've never seen a performance like that at this level before. Don't miss out on this."

I knew he was talking about me.

It was pretty cool to hear that. I got back on the bus and later, for a while, I was still playing JV. I was in one of the main lobby rooms one day and the varsity coach, Tom Fleming, walked by and said hello to me. I couldn't believe it.

Just before Christmas the varsity team was getting ready to make a trip to Boston to play two games. Two days before going, a kid from Philadelphia named Ken Cornell and I got called into the varsity coach's office. He said that he was going to be taking one of us on the excursion to Boston. I had never been to Boston. I was like, *Oh man, why did you have to tell both of us that you were only taking one.*

Two days later he calls us back in and I was thinking one of us is going to be really disappointed. Thank goodness it wasn't me. I had been called up to the varsity with all these superstar players. I got on the bus and I was so nervous. I had big-time butterflies fluttering around my stomach from two days back.

We played Harvard's and Merrimack's JV teams. That gives you an idea the level of competition Northwood was playing at the time. We played our home games on the 1980 rink, the Miracle on Ice surface, and for me, it was my own little miracle to be playing varsity as a raw sophomore.

Every time I stepped on the ice, I looked up at the rafters and thought about what happened there seven years earlier.

Meanwhile, back in Boston, I hopped onto the ice there and for pre-game warm-up learned what it felt like to be "Rudy," the famous unlikely walk-on character in the movie of the same name about the inspirational kid at Notre Dame. We took a 6–0 lead on Merrimack in the second period. There I was wearing a varsity uniform and I was beaming. It was probably the most meaningful moment in my life up to that point.

But there's more to the story. We got up 7–0 and I was still fastened to the bench. Not a single shift! Really? I figured out I had to be patient. So, in second game, against Harvard, this is where the protagonist in the movie *Rudy* beat me out. It was a tighter game than the Merrimack tilt, but we were still up comfortably. I still didn't get a shift.

I could have gotten down on myself, but I didn't. I took the positive from this and realized I should be encouraged that I was even on the team. I had not gotten a shift in two entire games, but it was the happiest I had been in my life.

You know, a lot of great things had happened to me in my college and NHL careers but probably the best moment for me was that time in Boston and then going home for Christmas.

It kept me wanting to play more hockey, to keep learning the game. I wanted to be recruited like Kurtz. I didn't know if that would happen but that's what I wanted.

This was my own little miracle at Lake Placid. It might not have created any national headlines, but it sure was front page news for me and my family.

CHAPTER 4

Last Dance with Mary Jane

AS CRUCIAL AS THINGS WERE for me on the ice my junior year at Northwood, there were also coming of age moments off it as well. My years at Northwood provided my life with structure and learning the importance of discipline in pursuing an education. But, of course, when you're living the so-called "college life" at a prep school with your parents a country away, there are going to be those experimental times in your social interactions. Perhaps the most memorable of these came at an off-campus party when a bit of peer pressure played a role in yours truly trying to keep up with the cool crowd. Details to follow as the season unfolded.

I had a very good opportunity to play on the varsity team just because of the way I finished my sophomore year. After my sophomore year at Northwood, I had decided it was crunch time and I think everybody knew that. The Christmas tournament with some varsity players was a great experience for me and signaled my time was coming.

Then I went home and worked really hard preparing to make the team. Running has always been my predominant method of training. My dad had me running since I was a young kid, about seven years old. That trend continues to this day. My history of exercise and conditioning proved invaluable and a lot of it came from my father. His hockey background was perfect to be able to share those types of stories with me. He understood how big a deal running was for conditioning.

Going into my junior year at Northwood was much the same as my sophomore year. I had a great off-ice training regimen leading up to the tryouts for Northwood in October 1988. I was excited about the possibility of things happening for me that year.

At the end of my sophomore year, I was the best player on the junior varsity. By the end of my junior year, I became the best player on the varsity team as well. Everything in between was a challenge. I had been cut from teams, I had quit hockey two years prior because of the negativity, the politics and all the other bull that comes with it.

But now there was no one else I could lay blame on. It was clearly laid at my feet. It was mine for the taking. I knew if I didn't make the team my junior year, my hockey career would be over. I didn't even know if I would have had a senior year at Northwood if I didn't perform well junior year.

In my junior year I was focused, and I grew in height. That was the one difference from the other years. I was now about 6-foot-3, 205 pounds. No one could tell where that height came from. My dad was 5'10", my mom was 5'6". There was no giant in the family. My dad's brother Mark was 6'4". But he was the exception when it came to size. No one knew or figured when I was 11 or 12 that I would grow to such a height.

So, I went out for the varsity team, and it became pretty evident to the coaches there was no way they were going to cut me. I was probably their best defenseman, but I was still very raw. At first, I was paired with Eric Gregoire, a good player from the Syracuse area. He was a very solid player and went on to play for Notre Dame on a four-year scholarship. When he looks back on it now, he says I made him look better. That was not the case. He was a good partner and helped me a lot. Good, calm demeanor. Sort of like with Éric Desjardins in my Flyers career.

He was very likable. Probably the kind of guy I would have liked around me when I was 13 years old. I'm glad I had the chance to play with him because he was a really good guy.

It was an amazing junior year. Offers were starting to come in from schools like Denver University and its coach, Ralph Backstrom. That's when I realized the kids back home playing junior were struggling and I was drawing scouts, some games 30, 40, 50 at a time in the northeast region of New York.

Craig Conroy and I became part of that Northwood "hockey factory." The start of my junior year was the start of the new version of Chris Therien that never looked back. That junior year defined who I was as a player, and it was the beginning of the confidence that carried through for the rest of my life.

It was a really important year for me. I started to come out of a shell that I had been in my whole life. That season was crucial for me—it was the year I was reborn, where I started getting stardom gifts for the rest of my life.

As upbeat as things were on the ice during that 1988–89 campaign, there were also some eye-opening events taking place off it.

One instance that absolutely changed my view of drugs took place at Northwood.

I had gone to an off-campus gathering in Lake Placid with a great friend of mine and a couple other kids who were not sports people. But I ended up going to a house occupied by some other Lake Placid students who did not go to Northwood. This is the first time I experienced marijuana.

The problem was the effects were so intense and so overwhelming for me that I had a horrible panic attack that lasted about three hours. When I got back to campus, I got back to my room and felt like the walls were moving and the ceiling was closing down on top of me.

What felt odd to me at the time was there were so many people smoking pot in and around the Lake Placid area, mostly because of the attractive outdoor atmosphere that it portrayed to many people. Some of this probably had to do with Lake Placid itself—the rock climbing and the mountain climbing, the kayaking—it's certainly a place that would be a natural home for people who enjoy THC.

The problem was, I think the stuff I smoked might have been laced with something. The reason I say this is because the same girl I went to the party with is still a great friend to this day and she corroborates what I suspected. We talked about that one night.

She also felt like she was on some sort of hallucinogenic trip. The more I think about that, it still scares me because I do know what the real effects of marijuana are. And that was not them.

That's why I tell people now, especially drug addicts: Please be careful. Know where you're getting stuff and who you're getting it from.

The best part of the incident was that it made me take a vow about my future life decisions. I looked at those walls in complete panic. The walls were dark oak wood walls and it was a gloomy, rainy day and I looked at that wall and said, "Oh God, I will never do drugs again in my life!" And I stayed true to that until I visited Denver in my mid-40s. I realized at that stage in my life that medical marijuana would probably help people with anxiety, not hinder them or make them feel like a paranoid fool like me in the late '80s.

But that night at Northwood was not a true marijuana experience and no one will tell me differently. What it did was allow me to be scared enough to never want to have that happen to me again. It goes back to me being raised in a sports household with a culture of hockey. It allowed for beer drinking with friends when you were older, but drugs in any situation were not acceptable.

I was disappointed in myself that I tried it no matter what the response was to my body. I really did feel like I let people down. And it was a dirty little secret that I kept inside for a long time.

CHAPTER 5

Coming of Age

FOR SOME NHL ENTRY DRAFT–HOPEFUL PLAYERS, the senior year is a time to possibly let off the gas pedal a bit. They've already proven what they can do and some, perhaps many, hang their hats on those accomplishments. Scouts have done their due diligence and kind of already know, barring unforeseen injuries, where a player is going to be slotted in the draft. That wasn't necessarily the case when it came to me.

Although I had put together two solid seasons at Northwood, I felt like I still had something to prove. So that's what I set out to do. Going into my senior year at Northwood I was definitely a different commodity than I ever had been in my life. I never really saw myself as the main man, and yet all of a sudden, I was. I was at a prep school that enjoyed incredible success at putting hockey players into the NHL and into college at all different levels, especially Division I. I was heading into Northwood for my last year after two successful campaigns.

It all started with the biggest event of the season, the previously mentioned All-Scholastic Tournament in Schenectady,

New York. We had lost my junior year, when we actually played a young Eric Lindros who, at that time, was just 15 years old.

He played for St. Mike's. They beat us. I do remember Eric at that point. Everybody heard a buzz about this 15-year-old kid. It was quite interesting to watch a guy with that kind of skill level at such a young age. I was a year older and didn't really get an opportunity to use that as a measuring stick against Eric at that point. He wasn't yet fully on the pedestal as he would be just a year after that. Again, that was a cool experience. That was a tournament you want to win, the one for all the bragging rights, the top major junior award.

Heading into my senior year, I was listed pretty high on the list of recruits. But I did not envision what was going to happen my senior year. When I went in, I saw a laundry list of post-graduates "on the board." There was Matt Collins, who ended up being great friends with Jeremy Roenick for many years. They played together in Boston. Also, a couple really good backliners named Ian Paskowski and Jim Pinti, who went on to play for the State University of New York at Fredonia.

We were the four top defensemen that year. You know, everybody loves to talk up the post-graduates that did not receive scholarships the year before. You would say to yourself, "Oh wow, these are the guys that are going to be really impactful players." And I was going in as essentially a true senior as a 17-year-old turning 18 in December. They were great, great hockey players and players heralded by US colleges. I wanted to still be that guy and I probably ended up being so, more so than probably anybody that had been there for quite some time.

At the pre-skate, the biggest name up front was Craig Conroy, a future standout player with several NHL teams, including the Canadiens, St. Louis Blues, and Calgary Flames. He was a guy, like me, who was trying to find his own wings. I thought he was a bit of a dorky guy, but in a real good way, a player we all liked. Smart, elusive. Here's a fun fact: Craig's dad played hockey for the Syracuse Blazers. When Craig was four years old, he served as the team's mascot.

That year Northwood had a stacked lineup and I guess I was considered the head honcho. To be honest, I still never thought of myself as "the guy." But any hesitancy in that department was about to come to a rather timely end. If anybody thought they were ahead of me on the Northwood depth chart, they weren't. For the first time in my life, I also just had a little bit of cockiness. After all those skates, I was pretty confident in who I was and how far I had come as a player.

But just when everything seemed to be going my way, I basically shot myself in the proverbial foot.

One day I was out in the lobby, with the headmaster's office directly behind. I was talking about tryouts (in probably too loud of a voice) and what I'd seen in trials with another kid who was on the varsity team. And I said, "You know, I don't think that kid is very good. I don't think he's going to make the varsity team." Well, the headmaster heard it. I didn't realize that the head coach, Tom Fleming, was in there, too. So, a few hours later I got called to the headmaster's office with Tom and the headmaster, John Friedlander, the former Green Bay Packer, a monster of a man. Both these guys were big SOBs, very intimidating guys.

There I was, thinking I was the star of the show and feeling pretty good about things. Maybe too good.

The bad timing of this gaffe was incredible. We were about to play St. Lawrence University JV the following week. As you know, St. Lawrence University was my dad's alma mater. He was a captain there.

Fleming and Friedlander brought me into the office, closed the door and, in his big Boston accent, Fleming said, "You know what, you don't talk about people like that. You don't talk about people trying out for the team or what you think of them. I'm the coach and that's the way things are here."

Mr. Friedlander sat there smirking at me. He called me some choice names. But he also said, "You're a good kid. I know that, but you fucked up." He said the punishment for this was that I couldn't go on the trip to St. Lawrence. I also had to call my dad and tell him that I wasn't going and tell him why. And I deserved it. I was a jerk, but I didn't think that incident was really in my character. Maybe I was thinking for the first time in my life I was a little bit too "entitled." Maybe it was because of my good junior year and I kind of expected special treatment.

I learned that lesson and I think I took it well. We played Clarkson's JV right after that. The schools are only about 15 miles apart. Before the game, they made me the captain of the hockey team. I believe I learned a lot from that about leadership. I had been there three years and had paid my dues. It only made sense for someone coming back to be the captain. Conroy was a co-captain. That was a proud moment for me, the captain of

Northwood my senior year. Schools were starting to contact me, and the offers were starting to come in.

The recruiting process is a story in itself. I was housed in a dormitory at the school's main building. This was well before cell phones, so the only real lines of communication were two pay phones. We had to wait in lines for phones…that's about as close as you can get—no offense intended—to being in jail! It was, for lack of a better term, horrendous. At night when I was in study hall the phone would ring: someone would answer and then yell, "THERIEN!" Followed by, "The Wisconsin head coach is on the phone!" Other times, it was John Walsh from Maine or Ron Mason from Michigan State. This went on every single night. Providence called me so many nights in a row they should have had a direct line sent right into my room. Sometimes seven times a week, sometimes twice a day.

The season got started and there was a buzz around upstate New York and points south that this might be the most dominant Northwood team ever. There I was, the kid who three years ago was literally stunned and awed by the 11 Division I scholarship kids that played on those teams, the future Winter Olympians who had gone on from there: Tony Granato, Mike Richter. I wondered aloud if I would be the next one on the list to make people say, "Look at the players that went to that school." Would I ever be on that list? It was important to me in a lot of ways because it validated the things I did not achieve as a younger person but were finally all starting to come together.

Why did it all come together? It all comes back to growth—and it certainly helped that I was the son of a hockey player.

My dad had me jumping rope when I was a kid. He made me run. He made me stay on my feet, always moving my feet. Even though he pushed me to do things I didn't necessarily like, it made me a great skater, a mobile defenseman. During my last year, my draft year (1990), Fleming used to tell pro scouts when they asked about me that he didn't know how to describe me, but "He's 6-foot-5, and he's quick." That was really a rarity for a guy like me, especially someone who was a bit on the heavy side as a 13-year-old. Like I said, it was all about the growth—mentally, physically, and emotionally. Because I went from a nothing and, in my own mind, became a something. But I was a something to other people, too. Forget the person side of it, just the hockey player. Think of it this way: You become a something when other players would openly brag about you, even in front of you. For a guy like Sidney Crosby at the NHL level, his peers (opponents) are like, "Wow, this guy is an unstoppable force, and we really don't know what to do with him."

For me it was newfound success, stuff that had never happened before. People had doubted me all those years and called me fat. I got beat up at school and had to fight through every single thing. Now, finally my draft year was upon me. I'm thinking, *This is insane. I could be drafted.* I remember reading a lot of magazines that year about guys being draft eligible. I didn't hear my name a lot and wasn't even considered for Canada's World Junior team. When I look at the guys who did play that year, I probably could have had an opportunity to go. I'm not sure if high school players had really caught on with NHL scouts just yet.

As for where I was mentally, this was just so new to me, and it validated me because it gave me a feeling of "you really had to work for something here." At that point I'm thinking, I'm proud of myself because I could have quit at so many crossroads and stopped doing the things I wanted to do simply because they were too hard. Or they were too demanding, or I wasn't good enough, or people put me down, or I was behind all these other kids But I never stopped working. I never stopped believing, even when no one else did.

The only one who might have believed in me was my dad. For me it was really brand new, and I knew what I had to do. I knew the bullying and the bullshit I had to put up with, the prima-donna kids, the prima-donna parents, the detractors, the haters.... There are lots of them and there still are today. When I see minor hockey now, it's an embarrassment the way the parents treat each other, the way they treat coaches.

My own kid gets judged now because he's my son. Is he the best player? Of course not. How do I know that? It reminds me of another kid I used to know. My son is my "mini-me." I couldn't be prouder of him.

Getting back to the final season at Northwood—we got off to an incredible start and all of a sudden I found an affinity for offense. I could (and did) score goals at will my last year. My shot was a rocket. I had an incredible shot. I could fly. We had those four defensemen on a power play with Conroy up front of me. That was a lethal power play.

I was the highest scoring defenseman Northwood has ever had. We went to the All-Scholastic Tournament at Christmas and played a team from Canada. A big team, a bunch of 20-year-olds with beards. They beat us in the preliminary round. They weren't going anywhere with their careers. They probably looked like they were going down to the US, play a hockey tournament, and drink some beer all weekend.

For me and the guys on our team, it was a huge tournament that we really wanted to do well in. In a way, to win that would validate us as the top prep school in the country again. We ended up going through the round robin and what do you know? We end up playing the same Canadian team in the finals. I had a dominant hockey tournament. You know, even though they had beaten us in the first game, we had gotten to the final game. We literally hammered this team, winning something like 7–1.

This was the championship game with quite a few scouts in the stands. At the end of the game, our goalie started a brawl by chopping somebody. It turned out to be a full bench-clearing brawl. Parents got involved, trying to get kids off the ice. I just wanted to get off the ice and get my trophy.

I was MVP of the tournament. But there was this big brawl. I got locked up with their captain and I didn't know if he really wanted to fight. I certainly didn't want to. I just wanted to get the hell home to Northwood and celebrate. It was a wild, wild finish, but this was like a Boston Bruins vs. Montreal Canadiens game in 1977. It probably lasted all of five minutes. Parents went on the ice breaking up fights. Fleming hated every minute of it. The Canadian kids had come down with real bad intentions. They embarrassed their team.

It was just an incredible victory for the school. It had been a major hurdle. In fact, I don't know if Northwood had ever won it to that point. That's how hard it was to win that thing. We went home to celebrate, no beers or anything like that. We were a pretty happy group of guys. A lot of guys felt it was just a dynamite experience. Great memories for sure that we would keep for a lifetime.

My senior year was about to come to an end but the recruitment for my services in college hockey certainly wasn't.

CHAPTER 6

Dreaming of a Big Man on Campus

SCOUTS LOVE HEALTHY HOCKEY PLAYERS but as soon as a prospect sustains a significant injury, things often begin to change. That's why I was more than a little concerned when I suffered a shoulder injury toward the end of my senior season.

It was February 1990. I was a kid who had been relatively injury-free for the better part of my young career. In the last tournament of the season at Northwood, a puck went into the offensive zone. I chased it in, lost an edge going around, and slammed left shoulder first into the boards. And man, did I hurt my shoulder. My whole anterior cruciate ligament was messed up. I couldn't really hold my arm up. I couldn't hit anybody. I just couldn't do anything.

Still, I managed to play every game in the tournament. I remember Coach Fleming saying, "If you can't go at a hundred percent, I'm not going to play you. You could be a late first-round pick or an early second-round pick in the draft coming up and it would be better not to play you." Anyway, I was able to play all four games. The only tough game we were going to play was in the finals and we had won every year for the past 10 years, so it was a foregone conclusion.

The shoulder did bother me quite a bit. And that's an injury that's gone on to bother me my entire life. I was never really a hundred percent again. Some days it felt great but even in my NHL career, my years at Providence, the Olympic team, my shoulder was always kind of sore. It was never right again. I guess that's just the way it goes.

It wasn't to the point where I couldn't play but I just never had full mobility in my left shoulder.

Recruiting offers were coming fast and furious. I had offers from just about every big school. We went to Harvard one year and Bill Cleary, who was the coach, had this letter in his pocket. He said, "I want you to read this when you're heading home." It was the copy of an acceptance letter to Harvard. It said, "We'll give you the real letter, all you have to do is say yes." I never realized it at the time but when you talk about Harvard University or another Ivy League university—I also visited Yale—I was not an Ivy League type of kid. I was an intelligent kid but more a survivor of the education system.

I played the game both in the classroom and on the ice. I remember the Harvard thing as being way cooler when I turned 40; that letter is still somewhere at my home in Canada. I just like to use it now to tell people that I got into Harvard and people think that makes me really smart. But you know what, a whole bunch of average hockey-playing kids got into Harvard.

I was recruited and very quickly had to narrow down the list of schools I was considering. Clarkson and St. Lawrence were legitimate candidates, but I had no interest going to my dad's alma mater. As for Boston University, I did not have an offer until late in the game. They had already gone after Scott Lachance pretty hard, and he became a good NHL player for quite a few years. Boston College did not offer Canadian kids scholarships and I was technically Canadian. When we played their JV, I thought it was the most beautiful campus, but I never had a chance to go there.

So how did I get down to my final five schools? They were the five schools I visited. I felt like Johnny Be Good in that movie with Anthony Michael Hall. It was very similar: every single trip I had the gold star treatment. It was unbelievable, with five-star dinners and first-class plane rides. The first trip I took was to the University of Denver. Coach Backstrom picked me up at the airport. I remember I was pretty nervous. I was so nervous, I went to the back of the plane and smoked two cigarettes with the regular passengers. They were like in their 40s and there I was an 18-year-old kid.

Northwood was notorious for smokers, and I was a guy who, if he wasn't playing, would go to the Butt Hut and have cigarettes with people. It was always my way of mingling. I loved to play Foosball in those Butt Hut rooms. I wasn't shy to have a cigarette here or there. I knew the Northwood teachers knew I would go out for a cigarette here or there. So, I smoked on the back of that plane to Denver, and it was pretty funny. Backstrom picked me up and took me for a tour all around Denver. We even stopped for a beer. Boy, how times have changed since then! Here's a legendary Montreal Canadiens player who became the coach at Denver. I don't know if I was ever serious about playing in the Mile High City but it's a great place. They partied their asses off, those kids, and there were a lot of Canadians on the team. Ralph ran it like a pro team. They were great people, and I had an unbelievably good time.

The second trip I took had me visiting the University of Wisconsin. Jeff Sauer was the head coach. So now here I was with former Northwood star Brett Kurtz. And the Granatos (Tony and Cammi) had played there. It was a different time, but the experience was similar to Denver. When I went out to Wisconsin it was one big party. I drank like a fish and partied like a rock star. I was impressed with Wisconsin and, like with Denver, I loved it there. A beautiful campus and I was deadly serious about going there.

From there, it was over to the University of New Hampshire, which had seen a bunch of future NHL players go through, including two-time Norris Trophy winner Rod Langway. They had four Northwood kids on their roster, among them the Morrow brothers, so that had some appeal.

I got there for a 48-hour visit just before Christmas. They had those food trucks. It was like minus-20 degrees, it was snowing, and I was freezing my balls off. A friend got into it with a student. He went off and the next thing you know a fraternity house emptied and there was a battalion of guys coming toward us. On our side, it was me and about seven recruits. We were sitting there eating sandwiches and we all got jumped, every one of us. It was one-on-four, one-on-five. I tried to get out of there, but I got the shit beaten out of me. Finally, the fight broke up. I had a bloody nose. I tried to fight the best I could. I said, "This is crazy."

I wind up getting to bed around 2:30 AM and I had to be up by 6:30 to catch a ride with the coach to Logan Airport in Boston. I got in the car. He looked at me and asked, "What happened?" I looked him in the eye and said, "Coach, last night I fell down a set of stairs because I had a few too many and banged my head on the metal railing." That coach looked over at me and said, "You're going to be a great teammate somewhere for somebody." Then he said he knew what happened, that we had gotten into it with the fraternity up the hill while we were at the food truck. I'm thinking, *Holy cow, this just happened four hours ago, and he knows every single detail from what had happened!* I was absolutely amazed how quickly he got that information. He apologized to me, to the Northwood people. It never really deterred me; I loved New Hampshire. But it was just too damn cold.

After that, the fourth stop was the University of Maine, which also has a storied hockey tradition. There were also some Northwood guys there, including my good friend Kent Salfi. On the visit, I stayed with him. The problem with Maine—and this was a hockey machine—is they didn't want the best and brightest. They just wanted the best, not the brightest. That's fine.

Coach Walsh greeted me and asked how I was doing. He asked what my SAT score was. I said I only took it once and I got like an 870 (out of a possible 1600). He goes, "That's terrific! That's wonderful, wonderful news." And I'm thinking, *It won't be hard to get into this place.*

That's what I loved about the Harvard story more than anything—that I had an 870 SAT score, and the coach gave me that acceptance letter anyway. So, all the people who have 1,500 to 1,600 scores out there but got turned down by your dream Ivy League university—if you can skate and shoot a puck half-decently, you could have gotten into a school like Harvard with a fraction of that SAT score. And I love that. Here's the reason I didn't go to Maine: When classes were out, instead of living on campus you lived with a billet parent and you would stay at their house for like two weeks. I attended a couple games and (author) Stephen King was there, which I thought was pretty cool. I had seen all his movies. Maine played Bowling Green in one game with defenseman Rob Blake—yeah, the future NHL Hall of Famer—and I saw him hammer home a goal from the point.

But it felt kind of gloomy there and it didn't appeal to me. Even though I loved Sean Walsh, I just didn't think the set-up in a real small-town kind of like Lake Placid was going to be an ideal spot for me.

That brings me to visit No. 5, Providence. My parents came with me on that trip. The coach, Mike McShane, treated us like royalty. That coaching staff had been the most assertive in terms of the phone calls. They were the ones most invested in me and cared the most. At that point, Providence was No. 1. My parents loved Providence, too. They had a great history, a good lineage of hockey people such as Lou Lamoriello, Brian Burke, and Ron Wilson. I really didn't have an offer in Boston except for Harvard. Playing for the Crimson wasn't really a reality because my dad would have had to pay for it, and he had already laid out a lot of money for Northwood. There was just no way I was going to see him pay another $20,000. And he told me he had sent me to Northwood to get a scholarship so he wouldn't have to pay for college.

The season ended. I brought a couple guys with me. The NHL had a fascination with size back then. Paskowski, my defense partner, and Brian Ridolfi, a forward, came along. I was really happy for them.

I go in and tell Reed and Fleming I've made my choice. I'm going to Providence. They were happy. One of the reasons I went to Providence was so that my mom and dad could come to my games. That's what ruled out Wisconsin. My dad had put so much time into me as a player so I felt like if I went to the WCHA in Madison, Wisconsin, it was not like he could just jump on a flight. In hindsight, that's the real reason why I didn't go to Wisconsin, because my mom and dad would not have been able to watch me play. That was so important to me, to have the availability for my mom and dad. It's not like it is now, where every game is streamed, like my daughter's basketball games are streamed on TV. I just couldn't do that. I knew Providence was about an eight-hour drive, which was a doable thing.

Here's another thing about college recruiting and it's something I tell coaches: Don't give up on someone. As soon as I committed to Providence, I didn't hear from them for a month. Not one call. I realize now they were just doing their job, recruiting the kid, they got him and now they don't have to talk to me. I got upset. I was like, *Is this how it really goes?* I had heard from these guys every single day and now I hadn't heard from them at all. So, what did I do? I went back in Reed's office and told him I might reconsider my college choice. I hadn't signed anything yet: it was just verbal. There was a February break that year. I called McShane and said, "Mike, I'm going to decommit. I'm not saying you are out, but I'm just saying I need to rethink everything. I haven't heard from you guys so I don't feel totally secure with my decision. I want to open that door again and it's just between you and Wisconsin."

I called Wisconsin and they were more than thrilled to go through and redo the recruiting process again. I just wanted this to be quick. I just wanted to get a check mark or validation. Sauer flew to Ottawa from Madison, Wisconsin. We had dinner at my house. We talked and he sold me the same thing he sold me before: You're going to play a lot, you're going to be a high draft pick this summer, and you're going to be part of a national championship-winning program. I still didn't believe it. Then McShane flew in the next night from Providence again. It was never my intention to play one off the other—a bidding war for my services. I wanted to make sure I was making the right choice. McShane apologized and said we should have kept the line of communication open. About five days later I made my decision. My mom and dad didn't point me to Providence; I just liked that they would have the opportunity to watch me play.

The rest of the year, I was just getting ready for the NHL. Northwood had just enjoyed one of its best years ever to that point. The Northwood years were a great experience. It was a whole different world. It was the first time I had seen drugs. Even now, when I talk to guys who were kids back then, we were sort of all the same kid. All of us were just wandering nomads, trying to figure out who we were. Some kids got into experimental drugs. The worst thing that happened at Northwood was during my senior year when three kids were involved in a car accident. It happened on a Sunday night on the way home. It was an absolutely devastating thing. It was almost surreal when you think of all the lives it changed. Just a horrible drunk driving accident. The kid who drove had to live with it the rest of his life. It was just heartbreaking.

I went back to an alumni event a few years ago. They hid the yearbook that year inside the old Butt Hut. They built a tribute to those kids and it's still there 30 years later.

I never really had a girlfriend. I don't think girls even liked me. I had a bad case of acne. From 16 to 20, I was like your average "pizza face." And they called me as much. Whenever my daughters get a trace of acne, they blame it on me, it's my fault.

Northwood ended and we had a great end of the year celebration. I was moving on. The big thing was if you had a car at school, you could only drive when you left on weekends. You couldn't even wheel around town. Those kids have memories of every senior getting shit-faced and walking home from bars. See, it's a small town and the teachers had a rapport with just about every business you could imagine. They had relationships with the bars, the hotels, and so on. They knew if a Northwood kid bought pot from someone.

I drank one time in three years at Northwood and almost got caught. One time. And graduation was the second time I drank. It lasted all day. Everyone had a good time and they deserved it. But then I went home and drank some more. This was before the NHL draft. Going into the draft, during and after, my friends were a little bit in awe of me. It's one thing to tell people you had an unbelievable career at a US high school. It was kind of interesting because no one believed me.

For me, the draft was the biggest thing that could happen in my life because it would be in the papers in Canada so everyone would know. This was the last thing I needed to have for my whole validation. Then again, this was before making the Olympic team, which pushed my celebrity even higher.

I was in a real secure spot but what I needed was someone to call my name out at the NHL draft in Vancouver. What I didn't know is that one day in June would define the rest of my life.

CHAPTER 7

Draft Day Vindication

UP UNTIL THE END of my final year at Northwood it always felt like I had to prove myself. For whatever reason, I didn't believe people thought I had the right stuff to advance, be it in the NHL Entry Draft or even at a Division I university. But all that was about to change in June 1990.

As the Northwood season came to an end, I was named most valuable player and the voting wasn't even close. Yet, since this was before the Internet age, word didn't always travel far or fast. Example: Our coach at Northwood, Mr. Fleming, was going to coach in the Hockey Night in Boston Showdown tournament as coach of the North/New York team. The Boston officials asked Fleming if he could bring a couple players that had not played before in the tournament. He brings me and future NHLer Conroy and the Boston guy had no idea who we were. He said to Fleming, "Are they good players?" Tom replied with, "Yeah, they're not bad."

Well, we literally mangled the competition. It was a great time and a good way to finish up at Northwood. The only focus I had now was the NHL draft, which was scheduled for that jewel of a city, Vancouver, British Columbia. While I waited, I worked for my father, who was in charge of the Canada Safety Council. I would go in there sometimes and he would give me projects to do. It involved everything from automobile safety to senior safety to safety at home. It was a non-profit job.

My dad actually made a business trip into a stop at Vancouver for the Draft. I was kind of unheralded with the crop of available prospects; a bit of a well-kept secret. I don't know what the majority of teams thought, but I had a meeting with one team, the New Jersey Devils. That was because former Providence icon Lou Lamoriello, the Devils GM, found out I was going to school there in the fall. He was the athletic director, the greatest representative of ice hockey you could find. Lou's only question was, 'How are you going to transform your game from high school to the much more physical NHL?' I said my dad played college hockey, and although I'm not exactly a heavyweight champion, I'll play the game hard and with integrity. I roomed with Lou's son Chris for two years at Providence. Years later I thought about the three Cups the Devils won. If the Flyers hadn't drafted me earlier, the Devils certainly planned to in the middle rounds.

Funny thing is, Marty Brodeur was taken by New Jersey in the 1990 Draft and defenseman Scott Niedermayer was taken the following year. They are two of the biggest pains in the ass the Flyers ever came across as opponents.

The Draft was a bit of a quirk. Under the rules of the time, as a Canadian kid who attended a US prep school, if I didn't get picked in the first three rounds, I would have to wait until the following year. I attended the Draft and ended up sitting next to Jason York, another Ottawa product. The first round went by— Owen Nolan first, Petr Nedvěd second, Keith Primeau third, Mike Ricci to the Flyers fourth and Jaromír Jágr to the Penguins fifth. What a draft, possibly the best of all time from top to bottom, after the legendary 1979 Draft, and certainly one of the two deepest in recent memory. Only the 2003 Draft rivaled or exceeded it.

The Flyers were just another team in my mind. There was nothing to suggest they were honing in on selecting me. Two rounds go by and in the second round, the Flyers took Chris Simon at No. 25 overall, then Mikael Renberg at 40, and Terran Sandwith at 42. As the third round started, they took Kimbi Daniels at No. 44 and Bill Armstrong at No. 46. I was sitting with a suit on, sweating bullets and probably smelling like a cattle roundup because I'd forgotten to put on deodorant. I knew the situation about my Draft status. Time was running out on my chances of being selected.

Suddenly, out of nowhere I heard, "With the No. 47 pick, the Flyers select, from Northwood Prep, Chris Therien." I went numb. I could not believe what just happened. When I heard my name, it was literally one of the greatest moments in my life. It was vindication. It was everything you would ever want wrapped up into one single thing and it shot right through my body. It was like someone magically made this moment happen. I knew it would finally give me the validation I so desperately needed.

Thank goodness the Flyers picked up a series of second-round and third-round picks. With an abundance of selections, I'd gotten on GM Russ Farwell's radar for the third round. They gave me a jersey for the cameras, No. 75. They didn't have any No. 90s left; they'd given those to the top picks, like Ricci. The latter-round guys got 74s or 75s, because those were the two years the Flyers won their Stanley Cups.

That night was great. My dad was very proud; I didn't care whether I was taken in the first round, the second, or the third. Just so long as I was taken. For a US high school player who had only been on the radar for about a year, it was astonishing to a lot of people. My agent said if I had not been picked in '90 I probably would have been a top five pick in '91.

It was just a wonderful experience and I got to do a lot of great things that made me particularly happy. As I tell my kids, everything we have is because of the NHL draft that day. That is one hundred percent true. It was incredible how time, in just a few short years, had changed everything. It was an all-time high for me. When I got back to Ottawa, that's what the buzz was about. It was almost like, *How the heck did that happen?*

When the draft ended that day, the celebration began. Talk about a small world—the guy I hung out with the entire night with was Nedvĕd, the second overall pick. He was playing for the Seattle Thunderbirds, which was Farwell's junior team. (Before he was hired by the Flyers to replace Bob Clarke. Actually,

Farwell unsuccessfully tried to trade up to the second overall pick to take Petr, but Canucks GM Pat Quinn turned down the Flyers' offer. Had Clarkie not been fired, the Flyers would have selected Jágr, because Bob felt—correctly, as history would show—that Jágr was the most gifted talent in the Draft class.) We shared stories about everything, including his defection from the Czech Republic. Time flew and suddenly it was dawn. We ended up back in Nedvěd's hotel room with another draft pick, Brian McCarthy, who'd been selected by the Buffalo Sabres. My dad was worried about me when I didn't come home to our hotel. This was before cell phones, so it was sort of a hit-or-miss proposition. I finally got word to him I was okay. It was all good and we shared a laugh over that one.

We spent the next day there and took advantage of all Vancouver, a beautiful city, had to offer. It ended up being my favorite city, finishing just ahead of my No. 2, Chicago. When we finally got back to Ottawa, the hometown celebration got under-way. I was joyous, heading off to Providence on a full scholarship with my career with the Flyers in front of me. I was still growing, and everything was looking good. I felt like I had a bright future in front of me. And I did, which turned out to be three years at Providence and a year with the Canadian Olympic team.

The summer of 1990 also brought some storm clouds on the horizon because that's the time I started pounding some beers. You must understand it was in the spirit of celebration and there were times when I was definitely overserved at local watering holes. Tracing my alcoholism back to my youth, people ask what it was like. I drank hard, my friends drank hard, we went out on weekends, and I probably had not learned to be the hardest-working guy yet. As far as dryland training went, we just got by on natural talent. It wasn't until I got to Providence and they tested me that I realized I had to step up the work a little bit.

As eye-openers go, my No. 1 reality check came about when the Flyers strength and conditioning coach Pat Croce had us in to spend time at the facility in Voorhees, New Jersey, and he gave us an idea of what it means to be a pro. There was a lot of work to be done. As Lou Lamoriello had said, "What are you going to do to transition your game from high school to the high-velocity, hard-hitting NHL?"

Still, I was 18 and it was the summer. I partied a little too much and put on a little weight. But my frame could handle it. I had the ideal body style for a defenseman—big legs and side-of-beef ass—perfect for battling big forwards in the corners and in front of the net.

I enjoyed what you might call my new celebrity status. A lot of people wound up with egg on their face because I had proven them wrong. I felt like I had climbed over the biggest hurdle. There were several in my life: the first was playing hockey as a kid, the second was getting cut and dealing with it, the third was quitting hockey for a year and skiing, and the fourth was my dad believing in me and sending me off to Northwood (one of the greatest hockey machines in United States history), getting cut again and playing JV. Then there was my rebirth, becoming a star at Northwood and becoming one of the greatest players they ever had along with Richter and Granato. The final hurdle was getting drafted, which allowed me to become a little arrogant. It gave me an air of confidence, a certain cockiness.

I treated the journey to the draft like it was my one and only chance. If I didn't make it to college, I wasn't going to make it. I put a lot of pressure on myself, and I think I got that from my father. I felt a lot of vindication, for myself, for my father. He believed in me and I believed in myself. Everything up to that point now felt like a miracle.

There were more pleasant surprises, and a few bumps, on the road ahead.

CHAPTER 8

Joe College Arrives

AT LONG LAST, my college career began. I was just playing off my talent on the ice. I hadn't totally learned how to work off the ice. Off to Providence I went, probably 6'5", 235 pounds. I probably had a little more weight on me than I needed at the time but again, I was a bigger-bodied guy, so when I put weight on at that age, much of it was in the right places.

First, there was getting on a flight from Ottawa to Boston and then taking a bus from Logan Airport to Providence. I stopped at a store right before I got on the bus and picked up a couple beers for the ride. That night I got picked up by an old Northwood teammate, Sean Doyle, who happened to live in Providence.

We went straight to this roaring Rhode Island party. It wasn't a Providence College thing, just a bunch of people from Rhode Island looking to have a good time. It was unbelievable. I remember getting drunk as a skunk, but that's what you're supposed to do when you're 18, right? I guess I was partying with about 200 people, and this was the night before I was supposed to check into my dormitory.

One of my roommates was Mike Heinke, the goaltender who played on the USA World Junior team and had been drafted by Lou Lamoriello of the New Jersey Devils in 1989. The other was Dean Capuano, who had been drafted by the Boston Bruins in 1990.

Now I had quite a personality going into college, and it was only going to expand from there. If there happened to be one "positive" from my drinking, you could say it helped draw out my natural confident personality. I do feel in many ways at the start that alcohol did give me confidence. Maybe it pulled out some of the stuff that had been ingrained in me as a kid. As much as the devil is in the details when it comes to alcohol, I often wonder if it didn't somehow help me find the person who was not the shy, nervous kid I once was.

A lot of my impersonations did start in college. That was a big step for me because when you're doing impersonations, you come out of your own shell. And for a kid who grew up in a shell all those years, I had finally come out of it. When you start doing impersonations, even your first year, it's a step in that direction. There was a little bit of arrogance to it, at least in public. Behind closed doors might have been somewhat different. I was still the shy, not-sure-of-myself kind of kid. Those feelings were starting to dissipate, and I was becoming more of a personality, one that people would look up to. But the process was slow, and things didn't really change all that much my freshman year.

College was a whole new experience for me. The Northwood years were great, but boy did I stay on the straight and narrow.

I did not want to jeopardize anything because of the money my dad was putting out. It was important to me to stay focused, and I valued that kind of stuff.

Things changed in a big way when I arrived at Providence. It was like someone lit a stick of dynamite. For kids who escaped Catholic high school, the first week was like the world's biggest drinking binge. It probably happens at every college in America, but this one had to be right up near the top. Those are the moments I look back at and I have no regrets. You're supposed to live and have fun. I tell my kids to go to college, have fun, have a party, enjoy yourself. These are supposed to be the best four years of your life. Even though I was only at Providence, I had a good time. Probably too good of a time.

Meanwhile, out on the ice, things were shaping up. My roommate, Dean Capuano, came from a big hockey family which included cousins Dave and Jack, a couple All-Americans at the University of Maine. Jack went on to coach the New York Islanders. Dean was from nearby and his mom used to host an Italian food party every Sunday, and it's still the best Italian food I've ever had in my life. She was just a great hostess.

As it turned out, my first year at Providence ultimately became a successful one. I enjoyed my classes and, in one instance, got a little help along the way.

One class, educational psychology, was not exactly a major challenge, maybe somewhere around the proximity of basket weaving. It was a classroom full of athletes, so what could go wrong? Well, the teacher of the course, Father Neely, was 91 years old, enamored by athletes and a bit forgetful at times. He put the tests (and answers) in a locked cabinet but left the key on the desktop. I remember one kid going up and reading off every single answer to the test. Every kid in there wound up with nothing less than a 98 score. Father Neely came back for the next session a couple days later and, being from the province of New Brunswick, said in a real eastern Canadian accent, "I've been here for 30 years, and this is by far and away the most intelligent class I've ever had at Providence College!"

I'm thinking to myself, *There's no way he didn't know he had left the key out.* I think he did. Right then I knew pretty much what my college education was going to be. Another professor was a die-hard hockey fan. He would be there at all the home games, cheering up a storm. He taught a theology class so I thought I would use my hockey-playing status as a little lever-age, wiggle my way through some of the work as it were. It didn't happen. This guy didn't care if I played hockey even though he was a psycho fan. Didn't give me one little bit of help.

I experienced two different ends of the spectrum in college. It seemed like my priorities were set: hockey and extracurricular activities tied for first, school second. I was at Providence to play hockey, more so than I was to be a student. If I wanted to be a student, I would have found a way to have my dad pay to have me go to Harvard. Providence was a hockey school for me, a means to the next level.

I was ready to roll and our coach, McShane, was a maniac. My dad liked him because he had coached at St. Lawrence in the early

'80s. I think he liked me because I was a high draft pick that he was able to recruit to Providence. We had a few excellent American players, including Mike Boback, a real stud on offense who came all the way from Michigan, which surprised me a bit. He could have gone to the University of Michigan or Michigan State; he loved that area, too. It was bizarre. He was a scoring machine.

We started off playing, oddly enough, the University of Ottawa. My defense partner, Shaun Kane, got jumped, a brawl broke out and I ended up taking care of about three guys.

While I wasn't producing as much offense as I had at Northwood, my overall play was sound. We had a very good team and eventually made it to the NCAA tournament. The highlight of my year came when we played our hated rivals, the fellow Jesuit institution Boston College. They were loaded during my years at Providence. Their goalie was Scott LeGrand, who later was my teammate on the Hershey Bears. It was 2–2 with a minute left, 3,500 people crammed into Schneider Arena, our home rink. Behind the BC net, Boback spotted me coming down the side and put the pass right on my tape. I slid it far side.

Well, the place went bonkers. It was the biggest goal of my college career and the building noise was insane. I think it validated everything coach McShane had wanted in terms of my presence being part of a huge goal. It was a monster win, the one that got us into the NCAAs.

For the season, my numbers (22 points in 36 games) really didn't translate into what I had done the year before at Northwood. But that was okay.

This was also the year I met my first girlfriend, Kristen, from Amherst, Massachusetts. She came from a great family, and I liked her a lot. My mom and dad were back in Canada, so her family was almost like a second one to me. Our relationship lasted until I had to leave to join the Canadian Olympic team for a year. But everything happens for a reason. I have nothing but great memories.

One of the other highlights of that first year was a three-game set we played at the University of Minnesota. This was the spring of '91. We drew something like 8,000 fans to 3M Arena at Mariucci and across town, the NHL's North Stars were getting only about 5,000 at the Met Center.

We won the first game and that was quite an achievement. Maybe some of those North Stars fans would have been there if the building hadn't sold out.

AT THE END OF MY FIRST YEAR in the fine state of Rhode Island, I was one of the Flyers' top five prospects in their system. There wasn't a lot of interaction with the team when I was a freshman. My reps were Pat Morris and Don Meehan of Newport Sports Management in Toronto.

There was nothing crazy with the drinking my second year at Providence, nothing that made me think I had issues with alcohol. I was just one of the boys; I was a hockey player. I was just a good old boy, recognizing that good things were happening in my life at that time. I was no longer the bullied, beleaguered kid with no confidence. Now I was feeling pretty good with where I was with my life.

It was important for me to have my family watch me play, whether it was live or on NESN (New England Sports Network). My entire persona was changing, and I felt good about myself.

Year number two at Providence we lost a lot of good veterans. They were a good group of senior guys, a lot of Canadians. McShane knew we had lost some veterans back on defense, so he decided to put Gaudreau back as my partner that year and he was actually a winger. He ended up being like a rover, a hybrid player, really good on the power play. Then we moved into a different stage. Robby Gaudreau, who was a senior when I was a sophomore, went to San Jose. Mike Boback was a 10th-round pick of the Capitals. Both guys were unbelievably gifted offensive players. Dave Berard, who was a backup goalie, is now assistant athletic director for the hockey department at Providence.

I wound up with 41 points that year in 36 games, which was a darn good ratio for any position. A lot of that production was because of Gaudreau. Overall, the numbers I put up in college were spot on in terms of my offensive production. They were about par for the course.

Gaudreau was a very good hockey player but one of the most miserable people I ever met. In all my years of hockey, this guy took the cake. He hated hockey. Good talent, not even six feet, low center of gravity, a wide-based skater. But everything this guy did seemed to be painful.

On the other hand, Boback was happy-go-lucky. A cocky guy but I admired his demeanor. He was a really smart hockey player. I thought he was better than Gaudreau, a far better passer. Gaudreau had a great shot, and I can't take away anything from his ability. He was a good NHLer for a little bit but not a hard guy to defend against.

Boback spent a lot of time in the pro minors but never really made it to the top. The problem was that he was not a gifted skater. At that time, if you were not electrically fast, there was a good chance you weren't going to make it. Those were the two best college players I played with.

We were top-heavy with our best players and our goalie, Heinke, could steal a game for us here or there. I was feeling a little more confident about my play. Back in my freshman year I had played in something called the USA Cup in Albany in lieu of the World Juniors. They had put together a team, a group of guys with mixed ages—36 down to 19 years old.

It was the first time I took the face shield off because it was international rules. In the first game, I got cut right under the eye, 15 stitches. It was a round-robin tournament and we played Russia. It was the first time I played for my home country, and I was proud to play for Canada. I forged some relationships I carry to this day.

We played Denver early in the season and that was pretty cool if for nothing more than that it was one of the schools I considered attending. The team played well but there were moments when it seemed we weren't all on the same page.

Case in point: We went to the Hockey East tournament, and it looked like we were going to win. Then came a rather dubious play that probably cost us the tournament. Gaudreau was part of a two-on-one and all he had to do was pass to his teammate because the goaltender committed to the initial shooter. The game would have been over, and I believe we would have gone on to win the tournament.

That's the problem with a guy like that. He was so selfish; he didn't care about anyone else. But he was so gifted, so you kind of had to live with how he acted. That's why college hockey has a problem because there are players like that. There are players there who really aren't as good as they think they are. That's what happens when there are so many players, I guess. You have a watered-down talent pool. When you have a really good player who's only thinking about himself, you're stuck living with him.

I tell guys even today, if you're getting recruited and you're going to college, make sure you know who is on that team. And it's so much easier now to do research with the Internet than it was back then. Gaudreau wasn't a bully or a bad person, he was just miserable. He looked at himself like a king and everyone had to sit around him.

We ended up losing in the Hockey East semifinals and didn't get to the NCAAs. The season was over. Gaudreau eventually left and signed with the San Jose Sharks. Later, I played against him in the NHL. I remember yelling at him and trying to make his life miserable in the game or two we played the Sharks. I made it a point to get after him. It was nothing personal, just hockey.

Coach McShane was getting the best out of us, and he was one intense guy. He was a yeller, a screamer. There was the time we were coming back from a game at New Hampshire. We lost and we were hanging up our gear before we got on the bus. McShane marched in and, in his big Boston/Rhode Island accent, announces: "I've got to talk to you. I have to say this right now—go home, take a look at yourself in the fucking mirror. And if you don't like what you see, get the hell out of my locker room!" What a scene: That speech, the animation, the look he gave everyone. He certainly had everyone's attention. I was sitting there laughing to myself as he's telling everyone to check to see the size of their balls.

Coach knew a lot of people in the hockey world and almost got a job as an assistant coach with the New York Islanders. He probably would have been a better NHL coach at that time but certainly not now. In the 2020s, everyone has to be treated with kid gloves. He could be mean, and his lips would start to swell when he was yelling at you. He did give me one lesson in life that I never forgot. He said sometimes before you sink your teeth into a prime rib, you have to sink it through a big pile of you know what. He's right. Sometimes you have to put up with some adversity before you get the glory.

I actually liked him. He's an interesting guy. He leaned on his good players. I believe he knew I gave an honest effort. I was right up there with Boback and Gaudreau as his best players and I tried my best. I think he knew that.

There was a story that bears repeating from our trip to the Land of the Midnight Sun when we played the University of

Alaska Anchorage. One night we ended up at a strip joint on our own. We saw him there and we immediately did an about-face before he saw us. I wonder what we would have said if both sides had seen each other.

Mike got to know my dad because of the St. Lawrence connection. It might have been somewhat of a factor for me going to Providence in the first place. My parents might have given me a nudge in that direction. We were looking at Catholic schools and, at the time, Notre Dame's facilities were not all that good. The religion part played into it, but my parents also liked McShane. A lot of good things came from that decision and Coach deserves credit for a lot of them.

Stan Moore and Tim Army were the assistant coaches and were extremely approachable. Stan served as a college head coach during three different stints at Union, Colgate, and Colby. Tim is a career hockey guy. He played at Providence and later became head coach for six years, along with a stint as head coach of the AHL Portland Pirates in the early 2000s. He also served as an assistant coach for 15 years in the NHL with Anaheim, Washington, and Colorado.

These were the gentlemen who guided me through those first couple critical years at Providence, ones that set the groundwork for my upcoming professional career.

As my sophomore year came to a close, there was a big decision to make: Should I stay in college one more year and keep myself eligible to play for Canada at the 1994 Winter Olympics at Lillehammer?

If ever there were a good time to sign a pro contract, that was it. The Flyers were offering me something in the $250,000 per year range to make it official. My agent (Morris-Meehan) was really pushing for me to leave. Of course, I ended up staying another year, which was a terrible mistake. If I could have done one thing over again, I would have left Providence after my second year and gone right to the minors for one year. But that being said, a lot of people wanted me to play for Team Canada, and for that to happen, I had to go back to school for my junior year.

The offer was in, and Russ Farwell was the Flyers general manager. It was a four-year contract for just over $1 million. I was 20 and wanted to leave, but my dad and my coach didn't want me to leave. Remember, this was at the time of the Lindros trade in June. The Flyers wanted me and after the trade, there was a little bit more of a push in my direction to sign. Ultimately, it was back to Providence for one more year. And a rather superfluous one at that.

CHAPTER 9

The Lost Years

BY THE SUMMER OF 1992 and with two years at Providence College behind me, I believed I had gotten all I could from the ranks of amateur hockey and was ready to move on to the professional game. But there were still other people who felt another year at Providence, plus a possible berth on the Canada Olympic team for the 1994 Winter Games at Lillehammer, Norway, might be in my best interests.

Russ Farwell was not in that mix. He told me enough was enough and it was time to sign a contract to play for the Flyers organization. In hindsight, the way the team was put together, I probably would have made the roster if I had left Providence after my sophomore year. This was one of those cases that I refer to now when speaking with younger people and say they should make their own decisions, be comfortable about what they want to do with their careers. As it turns out, Farwell was right—my junior year at Providence was a complete waste of time. My offensive numbers didn't match up with my sophomore year. I played with lesser talent and did not get better. I didn't care about any

All-American honors or stuff like that. My singular goal at the time was to get to the NHL.

To go back to college for a third year had a lot to do with a push from my parents. People at Providence, including coach McShane, wanted the decision to play made quickly in August of that year, but I couldn't shake that feeling that enough was enough. I had been on my own enough that I felt comfortable about turning pro, that my time had come. One of the reasons I did go back was my parents' vision of me playing on the Olympic team. It was a nice experience but, like the situation with Providence, devoting the entire 1993–94 season to the Olympics was pretty much a waste of time. I went there with an older group and although many of them wound up being minor league veterans, I still didn't play much. Not turning pro after the '92–93 season was dumb. It was shortsighted and I regret that. If I have one regret in hockey it probably would have been that I went back for my junior year at Providence.

When I did go back, the season left a lot to be desired. It was an ordinary cast of okay players. They weren't going to get us past Boston College or Boston University. I couldn't do it alone. We just didn't have the horses. I had a good year: it was fun in terms of camaraderie with the guys, and I was able to take more of a leadership role. They were all good people, including my good friend Dean Capuano. Chris Lamoriello, Lou's son, was one of my roommates. We would go down to see the Devils play. There were a lot of good memories from that time but from a pure standpoint of becoming better, the third season at PC did not serve a real purpose. That and the Olympics just took two years off my professional résumé. There was no dire ending here; it just slowed my progress. At the end of my junior year, I knew it was going to be my last one. That's not a good way to go in. You go in almost thinking you're going to finish your four years. I should have just up and left and not listened to anybody. I let other people push me into making that call. After the third season ended, I went home for a couple months and then committed to the Olympic team. I got a guarantee that I would be on the team. That was significant for me. So, off to Calgary I went that summer for the Canada training camp in preparation for the big event at Lillehammer.

I arrived in Calgary to join what was then the Canadian men's national team. For starters, Eric Lindros' brother, Brett—a real good kid that I enjoyed hanging around with—ended up being my roommate, along with Craig Woodcroft, who played at Colgate, and Russ Romaniuk of North Dakota (who was later briefly a Flyers teammate). The team had a lot of future and former NHL talent on it, including Paul Kariya, Petr Nedvěd, Chris Kontos, Adrian Aucoin, Corey Hirsch, and Todd Hlushko. The head coach was Tom Renney. From the moment I arrived, I never got the sense anyone really wanted me there and the feeling was mutual. I always believed I should have been in the professional ranks a year earlier or at least playing at the Flyers' American Hockey League affiliate in Hershey to prepare myself for my NHL career. Somehow, even though it's a great honor to play in the Olympics, for me it wasn't actually the career path. For me, it was a second wasted year.

My Olympic experience was a two-part event. The first, and best, part was I had the opportunity to see a lot of the world. We visited some of the most beautiful places on the planet as well as some of the real hellholes. Our first journey took us to Moscow for Russia's prestigious Izvestia Cup at Christmas that year. It's one of the top international tournaments in the world and gave us a glimpse of what kind of competition we might see at the Olympics. My dad came over on the trip with some of the other fathers, including Paul Henry, who was one of the general managers for Canada. He had a long history of being a scout and an advisor to many NHL teams over the years. Coincidentally, he played hockey with my dad at St. Mike's. Paul is a legendary figure and those in the know in the hockey world are quite familiar with this man.

Make no mistake, these trips had their lighter side with some rather humorous moments. One day we were walking through Red Square not far from the Kremlin. One of the guys, Dwayne Norris, who went to Michigan State, looked over at one of the buildings and he asked, "What's that?" Someone replied: "That's Lenin's tomb." To which Norris came back with another question: "Why would they bury one of the Beatles over here?" That was an absolute classic. Just an example of the collective great sense of humor these guys had. Later, we rode buses through the Alps, Italy, Austria, and Switzerland. It was a great way to see all the natural sights of Europe. It gave us a taste of European culture and the whole thing was on Canada's ticket. It was a good thing I had an Olympic guarantee, because if that were not the case I might very well have been cut. Coach Renney liked the guys who played for him in junior. He was probably nondescript at best. If you took a poll of guys who played for him, most would say they forgot him once they were past his watch. Renney favored the veterans and gave short shrift to the younger guys, which isn't that far off the track as far as most professional coaches go.

Ironically, I was playing in the NHL less than six months after the Olympics, whereas most of the other guys on defense never went on to anything. In fact, many of their careers came to an end. It's hard to completely disregard my Olympic experience because we did make it to the championship game, and it took a legendary (and, later, often copycatted) move by Peter Forsberg to give Sweden a shootout win for the gold medal. I was dressed for every game, but it was not what I had envisioned. It was more my parents' vision than it was mine. It was really what they wanted for me, and I did it to please them. Mind you, if being an Olympic athlete is one thing your parents dream about on your behalf, it's probably not the biggest sacrifice in the world to fulfill that wish. But for me, the last year at Providence and the Olympic year, in terms of preparation for NHL hockey, was not all that productive.

I did make a lot of memories, though. Our team traveled coast to coast, from one small town to another to feature and preview our team for the '94 Games. We would play in these small little barns in places like Cape Breton, Nova Scotia, or dinky towns in Saskatchewan. The whole town would make us dinner, including the opponents. It gave teams from countries such as the US and Russia an understanding, a true flavor, (or should I say "flavour") of what Canada as a country was and who the people were. From that standpoint, it did make me truly proud to be a Canadian. The guys I got to know were honest-to-goodness players, all in, so to speak. Hlushko, Aucoin, and so forth. Funny thing is, there were plenty of opportunities to go out on the town, but at that point I wasn't much of a drinker. I was never considered a big drinker by the people around me with the team. I was a normal guy still. My drinking probably didn't start in earnest until the 1998 season with the Flyers, in terms of partying harder than the other guys.

The highlight of the Olympic year for me was probably a game just before Christmas, a tilt against Russia, broadcasted nationwide on TSN. What people didn't know was this was only Russia's second- or third-line players. They were not the most hygienic people in the hockey world, basically eschewing the showering process after games. They would finish the game, ignore the shower, and flick their hair back with sweat. Then they would sit down at the dinner table with us, smelling like they just walked off the farm. We played the Russians in a sold-out building in Halifax. The game was tantamount to one of those must-see games on *Hockey Night in Canada*, and I ended up scoring my first hat trick since Northwood Prep. And, yes, it was the last trick I would register for my career because I just wasn't that kind of scorer. We won and I was awarded player of the game, a big thrill not only for me but also for my family and friends watching back home. That was the highlight of the year for me. Under different circumstances, the Olympic year might have been more helpful to me if the competition was held on NHL-sized ice rather than huge Olympic-sized rinks.

After the Olympics ended, I had to wait about a month to get my contract with the Flyers finalized. It wasn't until the middle of March that I was able to show up at Hershey for my first pro hockey game.

The journey was about to begin.

CHAPTER 10

Welcome
to the NHL

OF ALL THE YEARS TO FINALLY MAKE IT to the National Hockey League, I had to pick 1994–95, pro hockey's first great labor lockout.

It was as if the hockey gods had it in for me. Here I was, having paid my dues with an extra, superfluous year at Providence and a year dedicated to the Canadian Olympic team and now I was being sent back to the American Hockey League with the Hershey Bears after making the Flyers' roster out of training camp.

During training camp under new Flyers head coach Terry Murray and general manager Bob Clarke (who had left the GM post for Florida Panthers to return to Philly, replacing Farwell), I realized very quickly that the organization had their eyes on me for an NHL spot. When I came to the Flyers training camp in 1994, we had a new system being installed, and lots of competition for spots. Garry Galley, Dmitri Yushkevich (who ended up being my primary defense partner that year) and recently acquired Kevin Haller had spots locked up. The rest was up for grabs.

My competition included former first-round pick Jason Bowen (who had played 56 games for the Flyers the previous year), Stew Malgunas (67 games with the Flyers in 1993-94), rugged blueliner Ryan McGill, and depth veteran defensemen Jeff Finley and Rob Zettler. Others in camp included young offensive defenseman Milos Holan, former Detroit second-round pick Bob Wilkie, offseason signing Shawn Anderson (who, once upon a time, was the fifth overall pick of the NHL Draft), prospect defenseman Aris Brimanis and Dan Kordic. At the time, Kords was in the process of being switched from defense (where he first broke into the NHL with the Flyers) to wing, but also some reps on D at camp.

That's a whole lot of bodies in camp. A lot of these guys were pretty big, too, but I was the tallest at 6-foot-5. My biggest edge, as I saw it, was that I was an exceptionally good skater at the time for someone my size.

Lo and behold, on the first day of NHL camp, general manager Bob Clarke was watching us from overhead. Who did Murph match me up against in the battle drills? None other than Eric Lindros.

It didn't take a psychology degree to figure out what was going on. Right off the bat, they wanted to put me to the test against one of the biggest, baddest, and most skilled players in the world. Was I nervous? Maybe, but it was more the good kind of nerves; the kind that gets the adrenaline pumping and the competitive juices flowing. *Here we go*, I thought. Let's do it. I knew in that moment I'd have to absorb some punishment and stand in against one of the physically strongest players I'd ever face. Lindros didn't take it easy on me, nor would I have wanted him to. It was as physical a battle as I had on a rink at any point in my life until then. I was able to hold off Eric and eventually push him into the boards. Ultimately, I also came out with the puck.

It was after that that Murph and Clarkie said it was like having hit a home run for the organization to be able to find a guy who's able to get in a close-quarters battle and handle a player of Lindros's stature and ability.

People have asked me a lot over the years why I matched up so well against Jaromir Jágr. It was because Jags' game was based on his combination of lower-body strength and skill. I was one of the few players he couldn't muscle his way around. Keep a tight gap on him, and we were on equal footing strength wise. Give him time and space to come in full stride on a rush, and he'd make anyone— myself included—look foolish. It was similar with Lindros.

I didn't dominate Eric but I also didn't get manhandled. I also played pretty well in other situations during the preseason. It helped springboard me to the front of the young rookie defense corps that year who was trying to make the team and at that point there was no looking back for me.

I was told that I'd made the big team's opening night roster. Then the lockout came and screwed everything up. There was no NHL hockey all fall. Knowing that I needed game action to stay sharp, the Flyer sent me to Hershey.

What was Hershey like? Well, I was used to small-town life, having spent three years at Northwood Prep in Lake Placid, so it was no big deal as far as lifestyle adjustments were concerned. And everyone knew this was going to be temporary, that the NHL would resume operations at some point.

So I went down to Hershey, where I had played six games the season before, after the Olympics had ended. I wound up playing 34 games for the Bears, keeping a close eye on the news outlets for when the NHL might be open for play again.

I was averaging about a point every two games and I enjoyed my time down there. Former NHL assistant coach Jay Leach was Hershey's head coach, and he was nothing short of a maniac. I saw him hit a player in the head five times. That was Russian defenseman Vladislav Bulin, who had been drafted by the Flyers in 1992. Jay was trying to get him to do something and "Bulie" just couldn't understand him. "You suck," Leach bellowed. "Here's why you suck. Because you don't get it."

I'm thinking to myself, *Holy crap, man!* If that happened nowadays, there would be a firestorm you wouldn't believe. Coaches nowadays lose their jobs if stories go public about them being physically abusive to players. Even back in '94 this was really over-the-top stuff...a coach deliberately punching a player in the back of the head as he's trying to skate away. It was one of the most embarrassing things I've ever seen a player have to go through. Besides, he had been my roommate the summer before and we had come such a long way together. I felt really bad for him.

Then there was the story of the Hershey Bear mascot, Coco. I watched him get intimate with a woman on the team's training table after a night out at a bar. Actually, on that particular night it was one of the Bears' players who'd donned the Coco costume. It was one of the funniest damn things I've seen in my life.

The lockout finally ended in January and the NHL decided to play a 48-game schedule. Players had gotten back to their homes on a Sunday and then got called back to their teams. I was hoping to get called back soon because I felt like I had earned my spot, I had earned my stripes.

Besides, I was looking forward to moving to the big city, Philadelphia. I didn't have a great time in the minors as a player. The two or three weeks leading up to when the lockout ended, I was playing my best hockey. I was playing on my off side, the right, but still making my playing partners look good. It was a little bit more scrambly down there in the AHL and you hear that all the time. You're coming around the net and you're expecting your winger there, like John LeClair would be in the NHL, right there like clockwork. Here, sometime wingers wouldn't be in place, or the center wouldn't lend support that you needed.

So that's I why I believe I was better suited for the NHL game: because it was structured, and the skill level was higher. For me, it made the game a lot easier to play. I probably wasn't a great minor league player but that changed in the NHL.

I hoped the Flyers hadn't forgotten my performance in training camp. That was important to me that they remembered my capabilities. I figured they did. They still more or less had the same defensemen they had the previous year. There wasn't much top-level depth. Apart from adding Kevin Haller in an offseason trade with Montreal, the Flyers largely opened the season with the same cast of defensemen from the previous year. Garry Galley was a proven NHLer. Yushkevich was still young but clearly belonged. The rest of the cast included guys like Ryan McGill (tough as nails and a great teammate), depth defenseman Rob Zettler, and injury-riddled Stew Malgunas.

A few days went by, and I still had not gotten the call. It bothered me because I had made the team and was playing well in Hershey. It turns out all the guys were just getting ready. I remember coming back after a practice in Hershey to my apartment, which was just between the ones belonging to Dan Kordic and Neil Little.

The phone rang at 4:45 PM and I was half-asleep from an afternoon nap. It was Jay Leach on the line: "Hey, it's Coach Jay. You're going up to the big team. Good luck, pack your bags. If I were you, I'd plan to be there for a while. Good luck. We're going to miss you, but you've earned your chance."

I thought I was dreaming. I pushed the button on the answering machine to listen to the message and make sure it really happened. A tingly feeling was coming over me, things got real really quick. It hadn't taken four or five months to get my first NHL experience. The schedule came out and our first game was in a little over a week, an afternoon game against the Quebec Nordiques.

I went up to practice the next day and was welcomed with open arms. The guys were happy to have me back. They all remembered me from training camp. I believe I had left a positive impression. I was a good player in the development stage but also a bit of a character in the locker room. That helped build confidence about who I was and believing in myself.

Again, those were things I didn't necessarily have in my teens but did now. What an opportunity, what an experience. The Flyers coach, Terry Murray, and so many players came up to me and offered assistance. The other players who came up were Yanick Dupré and Patrik Juhlin. We practiced for a few days, and then it was go time. For me, I managed to get into two practices. I was at a hotel in Voorhees, New Jersey, near the Flyers' practice facility at the time, the Coliseum.

As for living quarters, after my first game, the assistant general manager John Blackwell told me I could get an apartment because I wasn't going anywhere. That's when you really know you've made it. It's not when you play in the league, it's when the team tells you to move out of the hotel and get an apartment. It's probably the sweetest music to your ears because you know you're going to be there for quite some time. It also affirmed that commitment to you, that you're not going to be moving back and forth with the minors.

It was a unique time for me. Everything had come together. Soon I was driving over to Philadelphia for that first game. I had a cell phone, a 1995 deluxe, and I was driving over the Walt Whitman Bridge when I called my mom and dad. I said, "We've climbed to the top of the mountain." Every step of my hockey life had led to the top of Mount Everest. Before I stepped onto the ice against superstars like Joe Sakic, all the things through the years that had gotten me here were on my mind. I looked back at all the pain that had come with it. Here it was, about to end. Everything I had wanted in my life was about to happen in the next few hours.

My dad was so proud. He said, "You did this." And I did. I got there. I worked, I stayed diligent, stayed true to myself, and was preparing for my first NHL game. What a feeling it was.

That opening game didn't go as planned. Even though our home building, then named the CoreStates Spectrum, was packed with loud, excited fans, we lost to the Nordiques 3–1. I finished a plus-1, so from a personal standpoint, it wasn't a total loss.

Coming off the bridge, after talking to my folks, I proceeded to drive past the Spectrum for the first time. There were like three or four thousand people out front trying to get tickets. Hockey was back and there was optimism the Flyers would end a franchise-record five-year drought without a playoff appearance.

I was in awe as I passed the Rocky statue. Talk about visions of grandeur. That movie was about the ultimate underdog. Nobody knew who I was, so I guess I could relate to that rags-to-somewhat-riches story. Most people were enamored at the time by Lindros, especially from what I had seen in training camp a few months before. In many ways, he did not have a very normal existence. Everybody wanted a piece of him. By some accounts, he probably didn't help himself either by being standoffish. But he did get hounded like I had never seen anyone get hounded in my life. I did feel bad for him for that.

That's why the fan base was so into the Flyers back then. This was the dawn of an era, supposedly a championship era. I don't know if I realized it at the time that day when I went to the game, but I certainly realize it now—that Lindros was a generational talent who was supposed to deliver the Stanley Cup, or maybe multiple Stanley Cups, to the city of Philadelphia. I will admit, initially I thought he was going to be our ticket to the Promised Land, to hoisting that silver cup. But later I realized it was never meant to be with this guy.

But that did not diminish the fact Lindros was a real superstar. People in Philly were really caught up with his talent, his looks, his nastiness on the ice. He was the total package. At 22, he was something to reckon with.

That first game was decided on a goal by Owen Nolan, and I thought the whole experience was pretty cool. It was a matchup between two of the league's powerhouses, and the Nordiques would go on to win the Stanley Cup in 1996 (after moving to Colorado and becoming the Avalanche). It was probably no accident the NHL wanted that marquee matchup to kick off the season. Toss in the fact that Lindros' refusal to play for Quebec back in 1991, forcing a trade to the Flyers, was probably still simmering beneath the surface.

Having lost to the Nordiques, we headed to Boston for the first road game of the season. I got to the hotel, grabbed my key, went up to the room, saw two beds, and really didn't know what was going on with the rooming situation. In walked Dave Brown, already one of the baddest dudes in the NHL. I knew Dave pretty well: we had gone through karate sessions the previous summer. He had taken me under his wing. He was into doing the right thing, being a leader, and being a good veteran for a younger player. I knew his reputation as being one of toughest guys ever to set foot in the National Hockey League.

We went into the room in Boston, and I asked him if he had a preference for which bed. I was a rookie, so I was eager to please. Brownie, who looked and sounded like a professor off the ice but was a killer on it, looked over at me—not knowing anything or if I had a girlfriend or whatnot—and said in this high-pitched voice, "Hey, I got just one rule. If you ever pick up a girl, don't you ever bring her back to this room. Ever!"

I'm looking at him going, okay, that's fine. Then I got up the nerve to ask him how come?

He said, "Because I'm not bringing home anything to my wife. I've seen shit jump from one bed to another multiple times in my career, and I ain't bringing something home from your bed to my wife!" I looked at him and it's Dave Brown. What else could I say but, "You got it, buddy." I did laugh. I didn't know what else to say. Those were the ground rules with Dave Brown. I sure as hell was not going to break those. He was easy to room with.

I will say one thing about Brownie: he played in Edmonton for a period of time in his career and won a Stanley Cup there. One of the craziest obscure facts about him is he had to sleep with the room curtains open for afternoon snoozes on game day. I thought it was insane. I said, "Why do you want the blinds open? I'm having a hard time getting to sleep with all the light in here." He replied, "It's so dark in Edmonton that you take any amount of daylight you can get." It was dark too early in the winter so he had to sleep with the curtains open to get more daylight in. Thank God I never played for Edmonton after I heard that story. That was Brownie in a nutshell, straight to the point.

We played Boston the next night and we lost again. But I came out of the weekend a plus-2 (have I mentioned I hardly ever keep track of personal stats?). We had two losses and nothing to feel good about. During the game, Don Sweeney skated by our bench after a big hit on one of our players and nobody said anything. After the game, Murray came in and said we had to start acting like a team. He mentioned Sweeney skating by our bench and nobody saying a word to him. It turned out to be wakeup call for us. In a lot of ways, it was a changing of the guard. The five previous seasons the Flyers had been a non-playoff team, a non-factor. That messaging had come from new GM Bob Clarke down to Murray and our new leadership group, with Lindros as captain.

That said, we wanted to be a tougher team. Not a bunch of guys to be pushed around, like the teams of the past had been when they had not gotten to the playoffs. Those years had been a big disappointment for a very proud franchise—one proudly owned by Ed Snider, certainly no shrinking violet himself. Thus, it was time for change and new pride in being a Flyer. It was an especially big opportunity for me, a big defenseman who could skate. I was already proud to be on the Flyers and I had only been there for two games. I loved the direction that things were going. It was a really good group of guys with just the right ratio of veterans. Craig MacTavish was there, a Cup winner with Edmonton, and Joel Otto, a champion in 1989 with Calgary. They were proven winners. I felt the foundation was set. We were ready to move forward, but they were not going to with guys like me and Garry Galley. We were good players, but they couldn't hitch their wagon to young players like us.

My first partner was Dmitri Yushkevich, and I loved playing with him. He was a tough Russian who played his ass off. But we needed something that was going to kind of fuel a lot of what we were doing. What was going to change the look of the Flyers? Even though we had Lindros, Renberg, and Brent Fedyk (who had a couple good years on that Crazy Eights line with Eric and Mark Recchi) that wasn't enough. I felt something was missing that was going to get us to championship caliber. Ron Hextall was the goalie and we used to drive to games together. I loved him as a teammate. But I think Clarke and Murray knew something was missing from that team and that was a number one defenseman. We needed a guy who was going to be a settler. We weren't sure when that was going to happen or how. We knew we could use an extra scorer and a defenseman, and Clarke had a plan. And it ended up being, in my mind, the greatest trade in Flyers history with the acquisition of Éric Desjardins and John LeClair.

We got to March and Clarke told us if we beat the Devils and Rangers over a four-day span, he would spring for a team trip to Hilton Head, South Carolina. Then we went out and beat the Stanley Cup–defending champion Rangers and the conference runner-up from the year before, the Devils. We went down south for a weekend of golf and relaxation. It was probably the beginning of a time period when I saw some of the funniest stuff I had ever seen.

The trip had some pretty comical people on it, including veteran Mark Lamb, who I thought was hilarious. The other acquisition we got during this timeframe was defenseman Karl Dykhuis from Chicago. Everybody who followed the Flyers knew he was a redhead, very fair-skinned. "Dyker" probably shouldn't have spent as much time in the sun as perhaps some of the rest of us did.

On this trip, it wasn't just two rounds of golf. It was a free-for-all alcohol festival. It was something else. Well, Dykhuis was out on the boat one day and everyone was having a great time, riding Jet Skis and so forth. Some guys were fishing, and some were just out drinking beers on boats. It was really a three-day getaway that we had time in the schedule to enjoy. I thought Clarke was trying to let the players know that hey, we like what we have going on here and want you to be rewarded for some of the things that are coming your way. At the time, those were some of the building blocks of that team, the core of that team being together for quite a while. He saw that vision and that's why he wanted that trip to happen. He was always into motivating stuff like that.

Lo and behold, we got down there and by the second day we noticed Karl was getting pretty red. MacTavish and Lamb were there, as was another veteran, Kevin Dineen, whom I really admired. Kevin told Karl, "Look, you better get like a 60 sunscreen on."

Karl said, "I already took care of it. I put the 30 on twice!"

Well, we all loved Karl, but we also realized he wasn't the brightest bulb in the lamp store. When it came to life skills, he was not exactly Mr. Manners, either. He was actually serious when he said he put the SPF 30 on twice to make it a 60.

Now here comes my part in all this tomfoolery. I had gone out and bought this portable mini sound system. It was '95, and I wanted to get all high-tech and everything. At home, I had a 40-inch TV and it probably weighed six hundred pounds. This little Bose system cost me about two grand, and I loved it. Back in Jersey, Dykhuis decided he was going to rent an apartment right across from me at the Main Street complex in Voorhees. He was like 50 feet away. He went out and bought the same Bose system. Ironically, both units were set up on the same infrared system, so I could control Karl's receiver on his Bose system from my apartment. As the year went on, I would come out of a bar at two or three in the morning after a game (if we had the next day off) and light up Dykhuis' apartment. I would shut my light off and turn up his volume full blast. His lights would go on and I would be cackling in the dark. This went on for months, every third night.

Finally, one day Dyker came into the locker room with a look of complete defeat. On this day, after the Garry Galley trade to

Buffalo for Petr Svoboda, Dyker walked in and all the defensemen are gathered in a corner. He said, "I think there might be a ghost living in my apartment." We went on like this for another two weeks. It was really funny. I kept telling the guys, "How could he not know that I'm doing it? Who else could be doing it?"

One night at 4:00 AM—during the days when drinking was actually fun and not the burden it would become on me—I turned up the volume again. Dykhuis showed up to the rink white as a ghost. After a good laugh, we had to tell him it was "Bundy" (my nickname) who'd been turning the sound on and off for the last two months. He couldn't decide whether to believe us or not. At first, it seemed like he didn't think it was possible I could do something like that.

Toward the end of his time here, he used to say that I teased him all the time. When Keith Jones got traded here, one day Karl walked to the back of the bus and plunked down next to him, which was a no-no because veterans are supposed to have an open seat next to them. Jonesy looked at him and said, "What are you doin'?" Meanwhile, I was sitting in the middle of the bus because I'm in the middle of my career. Jonesy has been in the league longer than any of us.

But Karl said, "I have to come back here because the team sports psychologist told me not to sit in front of Bundy because that gives him access to me. He'll see me and start giving it to me."

Jonesy said, "I understand. Now get the hell out of here!" Dyker wound up back at the front of the bus and the stories just kept on coming.

CHAPTER 11

A Trade to End All Trades

I HAD BARELY BEEN A FLYER in February 1995, but even just a handful of games had shown me this team wasn't going all that far as it was presently constituted.

The team was coming off a franchise record five straight years without making the playoffs, and everything seemed to be in flux. General manager Russ Farwell and head coach Terry Simpson had been relieved of their duties and Bob Clarke had been brought back for his second go as GM of the Flyers. In turn, he hired former Philadelphia defenseman Terry Murray to coach the team.

After a relatively slow start, it became apparent something had to change, and when it happened, boy did it ever. The National Hockey League schedule was starting late that season due to the labor lockout. During the down time, there were rumors the Flyers were looking to make a trade with the Montreal Canadiens for some defensive help. Speculation centered on Mathieu Schneider.

We knew at the time that Clarke was trying to put his stamp on the team somehow. Even though we had a couple bodies who were new, like me, we might not have been quite as good as some predicted us to be. We had the Swedish kid, Juhlin, who was highly touted at the time—he was one of Sweden's top performers at the 1994 Olympics and expectations were that he'd make the same sort of immediate impact in the NHL that Mikael Renberg did as a rookie—but frankly not as good as advertised under the Farwell regime.

Juhlin was a nice guy. His skills were obvious. But he was scared about venturing into the high-traffic areas of the ice where most goals are scored and the physical price is heavy. He was a good skater but not a pure speedster like a Pavel Bure who score regularly off the rush. He was responsible defensively but not a shutdown forward. So what we ended up with was one of the many players out there who could have success on the big rink in Europe and probably could be an AHL All-Star because he was more talented than the majority of players at that level, but who just another guy at the NHL level.

Renberg, on the other hand, fit right in and seemed to be developing into an NHL star. Another great guy off the ice. A two-way winger with good size and strength, good speed, and ability to score or set up a player. As a rookie, he soon knocked Fedyk off the top line and the trio of Renberg (on left wing), Lindros, and Recchi was a force to be reckoned with. Nowadays, I don't think many people realize just how good Mikael was his first three seasons in the NHL before injuries took him down a couple pegs. He wasn't just a good complementary player for Lindros, Recchi, and later LeClair. He was the real deal for a few years.

Honestly, though, we still weren't good enough as a team. Not until the blockbuster trade with Montreal. Clearly, in hindsight, that trade set the Flyers up as a contender for the next decade. Oddly enough, right up until the trade went down, all the rumors centered around the Flyers trying to acquire Mathieu Schneider—not Eric Desjardins—from the Habs.

But I think when you boil it down, Schneider might have been a nice player, but he wasn't Éric Desjardins by any stretch. So, the trade happened: Desjardins, John LeClair, and winger Gilbert Dionne to the Flyers for Recchi, who had just set the team record a couple years back for points in a season with 123. It ended up being a blockbuster.

When I first heard the deal had gone down, I was like, *Wow*. I couldn't believe that Recchs was gone. It was a surprise to me in many ways. He was a great, great guy. I loved him since training camp. He made everybody feel like a great teammate. But looking at it the other way, we were getting an excellent all-around defenseman in Desjardins and that was our team's biggest need.

I had played against LeClair in college when he was at the University of Vermont. Then I kind of lost track of him in the NHL after he had moved up to the pros. I knew he was a third-line center for the Habs who could also play left wing if asked. I knew he'd scored two overtime goals for the Canadiens in their win over the Los Angeles Kings in the 1993 Stanley Cup Finals—but I don't think anyone—Clarke, Murray, or even Johnny himself—realized that the Flyers had just acquired someone who'd immediately become one of the NHL's most prolific goal-scoring wingers of his era.

Desjardins, LeClair, and Dionne all had recent Stanley Cup rings, though, and that's never a bad thing to add to a team that's trying to learn how to win. Believe it or not, there were people back in 1993-94 who thought Gilbert (the younger brother of Hall of Famer Marcel Dionne) might be a better player than Pavel Bure. Well, he wasn't. It really wasn't a fair comparison, I don't think, ever for Gilbert. He was a good locker room guy and grew up in the shadow of his brother. Gilbert made an immediate splash as a good rookie in Montreal. He was never going to be a superstar. But he was a good player in his own right and a great dude to be around: fantastic sense of humor, and no ego. Even though it was for a short period of time, I enjoyed him very much as a Flyers teammate.

At first, we really thought the trade was going to be for Schneider. Then we found out it was LeClair, Desjardins, and Dionne for Recchi. At the time, I don't think people were all that enamored with the deal. They thought of Recchi as a point-producing machine. Mark was a proven 100-point scorer in the prime of his career. People were wondering, *What did the Flyers really get here?* The Flyers were skewered on the local radio talk shows and some of the newspaper beat-guys wondered if Philly had actually improved itself.

Just from talking with people around the club and putting my ear to the ground, I think the Flyers believed they'd be getting a No. 2 caliber defenseman in Rico and a third-line caliber guy in LeClair who might help create some space for linemates, because he was a tenacious forechecker and a big, strong guy who was hard to take off the puck. No one touted his slapshot (which flirted with 100 m.p.h.) or his uncanny ability to score on rebounds, deflections, and scrambles. Somehow, even playing with a stick blade that looked more like a shovel, he managed to handle and pass the puck. These were all things we discovered for ourselves after Johnny got here.

Recchi went to Montreal and had some success but when you look at it and some of the great moves other GMs have made, like with what Keith Allen did over the years, when you boil down that trade, I think it changed the fortunes of the hockey team for a decade. It made Lindros a better player, it made Renberg better after LeClair was moved to left wing, and the Legion of Doom line was created.

The defense was suddenly settled down by the addition of just one guy: Rico. For the remainder of 1995 and most of the 1995-96 season, Desjardins was paired with Kevin Haller, another former Canadien. Haller was a speedster on his skates. A religious and soft-spoken sort off the ice, Kevin had a nasty streak on the ice. He was no stranger to delivering two-handers with his stick, and he had a running battle on the ice with Mark Messier in particular. The new players formed an interesting dynamic. Those guys came in humble, ready to work. I remember the first game Rico played and thinking to myself while watching from the bench that he was okay. That he was a solid player, but it was just his first game. He had been playing in Montreal for a few years, and I was just getting started in the NHL.

As it turned out, Desjardins was everything he had been in Montreal and more in his career. As I got to know him, the person and the player, I always felt there was a pull toward him for me. I even thought in my first year it made sense pairing us together, but coach Murray would've told you I wasn't ready and he would've been right. You had to earn your right to go up and play with a guy like that. That was my goal. But I always thought we would be a good pair right away.

He clearly made me a better player, but you know what? When you talk to Eric about it, I was as important to his career as he was to mine. You can say what you want, but he will tell you the same thing. I was blessed that Clarke made that trade. It ended up with Desjardins being right up there with Mark Howe as the greatest defensemen in Flyers history.

When we did finally get put together, it worked like I knew it would. At some point, we probably were the NHL's best defense penalty killing tandem. A lot of the credit for that goes to Desjardins but I feel like I can take a bow, too. I'm not in the Flyers Hall of Fame. I have neither the accolades nor the goals scored of Desjardins, but I played a role in our effectiveness. When he said to me that I was crucial to his success, that was the best compliment you could ever have. It validated who I was. I wasn't just an afterthought. When someone like Rico, who is mentioned in the same sentence with Howe, talked about me in that light and said those things about me.... He once told me I was the best partner he ever had, and I made his career as good as he made mine.

Those guys came in and within two weeks the impact was immediately felt. Remember, it was just going to be a 48-game season, so every game seemed twice as important as teams raced to catch a playoff spot. Things quickly clicked for us. We transformed from a good, rising team into a really good team almost overnight. Those two major acquisitions, plus Dionne's positive personality, made a big difference. And Dionne added some depth to our lineup.

You can say what you want about trades like the one that brought Lindros here, but this was a trade that ranks right at the top in team history. LeClair was probably a lot more than people expected. He produced three 50-goal seasons and has borderline Hockey Hall of Fame credentials. Desjardins ranks no lower than No. 2 among all Flyer defensemen. Those were important moves and moves that Clarke made that were indicative of his style as a GM. He was always interested in the betterment of the hockey team. It was not about him trying to get players that were neither here nor there. It was about him trying to fit the right pieces together to build a very solid club.

Bob liked personalities and Johnny had a big personality. I know this because he was my roommate for almost a decade. And Rico was my partner for a decade. So, all other stuff put to the side, that's amazing. When you think about the combined years with those two that affected my life, it did so about as much as you could imagine.

You had the dynamic on the ice and off it. Johnny and I sort of had the same lighthearted approach at the rink and away from it. Éric was the consummate professional, both on and off the ice. I have the utmost respect for him and the way he handles himself. I watch people like Éric Desjardins and Rod Brind'Amour to see how they comport themselves. They are the players every GM wants and would want his players to be like. I certainly appreciated that.

I can't imagine what my career would have been like without them.

CHAPTER 12

Behind the 88 Ball

WHEN YOU'RE A YOUNG PLAYER in the National Hockey League on a team that's having a lot of success, it's easy to feel like the sky is the limit. I certainly felt that way the first two years of my NHL career.

Following the big trade that brought Eric Desjardins and John LeClair to the Flyers, our team never looked back. Bob Clarke made some additional, smaller moves that also benefited the team. For example, he acquired Petr Svoboda—a rock-solid defenseman—from Buffalo in the latter part of the season. Terry Murray paired Petr with Karl Dykhuis, and Petr helped provide stability to the duo. Suddenly, we had three good pairings that thrived together: Rico and Kevin Haller, Dimitry Yushkevich and me, plus Petr and Dyker.

As the season went along, I started thinking to myself that our team had barely scratched the surface; *Holy hell, we can beat anybody.* After starting out 3–7–1 through the first 11 games of the 48-game schedule—something that could have been fatal in such a short season—we rocketed up the standings and won first place in the Atlantic Division.

The Legion of Doom was quite a sight to see. They cycled the puck at will and scored in bunches. Meanwhile, Rod Brind'Amour kept other clubs from focusing all their efforts on stopping the Lindros line. Roddy's wingers were inconsistent, but he was very reliable.

Eric Lindros had a relatively injury-free season, except for a late season eye injury that kept him out of the first three games of the playoffs. He went on to win the Hart Trophy as the NHL's MVP; no one expected it to be the only time he'd ever win it. LeClair was named to the NHL All-Star Team as 1st Team left wing and Mikael Renberg was very narrowly edged out by Calgary's Theoren Fleury for 2nd Team right wing.

For myself, I felt like I was rewarding the faith the Flyers showed in me. I was named to the NHL's All-Rookie Team—something that I still get teased about in a good-natured way ("must have been a lousy year for rookies if Bundy made the All-Rookie Team!") and rarely mention unless I'm asked about it. I knew I still had a lot to learn about the NHL but, as a guy who was never going to put up a lot of points at the game's top level (I topped out at 24 points), it was nice to get leaguewide recognition as one of the first-year players helping his team.

Speaking of putting up points, when you don't score a lot of goals, you tend to remember the ones you do get. My first career NHL goal was scored on February 13, 1995; a power play goal in a 5–3 win over Washington. The game was best known for a big fight late in the second period that started between Ron Hextall and Rob Pearson, with various combatants piling up and a couple tumbling through the open Zamboni gate. That clip still makes the rounds on YouTube. I still get a chuckle when legendary Flyers announcer Gene Hart shouts gleefully, "We've got our first brouhaha!"

On April 2, we played the defending Stanley Cup champion Rangers on a nationally televised afternoon game from the Spectrum. In a game we won, 4–2, I scored a goal on a shot from the point. What was funny about this one was that Fox TV was spotlighting its various broadcasting "innovations": both the good ones like their in-the-net camera (which they used on replays of my goal, which was later reused on commercials for upcoming broadcasts) and the awful ones like those stupid "battling robots" animations. At least they didn't have that glowing puck gimmick quite yet. What a joke that thing was!

In the playoffs, we dismantled Buffalo in five games and then really became the talk of the NHL when we swept the Rangers in four. Suddenly, after five years out of the playoffs, we were proclaimed the favorite to beat New Jersey in the Eastern Conference Final and advance to the Cup Final. Detroit was the favorite to emerge from the West.

We went into that New Jersey series with sky-high confidence, maybe even almost cockiness. We had respect for what the Devils could do. They'd just come up one win short of the Cup Final the previous year, had an emerging superstar young goalie in Martin Brodeur, and Jacques Lemaire had installed a neutral zone trapping system that was ultra-frustrating to play against. But we had begun to believe our team was unstoppable.

Before we knew what hit us, we found ourselves trailing the Devils, two games to zero, after they beat us twice at the Spectrum. They trapped the hell of us. Scott Stevens got under Lindros' skin and took him off his game. We were collectively shut down in Game 1 in a 4–1 loss. It wasn't one of my better games, either. Game 2 started out well enough, with goals by Lindros and Renberg staking us to an early lead. But the Devils battled back to get the game tied, 2–2, by the first intermission. New Jersey then went on to control the rest of the game. We lost, 5–2, and were held to 20 shots.

Somehow, we managed to win the next two games in New Jersey, although we were pretty much outplayed in both games. In Game 3, we trailed in the third period before Brind'Amour forced overtime and then Lindros took a pass from Renberg and wired home a shot past Brodeur for a 3–2 win. In Game 4, we got outshot by a 34–19 margin but a go-ahead goal by Renny and a third period shorthanded goal by Brind'Amour put us in the driver's seat. Desjardins and LeClair connected for some added insurance. New Jersey's "Crash Line" got one of the goals back late in the third period, but we held on to win, by a 4–2 final score.

Through the first four games, the visiting team had won every time. Even so, we knew that we needed to take Game 5 at home to take control of the series. This one turned out to be a total heartbreaker. Two goals by Kevin Dineen got the game tied at

2–2 after we twice trailed by one goal, and then the game became up-for-grabs. Overtime seemed almost inevitable until, with 45 seconds left in regulation, Claude Lemieux beat Hextall on an unscreened slapshot from a stride inside the blueline. It was a blast of a shot but a save that NHL goalies would normally make 99 times out of 100. This was the one that went in. We lost, 3–2.

I won't lie. It was a total gut punch. Given the circumstances, it would have stung no matter how the puck went in or who scored it for New Jersey. However, the fact that the game was decided on a clear-sighted side angle shot from that much distance—and that it was one of the NHL's most hated players who scored it—added insult to injury.

Game 6 was almost a carbon copy of Game 2, except that the game was played in the Meadowlands rather than the Spectrum. We took an early lead—this time courtesy of a goal by fourth-liner Jim Montgomery—but the Devils shrugged it off and proceeded to take total control of the game as we got more and more frustrated at our inability to navigate the puck past the red line or get more than one-and-done chances on the few occasions when we did get into the attack zone with puck possession. We'd dump the puck in but couldn't get a forecheck going because Brodeur would gather it and outlet it tape-to-tape to a forward while the Jersey defensemen clutched and grabbed our would-be first forechecker. Rinse, wash, repeat.

Stevens knew he had Lindros right where he wanted him. At one juncture, a frustrated Lindros elbowed Stevens in the face as New Jersey broke out of their defensive zone. Stevens took a seat on the ice and had a trickle of blood running down his face but started derisively laughing at Eric, knowing that he'd taken 88 completely off his game.

By midway in the third period, we knew we were cooked. A late goal by Renberg assisted by Lindros and LeClair meant that we only lost 4–2 instead of 4-1. Who cares? We were held to 16 frigging shots for the entire game with the season on the line.

In hindsight, I don't think the Flyers ever again had quite the same mojo for the rest of the Lindros era. It wasn't only Eric's fault—there's a whole team on the ice—but the Devils showed three things over the course of the series.

First, they showed that Lindros and his line could be contained in big games even if they couldn't be totally shut down. Second, they showed that if you contained the Legion of Doom line, there weren't enough Flyers forwards beyond Brind'Amour who could pick up the slack. Lastly, they showed that if you put enough rubber at Hextall, a seemingly stoppable puck or two might slip through at a key juncture of the game.

This three-pronged reality of that 1995 Eastern Conference Final series became the league-wide blueprint for playing against the Flyers. The Devils got in our heads and stayed there for many years. To make things worse, the same basic script played itself out at some point in the playoffs each and every year that followed.

The Florida Panthers, another neutral zone trapping team, did it to us in a dreadful second round series in 1996 that still pisses me off to this day. We had no business losing that series, but we did, in six.

It was horrible hockey. Under the rules of the time, teams could change lines after committing an icing. There was also no automatic delay of game penalty for flipping the puck over the glass from the defensive zone (except if done by the goalie). It was up to the discretion of the refs to call delay of game if a defender put the puck over the glass deliberately, but it was rarely called. Add to that the fact that Florida did way more clutching and grabbing than even the Devils. Last but not least, goalie John Vanbiesbrouck covered the puck for stoppages every time he had the opportunity to do so.

The Panthers effectively slowed games to a crawl and kept us from developing any sort of sustained rhythm. They did the same thing to the Penguins in the Eastern Conference Final and got a trip to the Cup Final out of it.

Truthfully, though, we had no one but ourselves to blame. We fell into the all the same issues that did us in against the Devils. This time around, we led the series, two games to one, then lost two in a row in overtime. From Game 4 onward, we played a little worse each game than we did the game before. Hexy was the main reason Game 5 even got to double overtime because we could scarcely complete passes and we lost all semblance of composure. We got our asses kicked in Game 6, and that was the end of it.

During the 1995–96 regular season, we finished with the top record in the Eastern Conference and went into the play-offs as the No. 1 seed. Lindros, who had a career-best 115 points and 47 goals despite missing nine games due to injuries, did not repeat as the Hart Trophy winner but was a finalist again. LeClair notched his first of three straight 50-goal seasons.

Renberg, meanwhile, suffered what today would be deemed a "sports hernia." It was diagnosed during training camp and he underwent surgery. Two weeks later, he was back in the lineup for opening night in Montreal. That would be unthinkable today. Additionally, the surgical mesh procedure that Renny underwent to deal with a lower abdominal tear is nowadays considered largely obsolete.

For a few months, it seemed like Renberg was his normal self on the ice. By mid-December, though, he was not nearly as effective. He soldiered on a few more weeks before he had to be shut down. Without getting too graphic here, Renberg's abdominal muscles tore 100 percent away from the pubic area. He eventually returned part-time to the lineup but had to have half his body numbed in order to play. I don't think he was ever quite as dynamic or explosive again in the NHL as he was for the first two-and-a-half years of his career. He'd eventually get back to being about 75 percent of the player he'd been before; still good but no longer a star-caliber performer on his own.

Clarkie did what he could to strengthen our team. He acquired Pat Falloon (the former second overall pick of the 1991 Draft) in a trade with San Jose. As a stopgap when Rennie went down, Bob picked up Dan Quinn from Ottawa.

Later, Bob took advantage of an offer he couldn't refuse. Mike Keenan and future Hockey Hall of Fame inductee Dale Hawerchuk did not hit it off together at all in St. Louis—Iron

Mike took to trying to humiliate the player as a motivation tactic geared not only toward Ducky but to the entire team. Clarke was able to acquire Hawerchuk in a one-for-one trade for fellow veteran Craig MacTavish.

Craig was a highly respected leader and a still-solid defensive player for us. I'll never forget the night that Mac-T beat the ever-living crap out of Montreal's Marc Bureau after Bureau knocked Petr Svoboda unconscious with one of the dirtiest, sneakiest blind-side elbows I've ever seen. Referee Don Van Massenhoven allowed Bureau to stay in the game, knowing full well that payback was coming. Craig did it the old-fashioned way, dropping the gloves and laying one of the most lopsided ass-whippings I've ever seen in an NHL fight. By the way, Bureau later ended up coming to the Flyers a few years later and he and Petr coexisted okay as teammates. Marc was apologetic and Svoboda accepted it enough to be a pro about playing together on the same side for a couple seasons.

As valuable as Craig was to our team as a guy who had multiple Cup rings and helped lead the team, he was replaceable. First of all, during the offseason, we'd signed perennial Selke Trophy candidate Joel Otto. Joel was the ideal third-line center for our team; big, tough as nails, won a ton of faceoffs and worked very well with linemates Shjon Podein and (midseason addition) Trent Klatt. Secondly, Otto had a Cup ring of his own from his years with Calgary.

First and foremost, though, it's not every day that you can bring in a player of Dale Hawerchuk's caliber. Yes, he was aging.

Yes, he had a bad hip that would end his playing career after the 1996–97 season. No, he wasn't going to be the perennial 100-plus point scorer that he was with the original Winnipeg Jets and into his early years with Buffalo. But he was still one hell of a player.

Dale moved from center to right wing, playing with Lindros and LeClair during the lengthy stretches when Renberg was out. All Dale did was post 20 points in 16 regular season games. Even when Renberg came back for the playoffs and Hawerchuk moved to the second line, Dale was able to put up nine points in 12 playoff games.

I probably should have mentioned this earlier: My rookie season defense partner, Yushkevich, was traded by the Flyers to Toronto before the 1995–96 season. Philly acquired a 1996 first-round pick they used on Lithuanian winger Dainius Zubrus. In my second NHL season, I was primarily paired with veteran Kjell Samuelsson. Big Kjell had come back to Philadelphia as an unrestricted free agent during the 1995 offseason.

Sammy was a very solid D partner. I liked working with him. With players like Otto, Samuelsson and the tank-like Klatt added to our team, we now had the NHL's biggest lineup. Clarke supplemented our size advantage on most teams even further by adding big, sturdy (220-pound) checking center Bob Corkum to center the fourth line after MacTavish was traded. Even with Mac-T being traded to the Blues, we also had a ton of added experience with the aforementioned players plus John Druce coming aboard.

As a matter of fact, if everyone had been healthy, Terry Murray would have had to scratch a couple of capable veterans on a nightly basis. But it rarely works out that everyone is healthy at the same time. That's why Clarke loaded up our roster (no salary cap in those days, remember) for the playoffs.

Unfortunately, we were deeper up front than we were on defense. As long as our main starting six—Desjardins, Haller, Samuelsson, myself, Svoboda, and Dykhuis—were healthy, we could complete with the top teams. But whenever someone went down, there was a drop-off. This was especially true whenever Rico or Svoboda missed time due to injury. Dyker was erratic but generally played well with Petr. When Petr's stabilizing influence was lost, Karl tended to hit one of his stretches where he let one mistake snowball into two or three miscues.

I was still a young player, too, of course. All young players have stretches where they lose their way for a little while and have to snap back. It happens to veterans, too, but by then you can lean on your experience to know that the bad stretch will pass soon enough. You have an identity as a player and you can get back to the basics and work through the rough patch.

In hindsight, I think I had a pretty good second NHL season. I was a plus-16 for the year and I showed that I could kick in a little bit of offense from time to time, even though it was never going to be my forte. I did chip in six goals and 23 points in the regular season.

Actually, I had a two-goal game in a wild 6–5 win in Pittsburgh on December 17, 1995. What I remember about that game was that the bunch of Flyers fans made the trip to the Igloo in Pittsburgh. They really gave it to ex-Flyer Ken Wregget about all the pucks that were going in.

One guy clad in a Flyers jersey yelled, "Wregget! You were a fuckin' sieve in Philly and you're still a fuckin' sieve now! Even Chris Therien has two goals on you already!"

We all heard it from the bench. I cracked up as much as anyone.

As much as fun as the 1995–96 season was during the regular season, there were some things that, in hindsight, should have been red flags. First of all, the Devils still had our number whenever we played them. Secondly, when we had games against fellow Cup contenders, we found ways to lose them. There was one we lost in Chicago early in the season that stands out because it was our first loss. Another one I remember was a home game against the eventual Cup champion Colorado Avalanche (who had just relocated from Quebec) where Peter Forsberg and Joe Sakic were just a little better than the Lindros and Brind'Amour lines and Hexy let in two goals he'd have liked to have back.

We beat Tampa Bay in six games in the first round of the play-offs. Both Tampa wins were in overtime (Games 2 and 3) and a brief deficit in Game 3 was the only time all series that we had to play from behind in a game. In hindsight, it really wasn't all that even of a series from a hockey standpoint. But it was an absolute war from a physical standpoint—lots of fights, questionable to outright dirty hits and stickwork, and a slew of players getting banged up.

How much were we worn down by the first series? Not enough to justify losing to Florida. To this day, that series loss sticks in my craw. It was the Devils series all over again with all the same major reasons for losing except it happened this time against a lesser opponent than New Jersey.

When you win, you win as a team. When you lose, it was because your team collectively needed to be a little bit better. I need to emphasize this. At the same time, when the season is riding on the line, a team needs its best players to be just that. This is especially true when there's a superstar talent on one side.

Yes, I am talking about Eric Lindros. When we lost to the Devils in 1995, Eric had some decent games and big moments. But he never truly took over a game or dominated the series like he did in the sweep of the Rangers.

Same thing in the loss to the Panthers in 1996. Lindros was shut down completely in Game 1. He stepped up in Game 2 with a tremendous game and was also strong in Game 3. The rest of the series, No. 88 was just okay. Again, it's not entirely Lindros' fault that we lost three straight games after winning two of the first three. But the thing that separates the game's very best all-time players from the rest is what they do when all the chips were down.

In 1996–97, Lindros missed a lot of games early on in the season. He then came back to play at a comparable level to the previous two years. In the playoffs, he was a big reason why we dismantled the Penguins, Sabres, and Rangers in the first three rounds.

But when the 1997 Stanley Cup Final rolled around against an outstanding Detroit Red Wings team that I can admit was a better and deeper team than ours, we desperately needed Eric and his linemates to not only duplicate—but exceed—what they'd done over the previous rounds. Instead, Detroit shut Eric down virtually for the duration of a four-goal sweep.

At least the '95 series against the Devils had been highly competitive; win Game 5 and I think we'd have won that damn series. I don't know if we were going to beat Detroit no matter what in '97. But I do know it should have been a hell of a lot tougher and more competitive of a series.

When Terry Murray called it a "choking situation" for our team in between Games 3 and 4, it ruffled a lot of feathers. That was Murph, though. He was blunt and honest. He was also speaking the truth.

Collectively, we choked against Detroit. Our execution was lacking. Our goalies had letdowns that Detroit's Mike Vernon did not have. We found ourselves chasing games. It was a teamwide failure. No one gets totally absolved. That said, while there was plenty of blame to go around, I think the scathing criticism that came down on Lindros for getting nearly blanked in the Final (two assists in Game 1, pointless in Game 2, pointless in Game 3, pointless in Game 4 until a meaningless late third period goal) was accurate and merited. Being a superstar means playing up to the heightened expectations that your role carries.

There were almost two different phases to Eric's Flyers career, at least as I experienced it over the six seasons we were teammates. He and his family always had their squabbles with management and there was inevitably drama any time Lindros got injured, but it was never really a big issue or a major distraction to the other players on the team as I experienced it from 1995 to 1997–98. That was phase one.

I always found Eric to be pretty guarded, even around most of the guys on the team. Not openly a jerk, but a bit distant and a little socially awkward. He had his own thing going on, his own friends. That's okay. On the rare occasions when he actually relaxed a bit, you could see some of the things that made his brother, Brett, an easy teammate to bond with.

Most of the time, though, Eric kept us at arm's length. Worse, he sometimes seemed almost suspicious of the other guys on the team; as if we privately wanted to see him fail. It was never verbalized but you could sense it from the body language.

Whether he felt that way not, I can't say for sure. What I can say is this: With all of that guy's talent, we all knew our own success was tied to his. As such, we all wanted to see him excel for the benefit of our team. We'd all reap the rewards for it.

I do think, deep down, Eric kind of wanted to just be one of the guys when it behooved him to blend in with the rest of us. But he didn't really know how to do it, and I also think in was instilled in him that getting special treatment was an entitlement due to his talent.

But I really don't think he had a bad heart; I think he had good intentions about him. I've seen him show kindness and compassion in his charitable endeavors. I also think he cared about the success of the hockey team and wanted to win as much as the next guy did. But he did not know how to communicate; I don't think he ever really got along with groups of people. I don't think he was ever put in a situation where he was comfortable in groups with his teammates. Again, I played with his brother, Brett, on the Canadian Olympic team. I really liked Brett and I enjoyed my time with him. I got to know his mother and father very well, too.

Ultimately, I don't think the constant involvement of Eric's parents in his career did him any favors. These stories about letters being written to the general manager, his father trying to pick linemates for Eric, those types of things are abhorrent. Nobody wants to deal with them, nobody wants to hear about them. Nobody wants anybody but the coach making decisions and they certainly didn't want outsiders second-guessing a general manager, Clarke, a man who had won a pair of Stanley Cups and the Hart Trophy for the NHL's Most Valuable Player three times. For somebody to treat an NHL organization like it's a double-A minor team is an embarrassment.

My parents sat with a group of parents during a game in Ottawa one night. Eric was poised to break Clarke's team record for most consecutive games (18) with a point. It was the third period and Eric had not yet gotten a point. His mother was screaming in front of an entire fan base that the referee and the entire NHL had conspired with Clarke to make sure that Eric did not break Clarke's record. That insanity was being screamed in a Flyers away game in front of a multitude of other Flyers' parents.

Eric's parents, Carl and Bonnie, constantly wielded a strong influence over him in the professional sense; at the very least, it made for some awkwardness. Even so, for several years, it was nothing we couldn't usually work around as a team.

Phase two was where the rest of the team got sucked into the drama. It started with the collapsed lung in 1998–99 and the various concussion-related absences that Lindros had in 1999–2000. Oddly enough, the 1999–2000 team was the closest-knit squad I was ever part of during my NHL playing career. Sadly, at the same time, the relationship with Eric—within the locker room, as well as with the front office—fell apart beyond repair.

There are a lot of guys over the years with whom I've have had private discussions about Eric Lindros. Sometimes I tried to figure out where Eric was coming from; why he so often seemed like an unhappy person. Eric far too often ended up in the middle of needless dramas that created distractions instead of unity.

I knew Eric was a guy who grew up in situations where he was the best player since he was five years old. He was bigger, stronger, and better than everybody else in every game he played until about the age of 24. Even then, he was still the most dominant player in the NHL for a stretch of time here or there. But the way he played the game with physicality was not something that was going to be a sustainable style for Eric moving into the future.

Now my biggest frustration with Eric was not necessarily with his decision to skate the puck up the middle of the ice with the likes of Darius Kasparaitis or Scott Stevens looking to take his head off his shoulders. It was what had happened while he was the leader of the team as our captain.

John Worley was the Flyers' athletic trainer and when Eric decided to blame John for some of the missteps he considered malpractice, he called John out to the media. He argued that John was not capable of doing his job properly.

I don't know where the line was or wasn't crossed from Eric's standpoint. Because the trainers, or anyone else who was a regular around the team, were well respected and considered teammates. Eric lost the respect of the entire locker room when he did that to Worley. Unfortunately for me, Eric's only supporter, John LeClair, was my roommate. A series of events took place that, to me, ended the most tumultuous relationships between a player and a sports team in Philadelphia history. I know there have been a lot but there's never been a player that's been sold as the anointed one and the one who would earn the Flyers a third trip down Broad Street.

I loved the idea that Eric was here and that historically, generational superstars get the job done. Just take a look back at history: Gordie Howe, Wayne Gretzky, Jean Beliveau, Mario Lemieux, Sidney Crosby. Eric Lindros was a generational star that could literally transform the face of your franchise for years to come. If you look at every player up to the present time, every player hoisted the coveted silver Cup in the air after a grueling playoff competition in the past.

And in the process, he disappointed many former Flyers teammates. After the 1998–99 season, the one in which Eric attacked

John Worley, there was a complete disconnect between Eric and Bob Clarke. Clarke would openly say things to other players about Eric, putting him down. I think by then players knew the Flyers had catered to the demands of Eric and his parents.

I think Bob had felt that time was up. He wasn't giving a perceived prima donna who had attacked team trainers another inch of rope. The lead-up to this and the epic 2000 Eastern Conference Finals was what happened along the way. There were a few things that jumped out at me over the years that started with how Eric was perceived by his teammates. It was amazing.

One year earlier, when Eric got hurt in Nashville and had the collapsed lung, people don't know to this day what exactly happened. You couldn't tell by the way he landed on the ice. And I know behind closed doors there were tons of people who did not believe the case of the Nashville on-ice incident. Nonetheless, Eric had a collapsed lung and after his parents all but accused Clarke and the Philadelphia Flyers of trying to put him on a plane and kill him, it was roommate Keith Jones who found him in the bathtub.

Rooming with Eric probably felt like living with a sasquatch, but, by all accounts, Jonesy ended up getting Eric secured in a local hospital and making sure there were no other dire results than what Eric was already going through.

People were saying that Jonesy saved Eric's life. A few days later, Clarke casually walked by Jonesy's locker with about five guys standing there and said, "Hey Jonesy, let's start worrying about scoring goals and not saving lives."

All the guys standing there burst out laughing. That line has been quoted many times over the years. It gave a pretty good indication of the way and the direction people were starting to think about Eric.

Was Eric an underachiever despite being the Flyers' all-time points-per-game leader? I would have to say yes. It was becoming pretty clear after the 1996–97 playoffs and the blame game that went around that it was never really going to work out long-term. Even I sensed that after we got swept by Detroit in the 1997 Finals and the looming devastation that would come with it, the story was starting to end. I think that was felt by many as well.

It's not a secret that Ed Snider came to despise Eric Lindros. To be blunt, that's why Lindros wasn't inducted by himself into the Flyers Hall of Fame. It was only when it became a dual induction that also included John LeClair that Mr. Snider agreed to the idea. Lindros didn't get into the "big" Hockey Hall of Fame in Toronto or have his No. 88 jersey retired by the Flyers until after Snider's passing.

I can't say I really blame Ed Snider for feeling that way. To have somebody continually come after an organization and continually make demands about player personnel from ownership, it had to wear on a guy who was so proud of the Philadelphia Flyers franchise. I know Snider did not want to see Lindros celebrated. He thought Lindros was the worst thing that ever happened to the Flyers.

I think the part where Lindros lost all of us for good was when he went after Worley. That was truly unacceptable, whether that was Eric's own idea or based off the advice of his parents. No matter how you looked at it, you had a guy making $8.5 million compared to a trainer who was making a tiny fraction of that.

I think a lot of guys were sensitive to that, especially coming from the homes we came from. They were very humble homes; we were raised well and we never wanted to see anybody kicked to the curb over something that could have been worked out behind closed doors. When Eric decided to air his dirty laundry about that, I don't think anybody really knew what was going on, including Flyers management. The whole thing turned out to be a load that you would find at the bottom of a stable.

That truly came to a full blossom in the spring of 2000. There was so much bullshit going on with Eric in the 1999–2000 season that I think guys were tired of it. I knew going into the playoffs we had an outstanding record, we were first in the conference and without Eric we were a very determined team with a tre-mendous leadership group and a great veteran core. I was part of that veteran core. When the 2000 playoffs started, I don't think anyone on our team envisioned the thought that we had a long run in us, or that we could overcome the caliber of teams we had to play.

As things unfolded, we quickly realized we might be a team of destiny. We were on a mission because No. 88 was not part of our team. I believe there were a lot of guys on the team who were relieved by that. Certainly there were some who were discour-aged we didn't have that kind of talent in our lineup. I would say that 90 percent of the guys felt that his presence was more of a detriment to the group than it was an added bonus.

After we got through the first series against Buffalo, we did it with relative ease. Then we got to the Pittsburgh series where we fell down 2–0 at home before going on an epic four-game run where we came back and won two games in Pittsburgh. The high point was that historic five-overtime win over the Penguins at the old Igloo. Empty pizza boxes, destroyed bottles of Pedialyte, IVs, you name it. The locker room floor looked like a cross between the floors of a hospital emergency room and your local Italian restaurant.

When we won that seven-hour game, we knew we were going to win the series. Anybody that was in the way was someone that was simply in the way. Meanwhile, back in South Jersey, all hell was breaking loose. Word seeped out to Pittsburgh that Lindros had suffered another concussion, this time via friendly fire. Or maybe unfriendly. During a practice in Voorhees, spare part Francis Lessard leveled Lindros with a Stevens-like hit and pop! Just like that, another concussion.

There were rumors Lindros was going to try to make a come-back. The rest of us wanted no part of the drama that we knew would come with it. We wanted to just keep playing with the close-knit group we had in place. That brought us to the garden spot of the Garden State known as East Rutherford, New Jersey, home of the New Jersey Devils, the same team which had knocked us out of the 1995 Eastern Conference Finals. Now we were going at it again and that's when the fun—and the unnecessary garbage—started all over again.

It was probably one of the most pathetic things I had ever seen in hockey, and I've seen a lot of pathetic things, including my own disturbing behavior at times, which I say with a little wink and a smile.

After that first loss to the Devils in 2000, we had a players meeting. We knew we could do this. Our core leadership said we can beat this team. They didn't outplay us in Game 1. They just beat us on the scoreboard. Our goalie, Brian Boucher, was very young. We needed to play better in front of him. We did, winning the next three games.

Here's where things proceeded to go off the tracks. Eric decided then that he was good enough to play. A lot of guys were looking at each other like, *Yeah, we didn't see this coming.* We were up 3–1 on our nemesis and all of a sudden now he just happens to be ready to come out and play when we're one win away from the Stanley Cup Finals.

A lot of guys thought this. *Yeah, thanks for nothing. We'll do it ourselves. Where the hell were you the rest of this time?* After Game 5, which was a terrible no-show by our team, the final analysis was our best players really couldn't play after they found out Lindros was coming back. They were consumed with what was going on in the locker room—guys like Desjardins and Recchi. It bothered guys that Lindros was trying to come back and make this all about him. He had done nothing to be a part of this. Nobody wanted anything to do with him at the time.

After the Game 5 stinker, coach Craig Ramsay calls six of us into the locker room: Luke Richardson, Rick Tocchet, Mark Recchi, Craig Berube, Keith Primeau, and myself.

Rammer said, "Guys, what do you want to do? Lindros is probably coming back."

Two of us jumped up and I said, "No! Please keep him the hell out of the lineup, I promise you if this guy comes back, this ride we're on is going to go south."

Everybody concurred. But then it was put to us this way: When you are one win from the Cup Final, do you want Peter White on your fourth line or Eric Lindros? Problem is, I knew Lindros would never settle for sitting on a fourth line.

Lindros did come back in Game 6. We lost, but he played well. He scored one goal, but it was disallowed because time had just expired on the second period. He scored a third period goal that counted. The rest of us scored nothing, and we lost by a 2–1 score. Eric Lindros was not responsible for how the rest of us played.

Then came Game 7. A winnable game that we lost, 2–1. In the first period, Lindros was damn near decapitated on a Scott Stevens hit at the blueline. He was knocked out cold. All the energy was sucked out of the building. Guess what? When you roll the dice enough times, eventually they're going to come up snake-eyes. Our good fortune ran out.

You could call it a *fait accompli* that we would lose that final game, which we did by a 2–1 score in front of our own fans. We pretty much knew that Eric had a concussion, his dad was in the locker room after the first period shortly after the Stevens hit.

Craig Berube and I were sitting on the bench. Chief put his head down and was covering his face with his hand. Then he looked up. "Are you kidding me?" he said.

I almost replied, "I told you this would happen." I refrained. It wasn't the time.

Nobody wanted to see anybody get hurt. But when you decide you want to skate up the middle of the ice with your head down in Game 7 against one of the great predator hitters of all time, you're going to get what you're going to get. This leads me to what I thought happened to Lindros. Outside the numerous injuries which plagued him late in his career, it's my opinion he was healthy enough to make it back for the 2000 playoffs while guys on the team put their blood and sweat into it only to come away empty-handed. The entire 2000 playoffs were for the guys in Philadelphia that deserved a Stanley Cup and it was taken away.

Other guys had won a Stanley Cup with other teams— LeClair and Desjardins with Montreal, Tocchet with Pittsburgh. Never had there been a bigger disappointment than the looks on the guys' faces after that game. That's the best group of guys I've ever played with. It's a shame it had to end like that and a lot of players would echo that sentiment

I also think that Lindros' runaway freight train style of play ultimately hurt him more than it helped. Eric running kids over at 12 years old, at 14 or 18, didn't do him any favors. I saw a kid in Oshawa of the Ontario Hockey League try to take a run at Eric and the kid just fell off him. But the problem was, the level of intimidation that Eric brought to the ice every night, most of us knew was not going to be sustainable for him in later years.

To this day, it still haunts many guys on that Flyer team, certainly me. It's not all Eric Lindros' fault, but a team's best player can't be both that and also his team's biggest hindrance from a unit standpoint. That's how it played out.

If he had been 100 percent committed to hockey, been more open to criticism, worked to stay healthy and tweaked his physicality, he would have been the greatest player to ever lace up a pair of skates. That, in a nutshell, is what I think. And I could have easily lived with some of the minor bullshit along the way.

He needed to adjust his game and he could have. He'd already have created enough room for himself in the league, but Eric never made the necessary adjustments. He could been a great power forward, an elite passer, which he was, and a productive offensive player. He just needed to tweak his game and realize that running over people every night was not going to help his long-term health. Sadly, to this day, he's the one generational player who has never won a Stanley Cup.

CHAPTER 13

On a Tear
with LeClair

OVER THE COURSE OF A LONG PROFESSIONAL CAREER, you do have friends who are closer to you than perhaps some others are. I would say over the years, for me those would boil down to three favorites—Berube, LeClair, and Luke Richardson. They were guys who I enjoyed as much as anybody. I can say they were at the top of the heap, along with Mark Recchi and Rick Tocchet.

I always had an affinity and an admiration for the veteran core. I really felt in the late '90s that when Clarke reacquired Berube and Tocchet to come and play for the Flyers, that was the start of preparing for life after Lindros, in terms of re-defining leadership on the team. Those guys came in and really showed the old school Flyers way of doing things and clearly embraced the team concept that we had to the group. That is why we had such a great run in 2000 and quite frankly should have won the

Stanley Cup in my opinion. But it didn't happen. And you don't get any trophies for second place.

One of my great running mates over the years was LeClair. If I didn't devote a chapter to him, it would be a disservice. Johnny and I became road roommates after Shjon Podein was traded to Colorado for Keith Jones. There was an immediate attraction as far as fun natures went. Johnny was an old school kind of guy, and I had a lot of that in me as well. LeClair was a live-in-the-moment guy if there ever were one.

To say that we didn't go out after games and run hard would be anything but the truth. The two of us were, at times, inseparable over our decade or so as roommates. I will say that a lot of the drinking that I did was riding shotgun with my great friend, No. 10. There were always a lot of stories and a lot of laughs.

It started when we had a game and then we had a night off after. We would head out for beers to watch another late-night sporting event. One thing John and I enjoyed doing with our group was going out and hanging with the boys after a game. There was the faction of players who wanted go out and chase girls. But those were not the guys I hung around with. I cared more about the interaction and mingling among my teammates than I did about going to nightclubs.

LeClair and I had done a lot of work together over the years and we had a great relationship on the road. Some of the things I would do in the morning would be to relieve myself during a sit-down bathroom session, then turn the shower on maximum hot and leave the room. Johnny's alarm was set, and he would wonder what was taking me so long. When he opened the door and barreled in, all he ended up getting was a nose full of something out of a major city water treatment plant.

For some reason, Johnny actually laughed at something as ingenious as that. Another time we were in Washington, D.C., to play the Capitals. When we got to the hotel, I raced up to the room and took the foil off the bedside chocolates, put them under his sheets, and laid the bedspread back in place. Johnny got into bed that night in his underwear and was watching a movie with me as we often did. He rolled over to hit the hay, and he got chocolate all over the side of his body.

He looks over at me and said, "Hey, Bundy, can you believe the maid left the chocolates in the bed by accident?" He had no idea it was me who did it. I put my hand over my mouth to keep from bursting out laughing and almost fell out of my bed. We used to play tricks like this on each other all the time. But none was greater than Johnny's revenge from the chocolate incident.

One day I was driving a BMW down the road to the Flyers' practice rink in South Jersey. I was at a traffic light and cars were blowing their horns, creating a real ruckus. They were pointing at me to pull over: everybody was trying to get my attention. I was sitting there a bit perplexed, thinking that all these people couldn't be recognizing me from playing for the Flyers. I stopped at the light and lowered the window on the right side of the car to figure out what was going on. The guy next to me lowered his window and said, "Hey, Chris, you have a big sign attached to the back of your car. It says, 'I molest farm animals.'"

That was Johnny just being Johnny. And I think anyone could understand the fun he had with that one.

There was another time when Johnny had attached a somewhat offensive "sex appliance" to the grill of my car. And I mean a big one. I had no idea it was on there. I think either Richardson or Recchi finally brought it to my attention—after I had been driving around with it for a couple days. I laughed like crazy because it was absolutely hysterical due to the fact that I didn't see it. I wished later that I had taken a photograph of it because it was just classic.

I thought carefully about my revenge. I started by detaching said object from my car and sticking it in the grill of his car a few days later. Unbeknownst to him, that big fella was firmly implanted in the front of his vehicle. He drove around with it for almost a month. One day his wife walked out to the garage, turns to Johnny and says, in her deep Boston accent, "Ya got something rather obnoxious stuck in the grill of ya cah!"

We did a lot of drinking. And it was a kick because Johnny was a free spirit just like I was. He was a great teammate on the ice and off it. The guy was generous, thoughtful of his teammates, and in retrospect, I'm happy he won a Stanley Cup, even if it was with the Canadiens. It would have been such a waste for a guy with that kind of competitive level in front of the net to not win a Stanley Cup at some juncture in his career. Unfortunately, it didn't happen for his big center on the Legion of Doom, No. 88. But if anybody deserved it, it was Johnny.

When I was falling into full-bore alcoholism around 2003, he and I flew out to Las Vegas. My wife and I flew out commercial while the LeClairs took a private jet, because that's the difference between a 50-goal-scoring First-Team NHL All-Star left wing and a defenseman, albeit one on the top unit, with no goals.

I got so loaded the last day there before we were supposed to fly home the next morning that I got it into my mind to try something rather foolish. I was so blasted I decided to touch every painting hanging on the walls in the hallways of the Bellagio Hotel. It was a complete and utter disaster. I remember Diana had enough poise to call John and Tina and tell them that I was really loaded. She added that we really needed some help. John walked into the restaurant with a wheelchair and a couple Bellagio associates because I'm a really big guy, and I was hammered. I was about to ruin everything. I was scheduled to play golf the next day at the exclusive Shadow Creek Club and have dinner that night with my wife.

I made a complete fool of myself. And how embarrassing it must have been for that woman to have to deal with that. Johnny got me up to the room, packed my bag in a matter of minutes, jumped in a limousine at the front of the Bellagio, and had a Gulfstream waiting to fly us back to Philadelphia. We arrived back in Philly. It was Father's Day and thank God it was. I was able to avoid a nasty situation and bought myself another 24 hours to pull myself together. I just wanted the events of Vegas to dissipate as quickly as possible.

That's the kind of guy Johnny is. As much as he would go out and drink with me, we also had a lot of good times together and supported each other in tough times. I will say that even now, after the 2004 work stoppage, John and I ended up being work partners at LeClair-Therien Lines, a trucking and shipping service. We were a national and regional carrier. We did a good job with it, and it was something we were very proud of. It was something to do while hockey took a break.

We've been best friends for a long time. John and I partied together, gambled together, went to sporting events together, and we traveled together when we could. There was the time we went to Los Angeles for almost eight days because of the schedule, with games against the Ducks and Kings. We had a lot of time off and the legendary Roger Neilson was the coach. Anyone who knew Roger knew he loved sunshine and riding bicycles. This trip was perfect for him. And perfect for us. Johnny and I took a limousine to every game, and we had booze waiting in the car after every single game.

We won games and celebrated by going around in that limo, hitting all the big bars in Hollywood. We hung out with celebrities. We ended up going back to Goldie Hawn's house because Eric Lindros was dating her daughter, Kate Hudson. Anyway, we headed out to parties in the Hollywood Hills, saw some of the other players who had shown up as well. One of the great stories happened while we were hanging out, eating great dinners at the Ritz-Carlton in Marina Del Rey. When we went to check out, our bill was $14,500. I looked over at Johnny and said, "You've got this one, pal. Thanks for the great trip!" Johnny grinned and then broke out laughing as he threw down his credit card. Then we headed out to the bus.

Guys like LeClair, Richardson, Berube, and Recchi were all good guys. They were all with the Flyers because Clarkie believed in having good guys on his team. He was able to define what a good guy was and then bring that team together around those good people. Clarke always had unique guys in the locker room. He always liked John and me: he thought we were a couple of real deals. We weren't problem people or malcontents—just a couple of good character guys who'd answer the bell for the team, and I think he admired those traits.

CHAPTER 14

First Signs of Trouble

THE DISAPPOINTMENT OF THE FLYERS' FAILED 2000 Stanley Cup playoff run didn't put a damper on any feelings about my personal career path. As the summer was coming to a close, I had just signed my first big contract—four years, $9 million—after a holdout but it was a real commitment from the Flyers. Oh, and the offseason also marked the start of my "acting" career as well. Along with other NHL celebrities such as Jeremy Roenick, Scott Gomez, Kevin Weekes, and Sheldon Souray, I was hired to make a cameo in the soap opera *One Life to Live,* and it turned out to be a real kick.

Then came "The Trip."

It was my coming-out party defining my problem with alcohol. Don Meehan, who is one of the sport's top agents, decided to celebrate his 50th birthday in style by chartering a private jet to Scotland and Ireland with about 100 of his "closest" friends, agents, general managers, and players. The Flyers were represented by Clarke and team president Ron Ryan, along with players such as Richardson, Peter White, and me. And let me tell you one thing, the party started before we even landed in the United Kingdom. We began the trip by staying right at the legendary St. Andrews Club, and we got to play the iconic golf course. Quite a thrill.

After a week in Scotland, it was off to Ireland. Our golf itinerary included fabled Ballybunion and Old Head among others. It was golf by day, full-blown partying at night, and I went full-bore. I was drinking hard all night, all day, every day, on the golf course, in the wind and rain—it did not matter. So much so that by the time the end-of-trip banquet came around, I won the dubious "best drinker on the trip" award. Pretty much everyone voted for me and keep in mind there were a lot of heavyweight drinkers on this soirée. I was kind of embarrassed that I had won. I knew a lot of eyes were on me. Even though it was a social function and was supposed to be fun, it was not fun for me at all. I was thinking that anyone here would know I drink too much or certainly have the capability to drink too much.

At that point in my life, considering my history of alcoholism, that trip was a "bender," a binge-drinker's finest/worst moments. I could stop a bender. I had stopped benders all the time. If there was a night to go hard, I would go hard. If there were two days to go hard, I would go hard. If there was a beautiful summer weekend, I would go hard. But when it was time to go to work during the week, I would put on the work boots and be committed to my trade. The problem is when you do drink and you're a consistent drinker, it's going to catch up with you eventually. At this point it really hadn't caught up with me at all.

When I got back to North America after the trip, my agent, Morris (Meehan's partner), called me in and said he had been talking to a couple guys and they were really concerned about what they saw: a guy who drank too much. I drank so much one night on the trip that I fell asleep on a chair in the hotel lobby. My future teammate, Turner Stevenson, used a magic marker to paint horns on my forehead above my eyes. Lyle Odelein came in and said, "You better wash your face off"—that's how out of it I was.

I woke up in the lobby of another hotel, and it was all just part of one of those benders. It was a bit eye-opening. I knew Clarke always thought I had a drinking problem or at least drank too hard when I really went at it. Or it felt like that. He never really verbalized that notion to me. But I kind of felt like he knew my act a little bit. He overlooked it because I always came to play afterwards, no matter what. But I think we were coming to a day when my drinking wasn't quite as accepted as it was, in terms of the tradition and the history in the social parts of the sport. In certain groups, it was still accepted by certain people. Some people thought it was the coolest thing ever if you could drink 12 beers then go out and play hockey the next day. But how long can you maintain that kind of lifestyle when you're playing a professional sport?

It wasn't something to hold me back. The mantra "live hard, play hard, work hard" fit right into my personality at that point, and I lived by that standard. I truly did. As long as I was able to play, my teammates trusted me. But I was closing in on 30 and there were times when I wondered if this lifestyle might be affecting my performance. As for my teammates, if you have their trust, it doesn't matter what you do away from the rink. That credo is kind of what I hitched my wagon to.

After I got back from that trip, Morris told me a couple guys expressed concern and thought I might be drinking a little too much. This was coming from more mature, older players. That's when I knew I had to at least start investigating if I was drinking too much.

Right around then I had my first conversations with Holmgren, at the time the Flyers' assistant general manager. I walked in and told him I wasn't sure I had a problem, but if I'm here, I might. I just don't know the answer to it. He said, "Are you sick and tired of being sick and tired?" I said to him I didn't know. I certainly enjoyed myself drinking, but I didn't like feeling eyes on me. I wanted people to mind their own business and leave me alone. I was thinking, *How dare someone go to another person and say they were concerned about my behavior.* Plus, the guys who said it weren't teammates of mine. They were just observing from a distance.

But I had to find out if it was true. At that point I went to my first AA meeting in the late summer of 2000. I had been trying to negotiate that new contract. Meanwhile, when we got to Ireland and I won the best drinker award, something happened that really boosted my esteem. At the trip-ending dinner, Hall of

Fame general manager Cliff Fletcher (then with Calgary) came up to me and said he had been trying to "get me" for the past seven years. Then he added, "No wonder Clarkie won't trade you." For me, it was a great thing to hear and also said something about Clarke. It was a big statement by a guy who knows hockey inside and out. Fletcher appreciated me as a hockey player, but it was also amusing as it seemed to imply that Clarke must have loved my character. He was saying this was the reason they loved me in Philly, because of my character.

I got home from that trip and didn't believe anybody vilified me from what had taken place. I was the same guy I've always been, interacting with people. I've always loved people. That trip for me was the epitome of the ultra-man's trip. We're staying at St. Andrews with a hundred of the greatest hockey players on the planet, the best agents in the business, every single who's who of hockey. It was a really cool trip, but I wished I could have ended it differently because it left a sour taste in my mouth. As amazing as it was, the golf and everything, I wished I had acted a little bit more appropriately. I don't think I did anything worthy of any legal ramifications, but it was just how I carried myself.

Although not alone in that kind of behavior by any stretch of the imagination, the person I am now looks back on that with a certain twinge of regret and maybe shame. But it also might have been an awakening. When I think about the experience, that was point A for me. I went through other alcoholic experiences before in my career but really the trip to Ireland and Scotland had put me on the map.

The 1996–97 season was a strange year, in hindsight. Lindros missed the start of the season due to a groin pull he sustained at the World Cup of Hockey; won by Team USA (which included LeClair and Otto) in a classic best-of-three final against Team Canada (featuring Lindros, Brind'Amour and Desjardins). Every day in the early weeks of the season, it felt like the entire focus was, *When is Eric coming back?* in terms of what the fans and media talking about. I'd gotten a hint of what that was like one season earlier.

In Nov. 1995, we played a game against Florida in which Panthers defenseman Jason Woolley undercut Lindros with a low-bridge hit. Lindros suffered a sprained MCL—the third such knee injury of his still-young career. After that, on a day-to-day basis, there was nonstop drama until Eric returned to the lineup. Mind you, I don't blame Lindros for that. It was a legit injury after a rather dirty hit. But I do think there was too little attention paid to the fact that we held up fairly well as a team even without the reigning Hart Trophy winner in the lineup—LeClair, Renberg, Brind'Amour and Otto played some of their best hockey during that stretch—and I wish those guys got credit for how well they were playing rather than the first question every day being, *What's the latest on Eric?* When Lindros missed the start of the 1996–97 season, it felt like déjà vu. This time, we were playing just so-so as a team early on—I wasn't playing well from an individual standpoint, either—but it seemed like the first question asked every day was, *How close is Lindros to returning to the lineup?* rather than, *Why are you guys leaving winnable points on the table?*

Eventually, we got the ship righted. I remember that we had a stretch where we beat Toronto at our new arena, the CoreStates Center (nowadays called the Wells Fargo Center) and followed it up with a road win at Madison Square Garden over Gretzky and the New York Rangers. A couple games later, Dale Hawerchuk had a hat trick as we crushed the Penguins, 7-3. In some ways, it was a foreshadowing of how we would come together as a team in 1999-2000 without Eric. The main difference was, back in 1996, the team as a whole was happy to see Lindros eventually get back in the lineup. Within the locker room itself, there wasn't any meaningful drama at that point.

Lindros missed the first 23 games that season. To his credit, he played like gangbusters the rest of the season (79 points in 52 games) after his return, and our team hit another level along with it. This was the closest we'd ever get in that era to being truly the best team in the NHL. After starting the season with a mediocre 12-12-1 record, we went 33-12-12 the rest of the way. A couple weeks after Lindros got back in the lineup, Clarke acquired Paul Coffey from Hartford for Haller (Desjardins' primary defense partner since arriving from Montreal in Feb. 1995) and a 1997 first round Draft pick.

SOME SUPERSTARS AGE BETTER THAN OTHERS. They say it's better to retire a year too early than a year too late. But when you're a talent such as Hall of Famer Coffey, neither applies. Coffey had already won multiple Stanley Cups with Edmonton and

Pittsburgh, plus multiple Norris Trophies, by the time he was traded to the Flyers at age 35, so there was nothing really left to prove.

But that didn't stop him from making a significant contribution to our run to the Stanley Cup Final in the 1996–97 season. All you had to do was watch how he played to learn a lot. He was just a tremendous teammate. To have a boyhood idol dressing in the same room was a bit surreal at first. In my childhood he was winning Stanley Cups with the Oilers, and everybody wanted to be Paul Coffey, including me.

By the end of 1997, I had played with so many decorated guys. There were MacTavish, Otto, and Dale Hawerchuk—all either Stanley Cup winners or destined for the Hall of Fame. Hawerchuk and Coffey were two of the biggest superstars I ever played with. Add Mark Recchi (who'd return to the Flyers in 1999) to that list and you have three really dynamic talents. They epitomized the talent the NHL had in the '80s and '90s. It was a real honor for me to play with those guys and I did go to the '97 Finals with them.

It's no secret that Paul Coffey was first and foremost an offensive defenseman. He'd never been all that great about playing defense in his own zone. In his prime, he played just enough D to be adequate in that area but he more than made up for it with all the goals and assists he provided in joining the attack up ice. By the time Paul got to Philly, he'd lost just a little bit offensively and some of the poke-check plays that used to work with surprising regularity in his prime weren't quite as effective anymore. He went from an otherworldly presence in the lineup to merely excellent. But I tell you what, I was very proud to have him and Hawerchuk as teammates. Coffey had played with what seemed like all the big stars: Gretzky, Mark Messier, Lemieux, and Bryan Trottier. As a defenseman, Coffey was just tremendous. He won the Norris Trophy nine years apart, which tells you something not only about his talent but his durability. I used to see guys idolize Jágr when he was later in his career, and it was the same thing with Coffey.

We had a Finnish rookie on our team that year named Janne Niinimaa. The kid had outrageous talent; all the tools to be a superstar. He fell pretty far short of realizing his full potential, but he did, after his Flyers days, play in a couple of NHL All-Star Games. At any rate, Janne worshipped the ground that Coffey walked on. Niinimaa said that when he was growing up in Finland, most of the kids were Edmonton Oilers fans. He was, too. The difference was that, while most of the other kids idolized Hall of Fame right winger Jari Kurri, Janne's favorite player was Coffey. With the Flyers, Niinimaa was often paired with Coffey. To this day, Niinimaa says that being teammates with Paul was one of the most cherished memories of his career. I can relate. I felt the same way.

Terry Murray gave me some tough-love coaching that same season. Murph wasn't one to yell or show much outward emotion but he could be blunt in his feedback. Above all else, Murray spoke to you through your ice time. He didn't play favorites. Once, in 1995–96, he benched LeClair and Renberg for an entire period because he felt that the Legion of Doom line was cheating out of the defensive zone, overstaying shifts, and not backchecking in a game we were trailing. The message was clear to everyone: If Murray would bench two-thirds of the LOD, he'd bench anyone if he felt it was merited. (I will note, though, that No. 88 was equally guilty to his linemates in that same game but he remained in the game while Johnny and Renny rode the pine for the entire second period and the start of the third). The message registered. Above all, Terry Murray taught me how to become a long-time NHL player who could gobble up heavy minutes nightly. You know when it really sank in? December 1996.

In 1996–97, I had a rough first half the season. Murry told me several times that I needed to improve my play. I tried but the results weren't there. As a result, I spent most of December sitting out as a healthy scratch. I was scratched in 10 of 13 games that month, including six in a row to start the month. That was the first—and until the late stages of my career, the only—time I missed games for any other reason except injury or illness. I didn't like it one bit, but the message got through. Not long after that, I started to play some of the best hockey of my entire career, and my long-running partnership on the blueline with Desjardins began shortly after New Year's 1997. Our pairing carried over to the five subsequent Flyers coaches as a near-constant in the lineup.

As my game started to come around, I realized that Murray was right: there was another level to my game that I was capable of playing in tandem with Rico. I finished the season with a career-best +26 rating along with 19 points during the regular season. In the playoffs, I was plus-six. Seven of the 12 playoff points I posted in 99 career Stanley Cup playoff games came during our 1997. Yes, I put in the work. Yes, Rico was a fantastic defense partner; the best I ever played with. But I also owe Terry Murray a debt of gratitude for adjustments he taught me from a technical standpoint as well as showing some tough love coaching when I needed it. I learned how to be an NHL starting defenseman under Murph and that's something I am forever grateful for in hindsight.

In the 1997 playoffs, we steamrolled the Penguins, Sabres, and Rangers in five games apiece. For the '97 Final against Detroit, I thought we were going to do well. I was a little off on that one, since we were swept by the Red Wings in a tough series. The expectation was that Lindros would dominate and the other 22 players would just ride along to the championship. That simply wasn't the case. Defensemen Nicklas Lidström and Larry Murphy ended up being the stars of that playoff series. They took a real non-physical approach to Lindros and LeClair. We had some injuries and really had to tap into the depth part of our lineup.

As for me, I had an outstanding playoff season. I was second in the NHL in plus/minus. I seemed to get my points at critical times in games. There was a game-winning goal in Buffalo and a pair of assists in the series clincher against Gretzky and the Rangers in the Conference Finals. It was quite exciting for me, especially because I had been benched earlier in the year. The message from that benching was received; I turned the corner, and it became the first time in my career that I truly felt I belonged in the NHL. A regular mainstay, top-four defenseman and my play showed there was no doubt about it.

That's why I felt good heading into the offseason. The summer was a memorable one. I was getting ready for my second contract and hoping that things would go well. But by the end of negotiations, things became a bit contentious. When I got to training camp that fall, my agent told me not to participate. He said we're not even close on the numbers. He said he was going to hold true to what I was worth. I didn't necessarily like that stance at all. But Morris, who operated Newport Sports Management, was standing his ground, and it was a little weird for me because I had a strong relationship with Clarke. It was a fine line and Morris had to reassure me that this was just a process.

I also got married that summer to my wife, Diana. A lot of really great things were happening. After that great run to the Finals, the wedding preparations were getting into place. We had a modest guest list of only about 270 people (kidding, of course). It was an exciting time in my life. I felt like things were going in the direction that I wanted them to go. I was really happy with the life I was about to embark on with my new bride.

At that point I wasn't really down when the training camp stuff unfolded. It took a few days of waiting, but when I finally got the green light, I walked in and there was the new coach, Wayne Cashman, who had replaced Murray. Cashman walked up to me and said, "Welcome to town, kid!" That was the first time I met Cash. I was excited to play for him. He was a different bird. Really old school. The more old school you could get, the better it was for me.

The problem was, Cash was so old school that he didn't understand that there was even a new school somewhere in the middle of all this. Another problem: As someone who had been a long-time assistant coach but never a head coach before that (or afterwards), Cash struggled to run the bench during games. We figured it would get better over time.

It was perhaps my best training camp. I worked my way into the lineup pretty quickly with Desjardins. By then, the partnership was well underway. I looked forward to being part of the No. 1 defense tandem, playing against opponents' best players and logging ice time in critical situations, like penalty killing. It was a defining period in my career.

CHAPTER 15

Cashing In, Roger That

WHEN CLARKE HIRED CASHMAN, the implication was clear: The new coach was bringing a particular attitude and approach from his playing days with the Stanley Cup–winning Boston Bruins. Clearly, Cashman was a no-nonsense guy. Whether his style was going to work in the late '90s with this crew remained to be seen.

Don't forget, the Flyers were coming off a trip to the Stanley Cup Finals. And despite getting swept by the Red Wings, the general feeling was that there was enough talent in place to mount another serious run at the title.

Clarke thought Cashman would coach the same way he competed as a player. This much you can say—Wayne Cashman was loved by his players. There was no doubt about that. But I'm not sure coaching was really for Cash. I think he knew that right away. He struggled in game management and making adjustments. Wayne used to talk to me and Richardson, and I think he saw a little bit of himself in both of us. He was also from Kingston, Ontario, not far from my hometown, Ottawa.

Cashman had more character in his little finger than most people have in their entire bodies. I had a great time with Cashman, and with a new contract in my back pocket, I was ready to pick up my No. 2 defenseman role alongside Desjardins. In less than a year, my career had taken a complete turn. Some of it had to do with my fear of failure. That benching the previous season had left a mark. I was absolutely terrified of that happening again. Maybe it was a precursor of some of the pressure that was about to come in my career. But by no stretch did I feel any kind of threat. I had just experienced a great playoff and saw myself as someone who had a name around the league, someone the Flyers could depend on.

The new three-year, $3.7 million contract gave me a lot of confidence. One of the best parts of that contract had to do with one of my brothers-in-law. What I am about to say is not meant with any disrespect because he became a great friend and one of my drinking buddies over the years, but he had said to me, "You're never going to make a million dollars a year playing ice hockey."

I looked at him and I said, "Just watch." I told him salaries were headed in that direction and I was a candidate for seven figures because I was playing a ton of minutes.

But I love people who doubt me. I always put up with doubt my whole life. The more times I got it in my career, the more I was pushed up against the wall. Those kinds of questions about my ability only made me rise more to the occasion.

The 1997–98 season began, and maybe it was because there was a hangover from the preseason or whatever, but things never seemed to go Cashman's way. Clarke's faith in Cashman was pretty evident right off because he named him an assistant coach on Canada's Olympic team headed to Nagano, Japan, for the 1998 Winter Olympic Games. There was a point during the season when both Clarke and Cashman came up to me and said, "Be ready in case we need you for the Olympic team. You're on the list of the last guys that we are considering for the team. If there's an injury, you're probably going to be the guy that's going to go."

I thought that was quite an honor. I hadn't played a ton in the '94 Olympics at Lillehammer, and I thought it would be quite an honor to go to Nagano and play with guys like Gretzky. It would have been a cool experience. But there were no injuries, so it didn't happen. I missed out on that, but just being considered for a spot to me was an honor and made me realize just how far I had come in my career. It made me feel like I was one of the top defensemen in Canada, at least inside the top 30 at the time. No regrets. Just the fact my name was being tossed around was a great thrill to me.

Meanwhile, the Flyers were about to set sail into rough waters. This was around the time when Lindros started to act up. There had been problems in the past—bitching and moaning about coaches and players. Who he didn't like and who didn't like him. Lindros wasn't the only unhappy Flyer at the time. The arrival of Chris Gratton that offseason via a mega-million offer sheet as a restricted free agent and a subsequent trade to Tampa Bay (sending Renberg and Dykhuis) to reacquire the four first-round picks that went to the Lightning for not matching the offer sheet had an effect on our entire roster.

For one thing, Gratton's arrival displaced Rod Brind'Amour from the second-line center role that he'd played so well since Lindros arrived. Rod either played third-line center or had to switch to left wing to play on the top two lines. He did as was asked of him, and handled it professionally, but he was unhappy about it. Secondly, the departure of Renberg put 20-year-old Dainius Zubrus into full-time duty on the top line with Lindros and LeClair. Dainius wasn't ready for that promotion and he began to struggle.

For a couple of months, Cash even split up the Legion of Doom. Gratton had scored a big goal on opening night but it was his only goal in October. The fans started to get on him. As a temporary solution, LeClair moved to Gratton's left wing for about six weeks in an effort to get Gratts going. It worked for awhile, as Johnny kept right on scoring and Gratton's play also picked up. Brind'Amour moved to Lindros' left wing; although it wasn't Rod's preferred position, first-line left wing was a better opportunity than third-line center. Zubrus moved back down in the lineup, and a variety of right wingers (Vinny Prospal for a little while, Trent Klatt and others) completed the line.

We remained inconsistent. A lot of the structure that Murray imposed was lost during Cash's brief tenure as head coach. Coaches often talk about "playing the right way." Murray had a way of getting us to do that most of the time. Although it was not directly Cashman's fault, there were too many nights where we had too many players who did their own thing. Our goalie play was also inconsistent but in fairness to Hexy and Garth Snow, there were a little too much chaos on too many nights.

Then, in a Saturday game at Pittsburgh, things really started to get interesting. Lindros skated down the sideboards and Penguin defenseman Darius Kasparaitis raised his shoulder, hit Lindros up high and practically knocked him out of his skates.

The ironic part is, on the same weekend, the Flyers were about to make a coaching change. There were rumors Cashman was going to be replaced by Roger Neilson. I knew this might happen because Petr Svoboda and I had lunch in Haddonfield, New Jersey, the previous day, and he told me he had spoken to Clarke, who told him they were going to push Cashman down to assistant coach and bring in Roger to run the show.

Svoboda laughed and said, "Bundy, you're going to watch more video than you've ever seen in your life." He was right. Roger was already known as "Captain Video." So here we are, Lindros and Cashman out, Neilson in. The Flyers made it official on Sunday. Clarke was already upset with the way we were playing. He stormed into the locker room and told us to "get some wheels on your houses." He went around the room, taking potshots at everybody. He looked at me and says, "Poor Desjardins, having to play with you!" I was laughing deep, on the inside. I understood what Bob was trying to do.

A dozen guys must have gotten it. Clarke looked at rookie winger Colin Forbes and said, "You. . . What's the matter? Your wife's not letting you fight?" He then proceeded to really rip into Zubrus, Niinimaa, and Daigle; basically saying that none of them had their priorities straight. It was a rough one. But things almost had to happen like that. We came back to win the Sunday night rematch. By the second period, every hockey player in the building knew Roger would be coaching the team the next day. Oddly enough, Daigle scored to win the game in overtime (his long-belated first goal as a Flyer) and he proceeded to go off on offensive tear that was impressive for a couple of weeks and then disappeared as suddenly as it materialized. At the next game on Tuesday Roger was behind the bench. Who scored the first goal? Yours truly. A slapshot from the point that somehow eluded Hall of Fame goalie Brodeur. How the hell it went in, I'll never know. It was a good start for me with Roger, a coach I loved. He was my favorite coach of all time. His assistants under him, Craig Ramsay and Cashman, were absolute hockey lifers and understood the game like nobody else. I learned the most that I could with those guys.

Roger was an unbelievably good human being and, yes, was a pioneer in the use of video in coaching. He sure loved his defensive-oriented hockey and tried, with mixed results, to bring back some of the structure we had gotten away from we'd tried to open things up and freelance a bit under Cash. But I grasped his systems quickly and Roger had a lot of trust in me. Neilson's system was effective when played right.

It wasn't always highly entertaining for the fans or the most exciting way to play but it worked. We once played a home game against Washington—a 1-1 tie (remember those?) in which there might have been a combined five scoring chances all night. Each team's single goal was scored off a weird puck-luck deflection. Afterwards, Roger declared it our best-played game of the season from an x-and-o standpoint. He was right. Unfortunately, from an entertainment standpoint, there were a lot of zzzzzzzs in the stands, but Roger really wasn't there to put on a show.

Roger understood, however, that an 82-game season was a long haul. If you had a misstep in the marathon, the focus was on correcting it so you didn't keep stumbling. Roger was kind of like the absent-minded professor of movie fame; kind of an almost bohemian type. Structure-wise, we were getting back on track. However, the end of that season was not a memorable one. We lost in five first-round games to the Buffalo Sabres.

ANOTHER YEAR, ANOTHER DISAPPOINTMENT for a Flyers team that in my opinion should have been in serious contention for a Stanley Cup given the depth and talent on the roster. Like the 1997–98 season, hopes were high for 1998–99 but things once again seemed to get sidetracked by as much stuff off the ice as on it.

You could start with how the season ended. How do you give up just nine goals in six games and still lose? That's just pathetic. The season began with a transition in goal, with John Vanbiesbrouck coming in to take over the No. 1 post after the Garth Snow/Ron Hextall platoon arrangement was put to rest. Neilson had wanted "Beezer" and he was still pretty good, but he wasn't as good as he was when he took Florida to the Stanley Cup Final in 1996. In other words, he wasn't good enough to take the '99 Flyers to a championship.

And that's why I think that of all the money and all the goaltending decisions that Clarke made over the years, this one didn't quite make it. If he wanted the best free agent available, he should have gone after Curtis "Cujo" Joseph. They should have spent the extra two or three million dollars to get a guy who was still in his prime. He was incredible around that time and I'm almost certain we would have won the Cup in '99 or 2000 if we had him in goal.

Basically, a lot of 1999 was consumed by what allegedly happened to Lindros in Nashville with the bathtub, the collapsed lung, and the whole cause célèbre through the aftermath. It just kind of became too much for everybody. By the time we got to the playoffs, we were just a little bit off. I think even Toronto was a little surprised they beat us. After the final game, Ed Snider came into the locker room breathing fire, really upset with the penalty call that cost us the game. After referee Terry Gregson whistled LeClair off to set up the Maple Leafs' game-winner, Snider was ready to take on all comers. Ed just went ballistic.

His face was all red, and his eyes were glaring. "These bleepin' refs—where is Gregson from, Toronto? Who calls a penalty like that in a big game like this?"

Furthermore, Snider invited anyone to criticize the NHL and Gregson verbally and he would "pay the fine gladly." I understood the passion. I also understood that Toronto got all the calls. It was typical of the officials whenever you played a prima donna team like Toronto or Montreal. They were always looked after by the rest of the league, especially the top brass of the NHL. Commissioner Gary Bettman knew Toronto and Montreal were the keys to the Canadian kingdom. Toronto and Montreal get the breaks, the NHL moves them along.

It was a disappointing end to the season. I thought if we could have gotten past Toronto, we could have made a big play, but it just wasn't to be. Things started to fall apart in Game 2. Beezer let in a goal on a shot by Steve Thomas from the corner. I was on the ice, somewhere in the middle, and the puck hit Beezer's pad and went in. I wasn't sure if I had done something wrong. After the game, I went up to Roger and asked him if there might have been something I could have done differently. Roger just looked at me and said, "Bundy, a goalie can't let in a goal like that and have the team expect to win a game. A defenseman can't do anything about it." To say the whole series was a disappointment would be an understatement. I really felt it was another opportunity that got swept by the wayside.

I have no idea what happened that night with Eric in Nashville. I don't know if the accident happened on the ice or off the ice. I have to believe it happened on the ice. But whatever the case, he decided to go after the trainer, John Worley, who was beloved by the team. The trainers are teammates, they are equal to us. That's the way we view them—the equipment guys, the guys behind the scenes. When Eric did that, he lost many, many guys in that locker room immediately. First, he's a decorated hockey player making a ton of money. And Worley is a guy who's just trying to put food on the table and was loved and respected by the players. I thought to myself, *Man, you have to be a really bad person to go after a head trainer.* Just because it didn't work out the way you wanted doesn't mean you have to go after the guy. He called him out in public, put a big, red bull's-eye on him.

That's why people on the team soured on Eric, because of stuff like that... He had no qualms about throwing others under the bus or even trying to get people fired. Whether it was Eric's parents banging that drum, Eric was a grown man and had the ability put a stop to it. He didn't. Instead, he echoed it.

The right thing to do would have been to say, "This isn't right. I can't go after the trainer, he didn't do anything wrong. There's got to be a better way to do it." If the trainer did do something wrong, it should have been investigated, looked at accordingly, and handled. But John was an A-plus trainer, and no one was out to get Eric in any way, shape, or form. To believe anything else would just be paranoid thinking.

The other sidebar to that story is Eric's parents, Bonnie and Carl, said Clarke was trying to kill their son by flying him on the airplane home after he suffered the collapsed lung in Nashville. How ignorant and arrogant do you have to be, how misguided in life do you have to be, to publicly say something like that? It's really one of the most pathetic things I've ever seen. There wasn't a single player on the Flyers who didn't think it wasn't abhorrent, ridiculous to have to deal with.

We all got caught in the middle of it, too... No matter how many times we tried to say, "That's between the Lindros family and the organization. We're focused on hockey here," we'd get asked about it again the very next day. I don't blame the media. They were doing their jobs. I do blame Lindros and his family for turning an already bad situation into a circus. That was the underlying theme of the 1998–99 season, and I could see there were cracks forming in the foundation of the team through discord between the star player and the franchise. In many ways, it was a huge distraction. Murray's "choking" comment in the '97 Final may have started it, and I think that might have ignited something between the two sides. I think ultimately that's where the Flyers started to lose Eric and he lost them. Thing is, Murph wasn't wrong, and he wasn't talking specifically about Lindros so much as the entire team. To lose your best player at that point is really, really tough, and it's difficult to recoup that kind of magic that you thought you were going to have. That's why the season was so disappointing and certainly not shocking that we lost to Toronto. For me personally, I was improving my game and still learning how to get better. On a happier note, Craig Ramsay was a great mentor to me; he knew defensive hockey, and I learned from him. It was about the only positive development from that season.

Rammer is another hockey lifer, and one of the nicest human beings I've ever met. Very bright hockey guy. Never raised his voice; didn't believe yelling at a player or an official was an effective approach. Good teacher as an assistant coach. Ramsay's personality is very different than Cash's, but one thing they had in common was they were both probably best suited to the assistant coach role. Under Cash, we lost our structure that we had under Murph. Under Craig a few years later, we didn't really have enough assertiveness and accountability. I'll get to that soon.

CHAPTER 16

Land of Confusion

THE FLYERS' GREATEST SUCCESS took place in the latter part of the 20th century, with two Stanley Cups and seven trips to the Finals. But by the dawn of the 21st, things were heading in the wrong direction. Coming off the disappointing loss in the 2000 Eastern Conference Finals to New Jersey, the Flyers still had high hopes they could take care of unfinished business.

Instead, the start of the 2000–01 season went haywire right from jump street, although you wouldn't have known it as the campaign was about to begin. Everything seemed to be in alignment. Ramsay had taken over full time as the head coach, Mike Stothers was one assistant coach, and Bill Barber, who had done a terrific job with the Philadelphia Phantoms, making them into sort of Broad Street Bullies 2.0, was the other.

Only one problem: the NHL was no longer structured like that. There were still some nasty fights, and the biggest, toughest guys were still in the NHL. Barber had become in many ways a leader of a cult with the Phantoms. They were instantly popular and had won a Calder Cup with one of my future teammates,

154

Peter White, as captain. Billy had a lot of moxie as he took over as an assistant coach. I think he just wanted to travel by plane rather than ride that American Hockey League bus. Clarke decided to bring Bill in. Clarke was a great general manager and Barber is a great guy, although we butted heads a little. But he trusted me, and I played some good hockey for him.

The season started rather uneventfully with Ramsay coming in. We had a lot of veterans, and I had a coach who trusted me and would put me out in any situation—every big defensive moment I was out on the ice with Desjardins.

By the 25-game mark we were struggling for some reason, and we couldn't even stay much above .500. It didn't seem like Clarke really agreed with Ramsay's style of forechecking. Too passive perhaps. Fairly or unfairly, there was a growing feeling that Rammer was perhaps too nice—soft even—to be an NHL head coach. He was patient to a fault even when we needed a kick in the butt. There was no intensity at the First Union Center (now Wells Fargo). It was not livening up our building enough. And one of our broadcasters, Steve Coates (who is a good friend of Clarke's), told us that. Coates is one of the great characters of the Flyers. He made quite a name for himself over the years. But by no stretch of the imagination did anyone think that Clarke and Coates weren't close. Coatesy was always good to have around because he knew everything that was going on.

I stayed close to Coatesy. I genuinely liked him. I liked Rammer, too. But it became pretty apparent management didn't like the passive style Ramsay had. I always felt that Bill Barber was one of the most decorated men in the history of the Flyers organization and to have him serve as Ramsay's assistant was kind of a tough sell. Billy's a Hall of Famer and an intense competitor. Craig was well liked but he wasn't Billy Barber. It would be like making me head coach of the Detroit Red Wings and having Nick Lidström as my assistant coach. It wouldn't have made any sense at all.

I always believed Billy felt that way, too. We knew things were going to change if we didn't get that record well above .500 fairly soon. I walked in one morning and Tocchet was sitting in the hot tub. He said, "Hop in here, Bundy. Old 'Rammer' just got fired!" I asked him who was taking over. He guessed it was going to be Billy.

Then in came Barber. Mike Stothers, the other assistant coach, walked in and said, "You know what, boys, you better put on those work boots full time because he'll be here longer than all of you." The new coach made changes right away and it was a throwback to the '70s and '80s. He wanted us to play hard for each other, for our teammates. Be a pain in the ass on the ice. He switched the tunes in the locker room back to country music, some uplifting stuff. Billy was a character, no doubt about it. Right off, we won a bunch of games in a row. He told me straight-away I was playing some of the best hockey ever as a Flyer, which I didn't totally agree with. I was playing well but I was now 29 years old and that's getting up there in hockey years. But I was still in my prime, so I was going to play pretty well no matter what.

After Barber took over, we did play with a lot more energy. We really had no system in place at all. It was basically put your work boots on, and you're going to get good results. If it came down to backchecking, it was just outworking the other guy. I was structured with what I was doing with Desjardins and really didn't care much what Billy was doing. It's hard to change a system after you've been there for just 25 games as an assistant, but that's what I knew. Little did I know that about a year later, we would change systems after a game in the middle of a playoff series.

It was a screwed-up time; it was almost like we were living in some sort of "Slap Shot" reality. We had some characters come in, like Kevin Stevens and Gino Odjick. These guys were loose cannons in their careers. They were characters in here as well. Billy had an interesting relationship with both those guys. Gino had fought every proven and wannabe tough guy in the NHL over the years and was getting tired of that role. He rarely fought anymore by the time he got to Philly. In fairness, there weren't many people around the NHL anymore who wanted to piss off Gino. They usually kept their distance. Stevens was trying to rebuild his personal life and rescue his career, which was on the rocks. It started out well but Kevin, unfortunately, was not ready yet to stay on that path. I felt for him. My own life was going the wrong way off the ice. I was turning into a person who drank too much, although it was not yet affecting my play on the ice. I would always keep an eye on guys like that to see how it happened. In many ways, I became like guys who have current drug situations.

There were problems with guys, seen or unseen. I always wondered if something like that would happen to me. Little did I realize I was already on that path. I saw a guy like Kevin Stevens going through a lot of pain. He had that awful event in East St. Louis when he was busted in a hotel room with drugs (crack cocaine) and prostitutes. Ironically, his career with the Flyers came to an end from the aftermath of that incident, which occurred when he was with the Rangers. We played in Denver the night before he was scheduled for a hearing back in Illinois. He made curfew at our hotel after the game (we were staying over and flying out the next day to San Jose), then went back out again for a little more "entertainment." He missed his flight and made up some story. When the Flyers found out, it was all over. He never played another game for Philly again.

By the end of the year, things were well established with Barber's style. I love to do impersonations and Billy was easy, just go heavy on the Canadian accent and throw in a few clichés. I peppered with casual profanity. There was no such thing as analytics back then but if they kept an "f-bomb per sentence" ratio for everyone in the NHL, Billy might be the all-time leader. It's not just when he's angry. Billy adds "sentence enhancers" to even the most casual of conversations. It's kind of endearing, actually. I liked to poke fun and keep the room light. There was plenty of Billy material to use, a ton of it. Meanwhile, the Flyers turned the corner and somehow finished near the top of the standings. Billy won the Jack Adams Award for best coach of the year, which was incredible. It was surreal, who could have seen that coming?

Especially when we had no real system. He came in with a throw-back attitude and sheer will and made his players better.

The success caught everyone around the NHL a bit by surprise, but it wasn't sustainable.

CHAPTER 17

All Work, No Play

WE MAY HAVE had the talent. We may have had the work ethic. But we didn't have a blueprint for the transition from regular season hockey to the playoff variety. Some believe you can flip a switch and boost the energy level then all will be well. It doesn't always work that way. Hard effort can only take you so far, and the 2000–01 Flyers learned that lesson through blood, sweat, and tears.

This was evident in Game 6 of our 2001 first-round playoff series with the Buffalo Sabres. To lose a big game like that by an 8–0 score isn't easy to do. Literally everything has to break down. The forwards didn't come back to help the defense. In turn, the defense didn't know whether to play the body or the puck. The goaltending? Well, that's only the most important part of the game and when that dimension is a no-show, the outcome is predictable.

We were down 4–0 after the first period. Both netminders, Roman Čechmánek and Brian Boucher, were awful. And this was right after a season in which Čechmánek, a Vezina Trophy finalist and the Bobby Clarke Trophy winner as Flyers MVP, had outdueled Buffalo future Hall of Fame goaltender Dominik Hašek by an incredible 4–0 margin between October and April. How was this even possible? Maybe we thought Čechmánek's "magic" and dominance of the Sabres in the regular season was going to carry over, but it didn't.

Coach Barber came into the locker room after the first period and said: "It's 4–0. You guys are done. This game is over, and you have no sense of comin' back. And I'm going to tell you all something right now.... Next year I'm going to pick my own team. I'm going to get guys in here who are going to play hard and they're not going to blow an opportunity like this for everyone else."

We lost by that ridiculous eight-goal margin and when Barber won the Jack Adams for coach of the year, it just showed the difference between regular season hockey and the real chase for Lord Stanley's coveted prize. After our lousy start and then powerhouse finish, it seemed about right. But I reckon we would have turned things around that season, regardless of who was the coach. We just got started off slow because we went so deep in the playoffs the previous year. When we changed coaches, we still had our heads above water. Clearly, we had a very good hockey team. Billy came in and gave us some energy and some juice out of the gate, but it didn't matter. We would have rallied in the second half of the season; we had so many veterans that year. We didn't need a coach to motivate us. We could have figured out how to motivate ourselves.

The season ended on a terrible note. There was a bad taste because of the 8–0 loss. The offseason certainly was an eventful one, if for no other reason than the resolution of the Lindros situation. Eric had sat out the entire season, refusing to play for the team again even when he was eventually offered a one-year contract to return. He remained in limbo until Clarke finally had enough. He sent him to the New York Rangers for defenseman Kim Johnsson, winger Jan Hlaváč, and gifted but enigmatic prospect Pavel Brendl, plus a third-round draft pick.

In my opinion, we probably didn't get enough for Lindros, but you have to remember he had suffered a bunch of concussions and hadn't seen action since the Stevens hit back on May 26, 2000. But when the trade was announced, it kind of lifted a bit of a cloud that had been hanging over this franchise. Clearly, something was due to change. A proud franchise like the Flyers could no longer function with a reluctant superstar on its roster.

The morning of September 11, 2001, was gorgeous. Brilliant sunshine. Not a cloud in the sky. Comfortable late summer temperatures. A slight hint of a refreshing breeze. It was hard not to feel calm, peaceful and happy as I went to the Skate Zone in Voorhees, NJ, for practice. Otherwise, it seemed from outward appearances like just a normal day at training camp. That is, until the horrifying news unfolded that the United States was under attack in an interrelated series of terrorist attacks. Hockey—and most everything else—suddenly became trivial. Like everyone else, Flyers players could only think about the nightmarish story unfolded.

Regardless of our personal backgrounds, countries of origin or personal political beliefs, we were collectively devastated. It was hard to find words when the media guys asked us for reactions to what was going on with the hijacked airplanes that hit the Twin Towers in New York, attacked the Pentagon in DC, and the one that crashed in Pennsylvania. The one guy on the team who mustered a response other than "I'm shocked and sickened" was the one guy who should have taken his head out of his posterior and kept his mouth shut. I'm talking about Pavel Brendl. "Oh, that airplane thing?" Brendl replied when asked about the attacks. It wasn't that Brendl was deliberately being callous. Although you really couldn't blame it on a language barrier—the Czech player had been living and playing in North America for several years by that point—Pavel legitimately failed to grasp the gravity of what was going on. He was a 20-year-old kid who never thought about much beyond the confines of a hockey rink. He also didn't understand that the optics of his response were awful.

On Sept. 20, we had a home preseason game against the New York Rangers. During the second intermission, President Bush's speech to the nation was broadcast over the Arenavision screen. A decision was made—correctly—to forego the third period. Our players stood side-by-side with our Rangers counterparts and listened to the rest of the speech. Then we all simply shook hands and left the ice. Finishing an exhibition hockey game would have been ridiculous under the circumstances. We all felt raw and emotional and not one of us gave a damn about playing hockey at the moment.

The 2001–02 season began on time, however. Once again we were enjoying a measure of success. We had skill in a bunch of young players like Simon Gagné, Justin Williams, and Boucher and talented veterans such as Primeau, Roenick, and Tocchet. Then we picked up tough guy Donald Brashear from the Canucks in a trade for Hlaváč, so the toughness department was in good shape. No one was going to come after our skill players with "Brash" on patrol.

Johnsson was a good all-around defenseman; a nice addition to our roster. And Brendl was, well, different. Low-energy and pessimistic would be understatements to describe his personality. One time, we were trailing in a game. Trying to get some emotion flowing, John LeClair hollered, "Come on, boys! We just need to pick up on Pavel's energy and we'll be fine!" I looked over toward Pavel. He hadn't even heard what John said. He sat, inattentively, with a hangdog look on his face and his eyes half-open. I couldn't help it. I cracked up laughing.

Such was Pavel's career than when he scored his first NHL goal in 3-0 win over Washington on Oct. 30, he wasn't even on the ice when the puck when went in the net. He was going off on a line change, flipped the puck into the attack zone and was on the bench by the time it found its way past Olaf Kolzig. That would be Brendl's only NHL point of the season. A couple weeks later, he was sent down to the AHL. He remained with the Phantoms the rest of the season until he dressed in the final game of the NHL season.

Late in the season Billy was holding a video session. Brashear came in and, in an elevated voice, said, "Billy, what do we do when a guy is coming through the middle of the ice?"

And Billy replied, "C'mon, Donald, you just work harder!"

So, Donald was the first guy to kind of come in and push back on Billy. Brash said, "This isn't working. No one knows where anyone is going." The thing was, Billy had a playbook, and you can't have a playbook in hockey, unless your name is Fred Shero. It's too fast, there's no playbook. Actually, Shero created more of a guidebook than a formal series of set plays. It's too fast, there's no playbook. You might have pre-set plays on the power play that might work one out of 15 times because the other team's video wasn't working properly. But as for mapping out a game in advance, things just happen too quickly to take a football approach to the whole thing.

Bill had an NFL-style playbook. Nobody read it. When Donald said he didn't know where to go, Billy looked over at Stothers and said, "Hey, Stuts! Get Brash a playbook, he hasn't been here. He can review it and figure out what's going on." Those are the kinds of things we were learning under the Barber regime. Work hard, play with passion—we all understood that. As a player, Billy was an unbelievable goal scorer, penalty killer, and defensive forward. As a person, I love him. He's a cool guy. He was fun, entertaining, kept guys loose, and liked Johnny Cash and his style of music. But as a coach, it was one of the worst things I ever had to deal with at the NHL level. We needed more structure. With Billy in here, you could only work your butt off so many times. Then you need structure that would only make sense to you as a player. We never had that.

As the year came to a close, we got to the playoffs again: a date with the Ottawa Senators, a team not that loaded with talent but plenty of discipline. They did have Daniel Alfredsson, but the rest of them were hard-working, two-way types who seldom turned the puck over. They were very well structured. They knew defensive positioning and defensive responsibility. They might have been a boring team to watch, but boy did we walk into a buzzsaw. I thought we were going to win, especially since Ottawa had not had too much playoff success in the past. We thought we were going to come in and smoke them. Somehow, we won Game 1 by a 1–0 score when Ruslan Fedotenko produced a goal in and Čechmánek recorded a shutout.

Yet things quickly went downhill from there. Or maybe a ski run down the Matterhorn might describe it better. We lost the next four games in a row by scores of 3–0, 3–0, 3–0, and 2–1 in overtime. Now it's pretty incredible to lose four games in a row to begin with, but to score just one goal total in those matches? And two goals for an entire best-of-seven series? Pretty hard to do.

Out we go. You want to talk about the grandest of grandiose panic button moves—we pushed it. We pushed the biggest panic button you will ever see in your life in Game 4, where we were headed up to Ottawa. Coach Barber decided to scrap the 1–2–2 checking scheme—the defensive system also known as the neutral zone trap—and go with a "left-wing lock" made famous by some of the powerhouse Detroit Red Wings teams.

Now I'm not sure how many folks understand how that system works, but to be able to fundamentally make a system change through the course of a season is a difficult proposition. It's very challenging to get everyone to buy in because one mistake, one missed assignment could cost you a goal, screw up a game, and possibly keep you out of the playoffs.

Imagine then how difficult it would be to make such a change three games into a playoff series. He tried to explain it like he was trying to break down a Betty Crocker recipe. The problem was no one understood what the hell he was talking about. The Red Wings had a great deal of success with it, but it was geared toward different teams. It was three guys back and the two defensemen would hug up in the neutral zone, then the winger would go back and get the puck. Not really the kind of thing you would tell your forwards—who are not prone to hanging on to the puck in the defensive zone or making a play outside the defensive zone for that matter—in the middle of a playoff series.

That's what happened; that's where the frustration came from. That's why a few guys, namely Boucher and Primeau, came out and said they weren't guided in the right direction. There was a lot of built-up frustration. The ironic thing was that Billy had named Primeau captain after Desjardins stepped aside. Billy thought Primeau would have his back and advocate for him. That was not the case because Prims was an independent type of character. After what we had just gone through in a very awful exit, nobody was going to go out there and say the coaching was great. It was not good that year and everybody knew it. Management knew it;

Ed Snider knew it. It was a very disappointing thing, but it just goes to show you can coach one way in the minors where it's a little more hectic. You can have a guy like Frank "The Animal" Bialowas kicking the living crap out of everybody, but at the NHL level it takes more than "work harder" to expect better results.

You can work smarter: the problem was we just didn't have a roadmap laid out for us that we needed to have. Hard work can be effective to a degree but when we were facing a team as disciplined as Ottawa, we weren't going to win.

Billy got fired at the end of the season and this is where, in my mind, the hell begins.

WITH "GOOD COP" BARBER heading out the door of his Flyers coaching office for the last time, the players knew a "bad cop" was on the way.

Clarke didn't disappoint when he decided on Ken Hitchcock to run the show.

First off, when it came to people skills, "Hitch" left a lot to be desired. You're not going to go out and find many guys who say he's an amazing human being, not that you have to be a Sunday school teacher to be a successful coach in the National Hockey League. Most of the players knew the guy's back story: former sporting goods store manager who somehow worked his way up through the junior ranks to enjoy a multitude of success. Everybody in the locker room knew his reputation. He had won a Stanley Cup in 1999 with the Dallas Stars, using some of the best talent the league had to offer. Thing is, he thought he was the one who won the Cup and that was what we were staring at.

When Billy got fired, we knew something was coming down the pike that was somewhat anti-player. But it was really more pro-coach. Hitchcock thought he was the greatest coach who ever walked the face of the earth. He came in with that attitude.

There was a new assistant coach, Craig Hartsburg, who was cut from the same cloth as Hitchcock, and the other assistant, Wayne Fleming. If Hitchcock were to tell Fleming to jump off a building, Fleming would ask which floor to make the leap from. That was the kind of nonsense that we all were preparing to deal with. I knew that a guy like Hitchcock would get up in my grill the whole season.

This is how my tenure with Hitchcock started off at the beginning of the 2002–03 season. I already had a reputation for being a regular drinker. I came into a meeting the night before training camp began and my body fat percentage was something like 13.1 percent, which was slightly over the previous year's reading of 12.4 percent.

In his office after the meeting, it was him, the assistant coaches, Clarke, and assistant GM Holmgren. They asked me about my weight. My weight was the same as it was the year before, but my body fat was up ever so little. I really didn't have an answer. I said I was just getting ready for camp. I thought my body of work spoke for itself. But Clarke had his own theory on the body fat uptick: "Because you drink too much," Clarke said. "That's why it's up." So that's how everything started off that way and I'm thinking to myself, *This is just great.* I remember looking at those five guys who were staring me down, a brand-new coach who would never be mistaken for Rod "The Bod" Brind'Amour. Then there was the greatest leader in pro sports and his assistant—all big fans of mine but intimidating nonetheless—and the two assistants sitting there like they knew what was going on.

I looked around and said, "It's a shame you guys think that." I added that I liked to party when the opportunity presented itself, but I was not going to sit here and define what alcoholism is or isn't to those guys. That's when Hitchcock said we need you to lose a half-percent of body fat in training camp or I would not be playing in the opener at Edmonton. I looked back at everyone in the room and said, "Well, good luck in that game then." I continued that thought by saying I didn't know what kind of bull this was, but I was going to tell them one thing right then: I would be ready for the beginning of the season, or even the next day, so keep me informed. If they were satisfied with my game, which should be all that mattered, just let me know if I would be on the plane to Edmonton. And if not, then get rid of me if I was such a problem.

I stood up and walked out of the room. It was as high as I could hold my head. When camp opened the next day, Hitchcock had already forgotten about the meeting, and we proceeded from there, completely engaged in training camp at Voorhees, New Jersey, and pointing toward the first game of the regular season. Camp started and I actually had a very good preseason. Hitchcock tried to put in a new system. I could tell right away he was a very good Xs and Os coach but also very arrogant. Personally, I found it hard to comprehend that someone so overweight could be that arrogant at the same time unless you're a comedian.

Almost from the start, it just didn't work with Hitch. Players everywhere he went hated him. I think they liked the fact they were able to win games but if you ask anybody—and I've talked to many guys—there's not a single one that has a good thing to say about Hitchcock the person. They do like the coach, but they don't like his tactics. I can't begin to tell you how many times players have referred to him using a pejorative about his appearance. Even players on his own bench during a game! It goes without saying what players were catcalling with a degree of contempt from benches on the other side. Most of it was followed with a laugh from assorted listeners. It's amazing how someone like that can parade himself out there and not think he's going to get laughed at.

Yet we did appreciate his coaching knowledge. At the end of the day, I ended up getting along with Hitchcock my last season with the Flyers (2005–06). I was going through an awful lot at that time. The funny thing is, I'm not saying those guys who were in the pre-camp meeting were wrong, it was just that I didn't want to hear it at that time. I was still an important player. That's really what was lost in the whole thing. At this point I was still Desjardins' partner. He loved playing with me. Management and the coaching staff knew that, and yet they still called me in, gave it to me, and then just let me walk out the door.

You know, if it was such a big deal for them, why didn't they execute a plan of action to help me? Of course they didn't. That would have meant taking me away from the rink. No doubt, it would have left a hole in their lineup, and by the way, there was no way I wasn't playing in that opening game in Edmonton. That contention was simply laughable. They knew they were playing poker with me and using that no-play in Edmonton as a bluff. They knew it. I knew it. So I went about my business, getting ready physically and mentally in camp. It's the same every year: Work your ass off, be a good player by listening to your coaches. I was always that guy. I was taught as a kid to respect and listen to your coaches, but I was ready to cross that line because I had never dealt with someone like Hitchcock.

The worst part in the three or four years he was here was watching media fawn over him. It was embarrassing to watch reporters engage with him after games or practices. It made me disgusted that they could be so shallow and allow him to control the narrative. Guys hated it. Even his former players in Dallas were vocal with their criticism.

Despite all that, I played pretty good hockey. It's funny, after the 30-game mark I got hurt, and Hitch was asked what it meant to lose someone like Chris Therien. His response? He said that Chris was our "best defenseman" up to that point. I was dressing near Desjardins, and he said, "Did you hear that? He calls you our best defenseman and you have been our best defenseman." That was Éric Desjardins saying that to me. When I got hurt, they asked Hitchcock what guys had surprised him so far that season.

He came back with "the two guys who have surprised me most this season are Keith Primeau and Chris Therien."

After a blasting toward me about being a drunk right before the start of camp, he ends up calling me his best defenseman. Yet he never had me in his leadership group. He invited me in one time in his second year. He just knew I was someone who was never going to agree with him.

You know something? He was right.

CHAPTER 18

Here's to Your
Mental Health

THE TERM "FULL NERVOUS BREAKDOWN" should only be used in extreme circumstances, and for me, the end of my 2003–04 Flyers season certainly qualified.

The stress of the job on the ice, the daily micro-management by Ken Hitchcock, and the trade rumors about my imminent departure from the team conspired to put my life in constant emotional crisis mode. Of course, the easy way out was to turn to the bottle more than ever. Numb the feelings. Keep the foreboding thoughts in the back of your mind. Trust almost no one. A lot of it began to build at the start of the season when my status on the Flyers roster came into question.

I don't want to blame anyone for my alcoholism during this period of my life because at the end of the day, I was the one who put the bottle to my lips and nobody else. That being said, when you're put in a situation where the only thing you have to rely on is the drink and the main reason for it is the coach you're playing for, the logic is rather simple.

Hitchcock broke down every player he had. In my opinion it's amazing he won in Dallas. Any player on the Stars will tell you the reason they won is because of their absolute hatred of Hitchcock. They literally mobilized against him to win the Stanley Cup. I played in Dallas years later, and the stories were all the same. They were identical to the ones you heard in Philadelphia. The way I saw it, he always had a couple assistant coaches who were "yes" men, and during my tenure it was Hartsburg and Fleming. Because they never stood up to him, it was a waste of time to even have them around. The worst thing you can have around as far as an assistant coach goes is a yes man, and Hitchcock only had yes men as his assistant coaches.

As the years went by, as much as he would complain to reporters about me, I was still playing good hockey for him. Every single game, Desjardins and I drew the other team's top line. What was my reward for that? After our 2003 training camp I got sent down to the Philadelphia Phantoms for two games and Hitchcock had never spoken to me to tell me I would be the seventh defenseman on the team. He played fast and loose with the truth. I chalked that up to a nasty streak he had that no one could quantify.

Eventually the team was on a road trip in California at the beginning of the season. LeClair and I were there but not playing. LeClair was injured, and I was a healthy scratch. I can assure you that neither he nor I wasted a single second of fun on that trip. The Flyers were set to play the Sharks in San Jose. Team LeClair made a detour to San Francisco, and we hung out the entire night. It was easy to remember what night it was because we were watching the National League Championship Series in a bar when the infamous Steve Bartman reached over the fence to rob Moisés Alou of a catch, and the Cubs fans went berserk. Anyway, Johnny and I had a blast. The night started with dinner in Sausalito on the other side of the Golden Gate Bridge. I was having mixed emotions, feeling like I was getting the shaft, and LeClair was injured, so we just were looking to have a good time for a couple days.

Here's the topper: While the Flyers were playing the Sharks, we were watching the American League Championship Series on television. Johnny is a die-hard Red Sox fan, and I'm a big Yankees fan, so when Aaron Boone hit the big home run to win it, there was some good-natured bragging rights. When we got back to Philly, things only got worse. I had played in the season opener in Los Angeles on October 21, then was back on the ice when Montreal came to town on the 27th. So, I got sent down to the minors for a conditioning stint. Anyway, I got called into Clarke's office, and he had a look of disgust on his face. The Philadelphia Phantoms coach, John Stevens, was in there, too. Clarke said they had to send me down for two games because, even though it wasn't what he wanted, he needed me back and ready in the Flyers lineup as the season had not gone the way management wanted it to. It's always great to feel wanted, but why make it sound like I was part of the problem?

I went down to the minors, and we had a game against Scranton/Wilkes-Barre the following night and then another in Virginia. I played okay, just trying to get my speed back. I didn't feel great about my game. I really didn't care where I played as long as I was being treated fairly. However, the words "fairly" and "Hitchcock" really don't belong in the same sentence. When I got back Sunday, the Flyers had a day off following a tough game against Carolina. After the game, Hitchcock told everyone he was glad that the Flyers were going to have Chris Therien back in the lineup for the next game. I couldn't believe the hypocrisy after the way I had been treated. We played Montreal on a Monday night and guess who I was paired with? Eric Desjardins. We won the game 5–0. There I was playing in the top defense pairing two nights after I was playing with a bunch of American Hockey League kids down in Norfolk, riding a damn bus and 48 hours later I'm on one of the top defense pairings in the NHL. I was thinking what a joke the whole thing was.

To no one's surprise, I got what amounted to a hero's welcome back. Goalie Robert Esche stood up and said there wasn't one guy in the room who didn't trust me. They loved me. That meant so much to me. During games, everyone had my back because they trusted me on the ice. There may have been some occasions when I was a bit aloof or didn't do the right things, but my heart was always in the right place. When that first puck dropped, my plan was to give one hundred and fifty percent no matter what happened, and that's exactly what I did.

That's the way it went as the season continued along. It didn't get much better. Hitchcock kept pushing and pushing me. So, it figured that I would start drinking more and more. We went on the road, and I would bring a bottle of wine or two with me. The amount of stress and how to deal with it was becoming paramount to my career in the NHL. Under this regime, things weren't healthy for my body, mind, or soul. Sometimes it was hard to get up in the morning to get to the rink.

You talk about mental health in sports in general; guys have issues all the time. I believe at the time I was having a full mental breakdown. I was still doing my best to give one hundred percent and try to help my teammates win hockey games. After the new year began, I thought I was done with Hitchcock. The players didn't like him, and it was very difficult for anybody to get any kind of notion that we were all on the same page. It's funny, because Hitchcock is the kind of guy who, with the right people around him, can do some special things, as he did at the end of that season. For instance, Primeau went on an incredible run.

I was traded to Dallas on March 8, 2004. I'd become the longest tenured defenseman in Flyers history by that point in terms of games played. I was traded for a 2004 eighth-round Draft pick. Not a good feeling. The Flyers caught lightning in a bottle toward the end of that season and made a run. I was watching from afar, and to be honest, I didn't want Hitchcock to win. The Flyers made it to Game 7 of the Eastern Conference Finals before losing to Tampa Bay, ironically on a goal by ex-Flyer

Ruslan Fedotenko. I felt bad for my former teammates, but that's as far as my sympathy went.

AS EACH DAY PASSED through the closing stages of the 2003–04 season before the trade, my alcoholism accelerated. I had a feeling my days with Hitchcock and the Flyers were numbered. On a team with average talent, Hitchcock would be an average coach at best. But this Flyers team had the nuts, so it made him look good. He did nothing exceptional that made guys want to go through a wall for him. During games, opponents would shout insults at him right on our bench. He would flip off other teams' players, which is a no-no. I was always embarrassed by that. There would be verbal exchanges, too, which Hitchcock seemed to have a knack for. It never ended well.

One time during a particularly tense game, things came to a head on our bench. Roenick was coming off the ice after taking a shift, sat down, looked down the bench at Hitchcock, and said, "Would you just shut the hell up!" Or perhaps the language was a bit stronger, and there may have been a few words about Hitchcock's physique thrown in there as well. J.R. added, "Everybody is so sick of you." The coach just bowed his head and didn't respond. That happened a lot. I believe that's why Hitchcock played the media so well. He knew that the players didn't like him, and if the word got out from their end of who this guy really was, he wouldn't have lasted longer than a year.

My last game for the Flyers that season took place in the famous brawl game against Ottawa at Philly's then–Wachovia Center on March 5, 2004. The two teams accumulated a record 419 penalty minutes, eclipsing the old mark of 406. The Flyers also set a record with 213 minutes of their own. Even Esche got involved in a fight with Senators goalie Patrick Lalime. It was so bad that the NHL changed the rule involving "instigation" and mandated a one-game suspension for any violators.

Meanwhile, I didn't realize it at the time, but that first period shift would be my last as a Flyer that season. I injured my shoulder, went to the locker room for some ice bags when the fight broke out. I guess by that time there was a feeling they were going to trade me before the deadline. By that point with Hitchcock, I was done. It didn't matter where I was going; I would rather have been playing for Mystery, Alaska. That's the truth because I was so miserable. Ironically, they had a pretty good team. A few days before they had traded defenseman Eric Weinrich, so anything seemed to be on the table—everything was fair game. Why would you get rid of a veteran defenseman like that?

A week after that they sent me to the Dallas Stars for a couple draft picks. In that moment, after having played in Philadelphia for 10 years, I was like "Thank God." I didn't realize how much animosity I had toward the whole situation. I won't say that I wasn't to blame for some of the problem. I felt like a dog chasing its tail. What did I hate more? The coach and playing in a situation that was harmful? Or the fact that it was leading me toward alcohol as my only coping mechanism? It was very rough two years.

The move to Dallas was the springboard of my alcoholism. I was away from my family. It took a while to get used to unfamiliar surroundings—the time-worn line about old dogs learning new tricks. Funny thing was, when I returned to Philadelphia for the start of the 2005–06 season, things between Hitchcock and I somehow got better.

I don't think my play on the ice for the Stars could make up for what was happening off it. I believed I was still playing well before the trade, and I might not have been moved except I kept getting scratched. If I had been left alone, I would have been fine. Going from sitting out a game to playing with Desjardins was just ridiculous. It just shows the arrogance that was going on at the time. I am proud of the fact that I was never scratched from a playoff game in my entire career under any coach. There were times I had to sit out a regular season game but never one in the playoffs. Also, I'm proud of the fact I made the playoffs every single season of my career. That's a tribute to Clarke and his ability to build good teams. Also, Snider and his willingness to spend money to try to make this team a contender every year and give the fans something to cheer about. For that I'm truly grateful.

I headed for deep in the heart of Texas and it was an out-and-out free-for-all. I think we knew the 2004–05 lockout was coming, and every player was aware of it. We had meetings with NHL Players' Association chief Bob Goodenow, and he told us he didn't think we were going to play hockey the following year. To me, that was somewhat ludicrous. But it happened. Think about this: Under NHL commissioner Gary Bettman, the league has lost two full seasons (the entire 2004–05 campaign and half of 1994–95 and 2012–13). Think of it this way: Alexander Ovechkin was drafted No. 1 overall in 2004. He most certainly would have played a potential 82 games starting for the Capitals if that 2004–05 season had been held, plus another 34 in 2012–13. That's 116 more games. Imagine how much closer he would be to Wayne Gretzky's all-time record (894).

Can you fathom any business giving up two years of operations over a 20-year span? Hard to believe. Just amazing. I arrived in Dallas, and of course, my first game was against the Flyers. Just prior to the trade, Clarke called me into his office and told me, "We traded you. We moved you to Dallas." He sounded kind of disappointed he was making the trade, but at the time Snider didn't want to take on any more salary. And that was probably a first for him. I wasn't bitter because my situation there had become so bad that I told my teammates if you come down the wing in practice and take a shot off my foot, don't worry about it. That's when you know you are D-O-N-E.

As I mentioned, my drinking was getting worse. My attitude toward the team, because of the coach, was getting worse. I don't like to pass blame on my frequent imbibing but for whatever reason, it was becoming all gas, no brakes with the bottle. This was when it really got heavy. Not a day went by I wasn't thinking about my next drink.

The Dallas experience was short and bittersweet. I played 11 games in the regular season and five games in a playoff series against Colorado and the Forsberg-led Avalanche. Crazy as it sounds, I scored two goals in that series and that led the team. There weren't many sober days for me in Dallas. I was partying on a daily basis. I had a good friend down there, Ben Fanele, who had grown up with my wife. He became very much like a brother to me. We hung out together, and Shayne Corson, the ex-Montreal Canadien, was also part of that group. We laughed because he was an enemy of the Flyers over the years, yet we became very good buddies. This was his last roundup of a sparkling 20-year career, and he was trying to make the most of it. He was a great teammate and a guy I came to like a lot. I also found out he was a guy who, over the years, had anxiety and panic disorder. Boy, did we party hard together.

When the playoffs started, we knew we were up against it with Colorado. All things considered, I was playing pretty well. The fact that I led the team in scoring tells you the problems we were having on offense. Dave Tippett, the coach of the Stars, came up to me after the series and said he wanted to apologize. I said, "For what?"

Tippett's response: "Well, I said when one of your defensemen leads the team in scoring, you're not going to win a playoff series." I told him he was right and that's why we were headed home for the summer.

CHAPTER 19

Wasted Away in Margaritaville

THE ASSEMBLY LINE OF MARGARITAS I consumed the night before the last game of the Dallas Stars' 2003–04 season were bad enough. Throw in a handful of beers and you had a full-blown all-night bender. That's how bad things had gotten for me in Texas. No fault of the Stars, and there was no coach to resent now. I was just dealing with my own personal demons, wondering whether the 2004–05 season was even going to happen and, at this stage of my career, pondering my future in the sport. I was spending most of my downtime either in my dinky apartment or at a little Mexican bar called Primos. An average night? Oh, 15 margaritas after practice until the end of the night was my daily routine. Fanele was there with me, and this was only over a span of about a month, covering the 11 regular season games I played with the Stars.

Talk about weird scenes: My first game against the Flyers had to happen in, of all places, Philadelphia. What are the odds? What a surreal scene, playing my old team in the place I had spent the better part of a decade. It was so crazy that in warmups, my kids were down at the other end of the ice, and I was in the Dallas zone watching the Flyers get ready. It felt like I was in the Twilight Zone. I remembered I had played so many games for the orange and black. I had never been in this situation before. I was paired by assistant coach Rick Wilson with Russian defenseman Sergei Zubov. That was a great partner to have, a Hall of Famer. Man was that guy slick. The Stars also had another Hall of Famer, Mike Modano, a hell of a player.

The game started and it felt weird jumping over the boards and banging heads with guys I had shared sweat and beers with over the past 10 years. At one point, I was defending in the Stars' zone and I—just out of habit—almost checked a Dallas player. That's how second nature the orange and black had become to me. There I was in a Dallas uniform, and I almost banged into my teammate. That game was one of the oddest events in my life. Knowing my offbeat history, of course it would happen like that. The good thing was the fans received me well. They were very polite and nice. It was nice to get such a reception considering my situation was so bad. If I got booed by the fan base, I often wondered how much they were tying me—the longest cog in the machine—into a generation of Flyers players that had not won anything. Maybe it was more of a revolt against team management. We had enjoyed successful seasons, but we had not won anything. We got close; we got on the dance floor in 1997, but we were just not able to hoist that trophy. I always felt like we were a goalie away from winning at least one Stanley Cup.

Dallas, which had won the Cup back in 1999, still had a good nucleus. Billy Guerin was a great veteran player, and we became good friends. Dallas had a good locker room and my personality seemed to jell with a lot of the players. Robbie DiMaio was my roommate; I had played with him back in Philadelphia during my rookie and second seasons. He was probably one of the toughest small guys I ever played with. In the playoffs, my two goals felt like 10. It was the first time I ever felt like I had a real scoring touch, especially in the postseason.

Being on my own was a bit dangerous. When you're more than a thousand miles away from home and family, the personal hours feel different. It was the beginning of a full-on, no-consideration situation made primarily for drinking. It was almost like even though I got away from a situation in Philadelphia that I felt was so detrimental to me, I was still making the worst version of myself. What really happened was that this WAS me. I had gotten to the point where my alcoholism was getting worse. When the season was over and after I left Dallas, I went home and really thought that I was drinking more than I had before and it had become normalized in my day-to-day life. That was kind of scary from that point.

Still, I got the feeling Dallas wanted to bring me back. Stars GM Doug Armstrong called my agents (Morris-Meehan) and said he liked me so much he would like to offer me a two-year deal if the lockout didn't happen. The offer was a little bit less than what I was making but still a pretty good figure. They valued me enough to make that bid, and I don't even know if they were aware of how bad my off-ice situation was getting. My attitude had become: what they don't know won't hurt them.

That last game of the season epitomized what was wrong with my game plan. It was something like a 12:00 or 12:30 PM start. It was daylight savings time weekend, so move the clocks ahead—spring forward, right? The night before, we all went out drinking and the party went on until 3:00 or 4:00 AM. There were several Dallas players out on the town as well. The difference was, they beat me to the rink the next morning.

My alarm went off at 10:30 AM. Only problem was, it should have been set for 9:30 AM. Complete panic. I threw on my suit as fast as I could, hair completely all over the place, no time to shave, reeking of 20 beers and 15 margaritas. I raced out of the apartment, drove 50 miles per hour in a 25 zone, rushed into a Krispy Kreme doughnut joint, grabbed a handful of doughnuts and a coffee, and bolted for American Airlines Center. I showed up 30 minutes before warmup. Then I went out and played one hell of a game—maybe my best as a Star—which kind of shows you I was what some people might call a functional drunk.

The playoffs seemed to end in the blink of an eye. Tom Hicks, the owner, was a good guy and, like Snider, passionate about his team. After the last game, Hicks came into the room and called a team meeting. He looked everyone in the eye and said, "Guys, I just spent $69 million for a first-round exit. It will never, ever happen again on my watch." I was sitting there thinking to myself, *This lockout might be for real.* There was a lot of frustration hanging in the air. With the lockout looming, we figured the early part of the season would be canceled. I realized I wasn't going to be playing hockey for quite a while. The owners were pushing for a salary cap, and this time they weren't going to be denied.

That's where the line was drawn. It truly was the beginning of my alcoholism. It put me on a path that would take years to get out of. Alcoholism is a very painful disease of the body, mind, and soul. I never realized at the beginning of the summer of 2004 just what a ride I was about to embark on.

IN PRO SPORTS, there's an overused line about looking in the mirror to examine your own shortcomings when it comes to personal performance. Self-accountability for a player is the most important instrument in a coach's toolbox. The old adage is: Look in a mirror. Do you like what you see? If you don't, well, then do something about it.

In October 2004, I didn't need a mirror to know what was going on with me as far as being an accountable human being—a husband, father, friend, and teammate. Things were spinning out of control in my life and the irony was the problem needed a solution, but the only solution I could see was also the problem. That's because I had become a full-fledged alcoholic and felt powerless to escape the disease. To my horror, the only way I could cope with it was to drink more.

During the Yankees–Red Sox '04 ALCS, LeClair, Weinrich, and I went out to a local watering hole to watch Game 3. We didn't get out of there until well past midnight after drinking wine, beer, and shots. The next morning, we went out and skated about 10:00 AM in Medford, New Jersey. There were around a dozen guys, including some players and other people who worked with equipment, at the rink. I skated for about 20 minutes, and for the first time in my life, I had what I would call withdrawal symptoms. I was skating around the ice, and I felt dizzy. I felt like I couldn't swallow, and in some strange way, like I was coming out of my body. I was thinking, *Am I having a panic attack? Why is this happening?* It had never happened before, and I couldn't figure out a reason other than that I had been drinking the night before. There had been a lot of nights when I had been drinking the night before and nothing had happened. That was why this time was so different. It was the first day I admitted to myself that I was an alcoholic. *You're officially an alcoholic.* The subject wasn't open for debate. Besides, who was going to argue?

I came off the ice after about 25 minutes and said I wasn't feeling great. I went in the changing room and could barely get my equipment off, because my hands were shaking so badly. Somehow, I managed to get my equipment out to the car. The shaking continued, and I wondered if I could drive. I kept thinking, *I need to get home.* I didn't know what was wrong with me. This was a first. The thought persisted: *Is there something wrong with me?* I knew it was something chemical, that it had to do in some way with alcohol because I drank a ton. This was more than just your three-Tylenol hangover.

When I got back to the house, there was nobody home. My wife and kids were out. It was pouring rain, probably 50 degrees, and I got out of the car in my driveway not knowing what I was going to do. I don't know what made me do it, but I headed for the liquor cabinet. I found a bottle of Van Gogh vodka, probably a leftover from someone who had come to the house for a party. It's something I would never buy or drink, which tells you something about the desperate mode I was in. I grabbed a clear glass, filled it about halfway, walked out into the driveway in the rain, and proceeded to gulp down about six ounces.

What happened immediately was that it took away all the anxiety, all the pain, all the nervousness, all the shakes—all the withdrawal was completely gone. That's alcoholism in its truest form. If you wonder why alcoholics don't stop or can't stop, it's because most of the time they're dealing with the adverse effects of withdrawal. It's the worst feeling ever. For me, I wound up finding out withdrawal was something I couldn't take. The only thing I could do to make it go away was to drink through it, drink with it, and just let it play itself out. There's an old saying: "I drank myself sober." Well, that's exactly what I did. Just about every day from that point on. That's why I kept a bottle of vodka in my car all the time, because I knew a single shot would get me back on the right path. That's what started in the fall of 2004. I became a full-fledged alcoholic. I did not stop;

it went all the way through the lockout 2004–05 season-not-to-be. I drank more and more to the point where, in contrast to previous years where I suspected I had a drinking problem, now my actions were starting to confirm it. When you need a substance to help you with the same substance you're already dealing with from the night before, you officially have a substance abuse problem.

It was a very difficult and trying time in my life. I knew I would deny and lie about it, try to hide it as long as I could. I thought I was the guy that this kind of thing didn't happen to. But it did. The entire 2004–05 timeframe went like that. I got sicker and sicker. My weight went up a little bit, but it got to the point where I didn't even feel like eating that much. I got a little bit of food down through January, just to get some nutrition in me. I didn't skate after that. Most guys had kind of hung up their skates. My focus was to try to be somewhat disciplined through wherever it was going. It was bad because I was doing anything to find a party. It didn't really matter at whose cost. I can certainly tell my relationships at home were getting worse. They surely weren't getting better. Of course, things were only going to get worse. I mean what kind of person would want me and my problem? Why would Diana or our three kids want any part of that? They never wanted a part of that, and I don't blame them.

That had to be the worst year for her. This was worse than 2006, my blowup year. She probably realized she had three kids, and her husband the hockey player is an alcoholic. She probably thought, *I can't really do any reaching out now, because he doesn't listen to anything I say.* That's what a drunk does to the loved ones around him and the disappointment that comes with it.

I was hoping this lockout would end and be a silver lining to this period of my life. Eventually it did, but it was a little too late for me. By that time the damage had been done. My focus was shot, and my hockey career as I knew it would never be the same. Not the way I was drinking. I might have had flashes of competent play if I had another chance, but I would never be the player I once was, even though I was only 33.

I didn't believe that any help would get me out of this. I didn't think that it would even work. There was a persona that came along with it. My teammates were thinking, *There goes Bundy, the happy-go-lucky drunk.* They knew I came to play hard every night, but most people didn't understand the pain I was going through. I was really starting to hurt. The more I drank led to less gain in everything I did in my life. And it showed no signs of letting up.

CHAPTER 20

You Bettor You Bet

PROFESSIONAL ATHLETES ARE RISK-TAKERS by nature, so why should their approach to dipping their toe in the pool of sports gambling be any different? Michael Jordan, Jaromir Jágr, Pete Rose, Charles Barkley.... The list goes on and on. Gambling is certainly part of the fabric of hockey in general, and it's as prevalent as drinking. Who cares about losing hundreds or thousands when a superstar is making millions?

Gambling is something that has always been around hockey. Since my first year in the league, I had been using bookies to gamble on football. I would say in any given year there was at least half the team that gambled, as well as one coach and one person from team management. I'm not saying that in a bad way or to cast aspersions on anyone's character: I'm just saying it was prevalent. For whatever reason—whether it was competitive spirit, boredom, or the experience of sitting around wasting time watching games to see the outcomes and the guys' reactions to them—it was a big part of hockey. I would be remiss if I didn't mention this aspect of hockey because it was that prevalent.

I started off as a hundred-dollar gambler on a game, which is not a lot at the end of the day, because, as I mentioned, salaries are in the millions. It can spiral out of control, however, and it can get bigger, crazier over time. You always hear the random story about some guy getting his clock cleaned and then having to find a way to pay off the local bookmaker in South Philadelphia. These things happen but I will say one thing as someone who has been a gambler and been around that scene much of his life: I have never seen a hockey player that I played with ever gamble on a hockey game. The Rose story—allegations he bet on baseball—served as a huge deterrent.

Betting on hockey just never happened. It was always football or basketball, and it does happen. I believe it comes from the competitiveness of athletes and who they are. Sports gambling is one thing, and I will tell you that a team official used to try to gamble with LeClair and me in hopes we wouldn't gamble on games ourselves. The problem is, there were always 10 or 12 guys ready to put their bets in on Sunday mornings for late afternoon games. I knew that even though management had a sparkle in their eye about them, at least one of our management leaders knew there were times when players were up to no good. He knew through his connections who was doing what in the city of Philadelphia. He was pretty good at trying to monitor guys and keep an eye on them. It's true I was a drinker and a gambler, and yet I remained with the Flyers for the better part of 12 years, which in some respects is remarkable. I think that speaks for my character, and that others were able to see and recognize it inside me.

There were other guys who gambled, too. We loved gambling on football, but the highlights were trips to casinos. We always had tons of fun. We would go down to the casino some nights after hockey games as a team at the end-of-the-year party. As much as I liked the casinos, I did not frequent them a whole lot. When I did go, I usually hung out with a group of high-profile players. I would just sit around and watch them win or lose money.

The best story I have about gambling came in 1999. We had been eliminated from the playoffs and were at a Philadelphia airport bar at 7:00 AM. There were seven of us: Berube, Jones, Tocchet, and me, among others. Next stop: Las Vegas. That night I headed out to the casino, ran into a couple of the guys, and promptly lost 75 grand. The money was gone so fast you wouldn't believe it. I started off with one $75,000 marker and then I got another. I was loaded and being a complete rear body part. My brain said walk straight; my legs said let's go sideways. I was a sight to be seen, right down to the pair of sinister-looking *Mission Impossible* sunglasses I had purchased earlier in the day. They were selling the Ray-Bans as part of a promotion for the Tom Cruise movie.

There I was at the blackjack table and suddenly my luck changed. Talk about comebacks for all time.... I took that $75G marker and ended up turning it into $125,000 in about nine minutes. The pit bosses at the Venetian looked like they were ready to call security. They literally wanted me off the table because I was hammering them so badly. To top it off, Berube, who's not really a gambler, happened to be alongside me. I was so red-hot, wearing these sunglasses when "Chief" sat down next to me. "Put $5,000 in front of me, Chief," I said, "and let me do some work for you." In less than 10 minutes, I turned that $5,000 into $23,000. Things were going so well that the Venetian called the Las Vegas Gaming Commission to come down and check the *Mission Impossible* glasses to see if I had some kind of device in them. This really was going from *Mission Impossible* to mission accomplished. Every single guy on that trip watched it happen.

But like every true gambling story, there are moments of winning and there are moments of losing. Unless you gamble for a living, chances are things have a way of evening out, and so it was with me.

I went back three years later: same exact lack of sobriety, same exact traveling party, different hotel, and I lost $100,000. In my mind, for the two trips to Vegas, I was still up $25,000. Bottom line is, Flyers management didn't want guys gambling because they felt they were preoccupied by what was going on, causing a distraction from their focus on the ice. To that I say bunk, because there's not one bet I placed on a game that affected our level of play during games.

Except one time: Let's start off by saying this might be the biggest gambling story in a locker room in NHL history. Somebody said they had "a game of the year," a sure thing in betting parlance. It was a college football game—the University of Miami over Syracuse University. It was an ESPN game, and it was going to run in the 4:00–7:00 PM slot, right up until the start of our Flyers game. There were a few guys riding the exercise bike, the same crew from Vegas, and everyone had dumped their cash on the Miami Hurricanes. The pool of players grew to about a dozen. Eventually the group bet rose to around $100,000 that the entire group put in with this bookie.

I've never seen a collection of more dumb-ass guys going in to make it look like they were stretching in the weight room after each period of the game on TV. Miami, which had gifted quarterback Ken Dorsey that year, blew the game open and covered the spread. It was the first time in my life I have seen a group of grown men turn into a bunch of seven-year-old boys in a span of minutes. Everyone was getting ready to head for the bathroom if things went the wrong way and they lost all their money.

I can safely say, in my entire career, that's the only time I saw players actually care about a bet they made. Gambling is only a problem if you have an addiction and therein lies the trouble. A lot of people do.

SITTING AT HOME IN FRONT OF THE TELEVISION set drinking a few beers is one thing. Consuming several brews and then jumping behind the wheel of a Mercedes is simply a thoughtless, reckless act that puts lives in danger.

However, given my advanced state of alcoholism at the end of the 2005–06 preseason I was ill-prepared to make proper judgments late in the evening. A night at the end of the exhibition schedule provided a perfect example.

On the way home from Washington, D.C., we had a few beers in the back of the bus. There were a few "thirsty" hockey guys on that ride back, including Brian Savage, Turner Stevenson, Derian Hatcher, Mike Rathje, and me. When we got back to our New Jersey training facility, the Skate Zone, Rathje and I jumped into the Mercedes parked there because he lived not too far from me. It's about a 15-minute drive to Marlton. As I'm driving down a nearby highway, I see a cop on the left-hand side. I proceeded to accelerate a bit, make a right, and turn off the lights. It was the dumbest thing I could have done because it had "impaired" written all over it. The cop pulled up to me with the lights on, stepped out, came over, and asked me why I just took off. I came back with, "Well, we're hockey players; we were just playing hockey, coming home, etc." I don't even know if the kid heard me. He was a brand-new young cop, really green, but he decided he was going to run me through the roadside sobriety test.

I remember lifting up the one leg, that was fine; I touched my nose, okay there. Verbally counting letters backward and the whole test. I knew the last test was the "dilated pupils" one (a little birdie told me), and they can tell no matter how well you did walking straight lines and so forth—your pupils are going to dilate, and that's a clear sign you've been drinking. So, the guy said, "Your eyes tell me you've been drinking."

I looked at him and said, "Didn't I tell you we were hockey players? We just played the Capitals in Washington; we play for the Flyers, and my name is Chris Therien." I was thinking, *I'm not really a big name but hopefully it's enough to get us out of here.*

198

It was almost like the kid had some revelation. He went, "Oh, my God, you're Chris Therien!"

Rathje's in the passenger seat watching the whole thing. He probably was in no better shape than I was at the time. The guy said, "Look, I'm really sorry about this" and handed me back my driver's license. He added, "Have a good night. And if you've had a couple beers, do you think your friend would be all right to drive?" I smiled and said absolutely. Mike gets behind the damn wheel of the Mercedes and roars away toward home.

In all my years, I never got a speeding ticket, reckless driving, whatever. What's interesting is I never had a DUI stop in my life that ended with a ticket. Or even drunk and disorderly. The only bad thing that ever came from drinking was destroying almost everything else. But in that year, I was very cautious. I had other people drive, but on that particular night it never occurred to me to have someone sober behind the wheel.

What I do wish had happened is that cop would have brought me in, handcuffed me, and arrested me for drunk driving.

It would have changed who I was that very night instead of breaking into a brand-new NHL season as the drunk I was. I was about to embark on a journey where I was moving a lot of puzzle pieces and doing a lot of maneuvering just to try and get another day of fooling people so I could continue playing hockey. Frankly, it was exhausting.

Just a couple months before, I had gone up to Ottawa with my family to visit my folks. The lockout was over, and I was still very unclear about my future—who was going to sign me, did I want to get re-signed, and so forth. The bottom line was I wasn't even sure I could play hockey because my alcoholism had really taken over. The Flyers captain, Primeau, called me and asked me if I wanted to come back and play for Philly again. I thought in my heart if there might be a place I could play again it would be with the Flyers. Primeau said he wanted me to sign there, and that the team really wanted me back.

Clarke signed Hatcher, Rathje, and me—three defensemen with a total weight of about 750 pounds. I still wasn't sure of my abilities because of my drinking. As training camp started up, I headed into the locker room, and we signed some other good guys including Savage and Stevenson. All of us were kind of near the end of our playing careers in a very changing league, and the lockout didn't help anybody out, including Rathje and Hatcher. To miss a whole year and then try to come back no matter what the capacity.... It just wasn't conducive to success.

My journey in alcohol would ultimately get the best of me. Yet, I felt like the team wanted me. I already knew a bunch of players, including Roenick (subsequently a salary cap casualty when the Flyers signed Peter Forsberg), had gone in and told Clarke they would love to have me back. "We love him in the locker room," they said. "Whatever happened in 2004 when he was traded doesn't matter." Even Hitchcock, the guy I had butted heads with, was on board to have me back. He called me. At that point, I was a free agent and weighing my options. I was getting offered just $550,000, but I didn't care; I just wanted to get back in the league. Another incentive for me was that my former head coach, Terry Murray, was back as an assistant coach. As a former defenseman, he had been helpful with my growth back in the '90s. It was nice to have someone back I trusted. You can never have too many of those.

Working in my favor was that I had spent the offseason focusing on my training. I did a lot of running. It was amazing because I was drinking. I was running five, six miles a day. Only problem was, during the lockout I had put on about 25 pounds. I had to lose that weight and it wasn't going to be easy. My muscle mass had dropped off, and that makes it even tougher to get lighter. Muscle-wise, I wasn't as strong as I had been in my late 20s because I was doing so much cardio. I finally got my weight to where I wanted it to be.

Surprisingly, I came out of the gate playing well. Maybe I knew this was going to be my last rodeo.

Because it was.

CHAPTER 21

Beginning of the End

IT CAN HAPPEN TO US ALL, a moment in time, an epiphany as it were, when life can stop and change on a dime. For me, that vision took place on December 6, 2005, when, unbeknownst to me, I was about to take a left turn on a short road to the end of my hockey career.

The Calgary Flames were in town and the game was a textbook display of defensive hockey. Both teams wouldn't give an inch and the Flyers finally prevailed 1–0 in a shootout. In my mind, I starred in the game for many reasons. First, it was probably the best hockey I would play the entire season, at least of the games in which I did participate as a Flyer that year. Second, the Flames were the defending Western Conference champions, going back to Game 7 of the final four two years back before the lockout. They were still a bona fide contender. Third, I played the entire third period completely loaded. Drunk off my ass.

Competing completely on instinct. And it actually helped. I blocked a game-high four shots and skated 18:39 over 27 shifts without being charged with a giveaway when I had the puck.

The drama began when co-captain Primeau called me into Clarke's office over concerns about my drinking, and I walked out feeling I was alone. I never felt more alienated or more alone. All my close allies were gone. LeClair and Recchi were both in Pittsburgh by then. They were two of my best friends, people I trusted and could confide in. Berube also had moved on, and I was stuck with a bunch of guys who I loved, but they weren't the family that I had come to know. The guys who I had played with in the late 1990s and early 2000s were my family; those were the guys I knew were my greatest teammates. When Primeau brought me in, he lost me. The team lost me that day, too.

Was it their fault? No. It was all my fault. I'm never going to tell you differently. Even then, I logically knew there had to be an end point to playing only on instinct. Sooner or later, it would catch up with me. If you're going to tell people how it is, you have to be completely honest. Could they have gotten me help? Could they have pushed harder? What could they do? Are they going to make me stop drinking? If you wanted to be treated like a man, but then they decide they're going to treat you like a boy because you're not acting like a man, a lot of guys go sideways.

That game against Calgary, for the first two periods, I was playing beyond good. I was playing my best game since before the lockout. I had been drinking the night before. However, all day long, I went without that drink because it was game day. It's just not conducive to playing at your optimum ability at a professional level. I was still playing top four minutes, 18, 19 minutes a game.

By the end of the second period against Calgary, I was starting to shake pretty bad. I don't know if it was the start of DTs (delirium tremens), but it sure felt like it. I was like, *What am I going to do?* I didn't know what to do because the game was so tight: it was 0–0 after the second period. One period (or more) to go. How was I going to get through it?

So, I took my skates off and did the only thing that an alcoholic can possibly do: I walked into the dressing room where the players hang their street clothes, took off my Flyers jersey, grabbed my car keys, and headed for the long tunnel that leads to the players' parking lot. I hurried past two security guards in my socks and flip-flops and avoiding eye contact. I ran out to my car, where there was always a water bottle filled with vodka. I grabbed the bottle and chugged the entire eight ounces.

Immediately my body became calm. I went out in the third period and played the best period I had played in a Flyers uniform all season. This was a departure from getting booed by Flyers faithful most nights. Some nights I would fall down out of the blue, and people wondered why. I had always been a plus-skater for a player my size. Now I'd lost nearly a full stride compared to where I'd been before. I wasn't THAT old. Why did it happen? Well now you're finding out why. I wasn't really that bad, my abilities hadn't left me. I was just a goddamn drunk.

That night forever changed me. It changed who I was because I felt like I had violated the oath that I had held true to—namely the principles of the sport I loved so much. I felt like I defied that trust. I had mistreated it. But it was an amazing win for the team. The funny part of the story was that we were slated to play a couple days later, and as I walked into the locker room the day after the Calgary game, Hitchcock told me to get my sweats on and pay him a visit in his office. I was thinking: *Do they know I was drinking? Somebody must know.* After all, he would never call me in to tell me how good I was playing. It was always something about making a bad play or not having a good run of games.

I got my sweats on and went into Hitchcock's office, where the mood seemed strangely light. Hitch looked at me and said, "How come you play so well against great teams, and not so great against the lesser ones?" I was thinking this scene either has to go in a book or *Ripley's Believe It or Not!* Either the coach had no clue about how out of control my drinking had gotten, and if he did know, I don't know why he said nothing.

Thing is, I was so good in that third period with eight ounces of Cold Spring Vodka rolling around my insides, that the wrong sort of thoughts started turning in my head. Sadly, for me, I thought, *Well, maybe this can work. Behavior like that might get me through the rest of the season. Maybe I could even bring it into the locker room and have it there "in case of emergency."* It was never really my plan to do that and never my plan to drink, period. But as time went by after that I found myself drinking even on the way to games. I was having three or four ounces in the car, stashing the water bottle in my suit coat, and mixing it in with other stuff in my stall. It was unbelievable and at the same time really sick.

Whenever I drank beer or wine within limits over the years, I was okay. But when I overindulged, I felt bloated, loaded on wine or beer, I felt like I was putting on weight, which became a problem. It became a problem for a lot of different reasons because I was in a sport where I didn't want people noticing that I was putting a lot of weight on. Back in the 2003–04 season, things were almost as bad, and it was almost like people knew something was wrong with me. They just kind of left me alone.

I had a lot of regrets about taking that path and I did for years after. Who knows how much longer I could have played if things had been different? I talked to some other guys and found out they were drinking before the game and were loaded the whole game. And I'm not talking about one or two guys, I'm talking a lot of guys.

These are the things that happened to an alcoholic like me in the National Hockey League. It shaped who I was. On February 4, in a home game against the New York Rangers, I was still getting over a major bender the night before, and by that point I was drinking on game days. I was just skating on my second shift when I went back to get a puck behind the net. Esche came out to play it, my head smacked on his shoulder, and to compound the calamity, I was still half in the bag from the night before. I had an awful concussion and was instantly sick. The nausea stayed with me all night.

The worst part was that it was my last shift in the NHL. When I got booed, I was thinking, *Good, I should have been booed*. Thank God for the fans of Philadelphia. If it had kept on going, I would probably have hurt myself or someone else. I was getting to the point where I had no consideration for the game. Some nights on the ice I was reckless, not mentally plugged in at all. I have no regrets about what I did, but, paradoxically, I also have a lot of regrets about what I did.

EVEN IF I HAD NOT SUFFERED a severe concussion in a collision with Robert Esche, the end of my professional hockey career was clearly in sight. Why? Because my drinking had taken a turn for the worse. No doubt the injury exacerbated the problem, but it would be naïve to say the concussion put me completely over the edge. That turn of events had already taken place.

The team went on the road after that game, and I went home. Diana had been at the game that day, and she knew I was in bad shape. I was pretty banged up, experiencing all the worst concussion symptoms, such as seeing double. To top it off, I was extremely hung over as well. I had to sit in the dark for the next three or four days. I was vomiting, had bad balance, and was feeling sick and dizzy. And, amazingly, I continued to drink and drink and drink on top of the concussion. I hated how I felt. I just wanted to be numb.

The following week, head trainer Jim McCrossin sent me in to have my head looked at. I had to go through the baseline test again and an anxiety test. I don't know who threw that in there, but it must have been someone who knew my personality well. Sure enough, the test came back that I had very high anxiety. The team then sent me to a psychologist in Philadelphia recommended by team doctor Gary Dorshimer. I began to see a psychologist for the next three months, sharing my problems.

At the same time, I just found out Diana was pregnant with our fourth child, our son Christopher. It was amazing that happened because we were at a point then where she was getting very frustrated with my level of drinking, which was out of control. It really skyrocketed that year at the Olympic break in February. I was already concussed. We had a vacation house north of Montreal and decided that we were going to go up as a family during the break. The last game before the break was in Ottawa, so I caught a ride on the team plane and then met my family at my parents' house.

I didn't realize that would be the last time I would spend with my sister. It was three or four days of complete drinking: at the bar, shots, beers, everything. My sister, Sarah, and I had some real heart-to-heart talks. She had stressed to me how much she hated my drinking and how I was really starting to ruin all the good things in my life that mattered. I was in agreement. How could I argue? We even shed some tears. However, it didn't slow my drinking, even in that moment of awakening, that moment when someone was reaching out and telling me this wasn't the best version of myself.

She said she hoped my head was okay, but really hoped that my drinking situation would be better down the road. She felt that a lot of other things had come along with the drinking. The concussion had not improved. It got to a point that, even after the Olympic break where I had gotten back to Philadelphia, I almost didn't drive a car for the next four months. I got rides to games from a neighbor of mine. I felt extremely uncomfortable in that situation, because I did not feel good getting behind the wheel of a car with the headlights on. I would rather have been buried in a room in the dark.

Talk about everything coming to a head. My career looked like it was coming to an end. I was drinking like a fish every day, with a steady intake of vodka. I was a guy who was at home, essentially living alone. My family did not want to have much to do with me. I certainly wasn't going to bring any kids in a car if I ever drove during the day, and Diana had had enough of my act. It went on for months and months, and my career was over. I know Clarke was not happy with me at all. I think he thought I could have come back, but the problem was I was so sick.

I was so out of my own element that I didn't even want to be around people. I was just flat out scared to go in and say I needed help. That ended up being my mantra in recovery. It's like I tell people all the time: the hardest thing to do is to truly ask for help. I was absolutely scared to death to go in and say I needed help. Maybe if I had gotten help, I might have been able to play again and help the team. But that would have come with me having to tell the whole world, including my family, to totally admit what they already knew and then share that with my mom and dad who really were not aware as other people were. Some people knew, some people didn't.

That was the hardest part for me, getting to the nitty-gritty of it, which was coming out and admitting I had a problem. Unfortunately, as far as my hockey career was concerned, it came far too late.

By the end of the vacation trip in Canada, my sister and my wife had gotten into a huge fight. Diana had accused my sister of enabling my drinking, when all she did was try to tell me my drinking wasn't good for me and that she would have liked to see me stop. That's the demon with alcohol, it causes so many problems for the family, not just the individual. So even though people had no idea what I was going through mentally and physically—where my mind had taken me.... Where my body had taken me.... I was a person who was running alone in life at that time. One of the biggest reasons was I just didn't want to burden anybody with what I had, which was the disease of alcoholism. I didn't want it to be a problem for the team or the organization and have it become something they would have to absorb. I just wanted to go off into the sunset and be left alone at that point. I knew my career was over, and it was.

But I felt like I had let a lot of people down, including Clarke and Snider. I wasn't going to be a difference-maker; I knew they weren't going to win a Stanley Cup whether I played or not. But what I prided myself on so much over the years was being a complete person and a conscientious player at all costs. Quite frankly, at this point, the alcohol had taken over, and I was no longer able to control my situation.

That was the truth, the reality of the situation. In the end, alcohol takes control of you. It takes control of everything you love, everything you cherish, and everything that's near and dear to you. It crumples it up like a piece of paper. That's where I was at: sad and alone. Some days I would just drive around and around and around. Even before that, during the lockout, LeClair and I started the LCL Lines moving business. I would be drunk most days during the lockout. From the beginning of the 2003–04 season to the end of 2005–06 was the period of my most prolific drinking. It's a wonder I can even remember half of what took place those years.

It's what earned me a seat in Alcoholics Anonymous. More importantly, it pushed me into rehabilitation, where I ended up in July 2006. I was coming to a crossroads in my life, but my journey to a clean, sober existence still had a long way to go.

CHAPTER 22

Loss of a Loved One

BE IT HOCKEY OR HORSE RACING, the professionals in their respective sports have a sense that they're expected to perform at the highest level when called upon. Some can excel under pressure, others can't. Maybe that's why the ice guys buy into the equine set to see how these magnificent creatures handle the spotlight. In my case, I was able to compete with the best on the rink but off the frozen pond was a different story. It most likely contributed greatly to my alcohol troubles.

Things took a severe downturn starting in the spring of 2006. In May, just a few days after the Flyers were eliminated from the playoffs, we wound up at the Kentucky Derby because I owned a piece of a horse named Flashy Bull, who finished 14th. I went to the party the night before, and let me say this, they serve more than mint juleps on the eve of the big race. I was obliterated. Other Flyers eventually arrived in Louisville including Derian

Hatcher, Brian Savage, Turner Stevenson, and Mike Rathje. They showed up in Rathje's Winnebago the morning of the Derby, and we did not limit ourselves at all. Especially me. I was so loaded that I could barely walk around the paddock.

After I got home, I heard about how excited my sister had gotten about the race and having a little piece of the horse in the Derby. Mom, Dad, and my sister went to the local track to watch the race. Interestingly, I was about to embark on the endgame of many things. The Belmont Stakes in New York was on Saturday, June 10. I had a small piece of another horse. My dad had come down from Ottawa to watch the race. My mom came along for the ride but stayed in New Jersey that day and watched it from there on TV. At the track we ran into Colorado Avalanche coach Joel Quenneville, who was with some other people. We spent about an hour talking to him, and that conversation was very smooth because of our hockey connection. I spent half the time wandering around the track trying to buy heavy liquor, because I was a full-fledged alcoholic by that time. I needed it to function properly. At that point, the alcohol was the only thing that kept me straight. That's where my life had gone to that point. My horse did not win.

The ride home was no pleasure cruise either. I resorted to the old water bottle (filled with vodka) trick to get by, because I didn't want to get involved in a withdrawal situation. Things were not going my way, and so I wasn't emotionally strong for the next morning when the bottom dropped out of my world.

The telephone rang at about 10:30 AM. It was my cousin, Krista, who said, "Your sister collapsed in bed this morning." She was only 32 years old and there was nothing to suggest in her health background that this could be anything serious. Krista said she had fallen back into her bed like she had fainted. She added that an ambulance had come and taken her to the hospital. That was all the information I had received.

My hands immediately started to shake. I knew something wasn't right. If anything, something was very wrong. Nausea swept over me, just from the sudden shock of getting this news. I calmly looked for Diana and told her the situation that was happening. Of course, she told me I had to tell my parents, who weren't going home until Tuesday. Now I had to tell them that something had happened to their daughter. They had an eight-hour drive back to Canada. It was as stressful a time in my life as I can compare to anything else. I wasn't capable of handling any emotional situation, let alone something like this.

After about 20 minutes, I summoned up the nerve to go upstairs and to say something was wrong with Sarah. I told them about the collapse on the bed. From all accounts we had heard that everything was okay—she was in the hospital—and I was going to try my best to get them plane tickets home. My parents are the kind of people that, after they heard the news, they tried to explain it to themselves. My dad said she had been working too hard, and my mom said Sarah had experienced a fainting spell about a month earlier at a family barbeque back in Ottawa. But there was still nothing to suggest that anything was seriously wrong.

She was in decent health by all accounts. My mom and dad decided not to take a plane; they were simply going to drive home. I asked my mom before she left to not answer any phone calls from anyone except me on the way home. I did not want any misinformation going out. I didn't know what was happening myself, but I didn't want them getting any calls to make the trip any tougher than it was already going to be. I couldn't go with them because I didn't know the situation and didn't want to get in the way.

As the day went on, my uncle Mark, my dad's younger brother, was the one I wanted to be the liaison between the hospital and the family. Later we learned she had lost consciousness, but there were not a lot of answers I could get that day. A friend from south Jersey came over to the house to commiserate and that helped. I decided to leave for Ottawa on Monday night. The doctors had tried a medically induced coma on Sarah with the hope she would awaken in a couple days.

But we realized she was never going to wake up again. Sarah was gone.

When she had collapsed onto the bed, she had lost too much oxygen. It was about Wednesday evening when I finally went into the hospital to confront the doctors and get an honest prognosis. The doctor said her chances of coming back were one in a million. I was upset with the way we had been treated. The doctor acknowledged she had suffered severe brain damage, and her brain was not able to operate the motor functions of the rest of her body. Essentially, she was brain dead. We had two days to make a decision about what we were going to do.

This was where I saw my parents shine like I had never seen them shine before. The courage, integrity, compassion, love, and pain they were feeling at that time…. And still to be able to make rational, hard decisions for everyone else was one of the most inspiring things I've ever seen in my life. Whenever I think of Sarah, I think of my parents and what they put into that ordeal. They had lost their only child living in Canada with them. The decisions they were about to embark on were the hardest calls you will ever see somebody make, but something that lets you know how great your parents truly are in that moment.

IN MANY WAYS IT WAS THE PERFECT STORM. Here I was in Canada, mourning the death of my sister, Sarah, and the only way I knew how to cope was to nurse on a vodka bottle while sitting in my parents' basement with the lights off. Food or any kind of normal sustenance was out of the question. Reality began to set in. Somehow, a funeral had to be planned. There was a moment of reckoning, an instant where I had to reconcile with myself. I was at a point about as emotionally low as a person can go. It was that bad.

By Saturday, I was finally out looking for something to eat when my father called my cell phone and told me to please come home. We were going to gather at the hospital with the family because they were going to make the difficult decision to take my sister off life support. That would be her final moment of existence. The plan was to donate her organs, but because her passing had been ruled a cardiac-related event, doctors said that couldn't happen. However, my mom and dad called the Gift of Life organization in Ottawa and asked if there were any possible way Sarah's organs could be donated so that someone else could live a quality life.

At her room in the hospital, just before they turned off the machines, I kissed her on the cheek and touched her face with my hand and said I loved her. I told her I would see her again someday. I said it was going to be okay and promised her that every day going forward I was going to live my life in the nature that she would want me to live it. It was the most heartfelt moment I ever had in my life. It felt surreal; it felt like it really wasn't happening to me. My mindset was that stuff like this only happens to other families, not one like ours. But it did happen, and what an awful day it was.

Because of my parents' commitment, Sarah became the first person of cardiac death in Canada to have some of her organs transplanted, including the corneas from her eyes. She became a medical pioneer in the country of Canada. The rest of it was abhorrent; the worst day of my life. I looked in my mirror and said, "My sister is dead now." Reality was upon me that this really did happen. My mom and dad, not knowing how bad my alcoholism was at the time, asked me if I could prepare a eulogy.

The funeral was on a Thursday. It took me days to write the eulogy, I just couldn't find the right words of what I wanted to say and what I wanted to celebrate about Sarah's life. I was in a battle—my head was a mess from constantly drinking vodka, and yet I wanted to be sober. Snider called and reached out to me; he sent a beautiful bouquet of flowers to her funeral. Also, a lot of my teammates got in touch. The support I had from my friends and teammates and the Flyers organization was an amazing feeling. It's one that I will remember and cherish. Just hearing Snider's voice on the phone was amazing. His voice was one of concern and empathy for a person who just went through hell. It was nice to know that someone cared.

Meanwhile, I continued to struggle with the wording of the eulogy. I told my mom about this. My mom replied, "Just remember her smile." And I did. This conversation was around 9:30 AM. I went to a Starbucks nearby and sat outside. The tears just started to flow out of my eyes. Uncontrollably. It was quiet, and I could hear myself gasping, the tears flowing down my face. At that moment I was able to put pen to paper, and it almost wrote itself.

The morning of the service I still had to take a measure of alcohol to steady myself. I wanted to be sure I wasn't overcome with the shakes. I delivered the eulogy with the words that expressed my love for her. There were about 500 people coming by the front row of the church, expressing their condolences. There were handshakes and hugs, and it was great to see so many people we had grown up with as children. People we hadn't seen in years came there to remember her.

It was a solemn and sad day. I felt like my eulogy lifted people's spirits, recalling what an amazing person she was. It was from the heart and the emotion in my voice embodied that. I knew in that moment she would be up there winking at me. It was at that point where time almost stopped. I spent a few more days at my parents' place before I went back to the US to be with my family back there at my home in Marlton, New Jersey. I knew the next phase in my evolution would be to take a step forward in getting myself sober. Not just for the memory of my sister, but for the family that I had and loved dearly.

SOMETHING HAD TO CHANGE and that was clearly evident from my soul-searching week in Canada. Losing my sister at such a young age reminded me how precious life is and how fragile it can be. Here I was sabotaging all the good things I was blessed with and not really thinking about why.

My friend Ben was there and offering me support throughout this difficult time. He was a great buddy of mine right up until 2017 when he passed away after a brave 10-year battle with cancer. He was like a brother to me: I loved him like a brother and so did my family. About three days after the funeral, Ben drove us back to New Jersey, and I was still in the same shape I had been throughout the week. Or maybe worse. I had to accept the fact that my sister was gone. It was about the worst piece of bad fortune a person could ever have. I constantly thought about the pain my parents must have been going through, which was unimaginable to me—and there I was in a complete alcoholic trance, dealing with a range of emotions I never had to deal with before.

I returned to New Jersey to see my children for the first time in what seemed like forever. They were still young, and we did not want to subject them to the sadness surrounding their Aunt Sarah's passing. We presented to them a different scenario, since they were quite young—just three, five, and eight years old. They were just sad because Aunt Sarah wouldn't be there anymore, and they were sad because their dad has lost his sister.

As for me, I was more concerned with my overall demeanor and how I was going to rectify myself of the alcohol that was flowing through my blood on a daily basis. I had called the NHL prior to my sister's collapse and made a connection with a psychologist, Dr. Brian Shaw, who was affiliated with the NHL. That was in late May when I had a friend actually call and tell him I had a problem. When Sarah collapsed, I had to call the league back. I said, "You aren't going to believe this, but if you could kindly give me some more time, something's happened to my sister, and I'm not exactly sure what yet."

The NHL doctor told me, "Whatever you do, don't stop drinking. You could have a seizure."

Well, telling an alcoholic to not stop drinking is like telling a race car driver to have the brakes removed from his Ferrari. By the time I got back from Canada, Dr. Shaw was already aware of what had transpired during my week up north. It was the destruction and falling apart of a family over alcoholism and my sister's death. I knew there was really no choice but to fall on my sword and get the help I so desperately needed. For me and for the family I loved. Diana deserved far better than this. The whole recovery process had almost nothing to do with me but everyone else.

I figured along the way that my recovery would just fall into place. It would be easy. I would just stop, and the problem would go away. But I now believe it takes 10 years from the time you admit you have a problem to the time you get sober and figure out your path forward. There I was, so I called him and said it was time. There was no getting around the fact that I needed help, and I needed it soon. On July 8, 2006, I got up and had not eaten in three days, no food at all, strictly alcohol. A friend of mine from north Jersey picked up my wife and me and drove us to the Caron Treatment Center, one of the biggest in the country. I knew I was going to the right place. The NHL Players' Association had taken care of it, and they had Dr. Shaw book me.

When I left the house that morning, I had almost two liters of vodka with me. We left around nine, and by the time we got to Caron around 11, I had consumed the entire bottle like it was water. I showed up at the front door thinking this might be the lowest point in my life. Here I was getting dropped off at a rehab for alcohol, and it didn't seem possible that this could be happening to a successful hockey player. We weren't supposed to end up in rehab; we were supposed to fix these things on our own.

The problem is that really isn't the truth. When I went in, I gave my wife a hug, said goodbye, and gave her my cell phone. I had nothing at that point, no means of communication. I went into the nurse's office, and she said they were going to have to do blood-alcohol and breathalyzer tests. They did the breath first to figure out what I would need for medication to help me with the withdrawal. My blood-alcohol level was a .63—almost eight times the legal limit for getting behind the wheel of a car in New Jersey.

If I had been operating a motor vehicle, I would not have been a threat to myself but to every single person who happened to be on the road that day.

CHAPTER 23

Skating Away from Skating

I NEVER PUT A LOT OF THOUGHT into what my life would be like without playing hockey and it's probably just as well because alcohol had been clouding my judgment literally since the first day I got paid to play. After completing my stay at Caron, I had reached a day of reckoning. I was 35 years old, had another whole life in front of me, and wasn't sure what the plan was.

My time at Caron was a good one and left me hopeful I was starting a road to recovery. During those 30 days, I met a lot of good people and lots of people from the Philadelphia area, which was cool. Before I got in there, they had to let people know a sports figure was coming in, and that person was Chris Therien, so please give him some space. At that point in my life, I was happy to talk to anybody, to make a new friend, and to try to leave what was left of my past life behind me, at least for the time being.

I went through that month and met a real nice person, a young guy from Moorestown, New Jersey, who was my room-mate. He had a heroin problem. It was the first time I was introduced to anyone dealing with drugs. That was the shock I received when I first went into rehab, that there was a world far different than the one to which I was accustomed. There were people in there addicted to heroin, methamphetamine, and so many other types of drugs. It was the beginning of a new drug age, which now has evolved into fentanyl and the like, especially with young people.

One day one of the head guys came up to me and asked what I was in for. I looked at him and said, "Alcohol."

He replied, "Okay, what else?"

I said, "No sir, just alcohol, nothing else."

To which he responded, "Oh, a purist. You guys don't exist anymore."

I found that kind of interesting because I never really thought of doing a drug. I was raised in the environment where drugs are bad but go out and have a beer because drinking is fine. That may be true for some people, but it was not true for me, ultimately, at the end of the day.

At Caron, I took a lot of great notes: I really educated myself and did not waste time. I continued to work out in case I decided I wanted to go back and play in the NHL again. When I finally got out of Caron in early August, I realized fairly quickly that I probably wasn't going to play again. New Jersey general manager Lou Lamoriello had asked me if I had any interest in joining the Devils because I roomed with his son at Providence. Lou had a soft spot for me because of what had happened to me that summer, with the alcohol rehab and the news my sister had died. To this day, I appreciate his outreach to me. To be honest, I thought it was brave of Lou, noble even, to consider me. I also had a tryout offer with the Columbus Blue Jackets. The Flyers had moved on from me. I don't blame them at all. I wish I had done the work the summer before, not the summer after.

By all accounts, my hockey career was over. I was fine with that. Because of Sarah, I wasn't in a place mentally where I was going to be the best version of myself. I might have been sober; I might have stayed sober for as long as it took. Frankly, I don't know how long it would have been until I started living again. To have done that with a new team in the fall would have been wrong. I don't think it would have been a good situation for the Devils or the Blue Jackets. I didn't have a whole lot of belief in myself because of the damage I had done.

When I got out of the treatment center, I felt more alone than I ever felt before. That became abundantly clear as training camps started to roll around just about a month after I got out of rehab. Camps were opening again, and players were reporting. I was alone, just three weeks sober. I had no job, my sister was gone, and my wife was ambivalent about our relationship because of my alcoholism. Plus, I had three kids who just didn't understand what was going on. I was kind of in no-man's land. It was a difficult time for me because getting sober was a hard thing to do and so was being sober. Everything changed, and I think a lot of things that people go through, you're not really accustomed to going through them.

When you get home, you feel safe, and that's when you believe real change is going to happen. I looked around, and it seemed like everyone I played with for any length of time was also leaving the game: LeClair, Primeau, Stevenson, and Savage. We were all about the same age; we all kind of finished together. The retirements weren't by design; it's just the way it went. The NHL was turning into a younger game, making it even harder for the veterans to play with the new rules on limiting clutching and grabbing. The way I saw it, physicality was leaving the game. That was the beginning of the new era of hockey. I never thought the product got any better from that point on. People thought hockey was awesome up until 2004 and the lockout. Now it's hard to find people who will say that about today's game.

Fall began and I was attending some Alcoholics Anonymous meetings. But through these sessions, I was playing on my phone and not really engaged. At the same time, I was thinking, *These people really aren't for me.* I couldn't relate. *What's all this God stuff they're talking about? What does God have to do with getting sober? Or staying sober?* Actually, I thought it was kind of pathetic. To me, it was as simple as putting the bottle down and not drinking. It's up to you. That was the athlete in me formulating that opinion, the competitor. It was more like me versus the alcohol. But even at that point I didn't realize I wasn't strong enough to beat it fully. I don't know if an alcoholic ever becomes engaged enough to beat it forever. So that's why you have to have a daily reprieve from it, where you start to feel better about yourself.

I didn't do myself the service I needed to do. I was going to Alcoholics Anonymous meetings. In the meantime, Paul Holmgren was about to become the new general manager of the team after Clarke resigned the position early in the 2006–07 season. I had no job with the team, and I wasn't looking for one. Homer shared some wisdom with me. He said part of the recovery was to admit to the mistakes you made and apologize to those you let down. He told me I should probably apologize to Clarke. I agreed I should go into his office and apologize to him. That's what I did. I walked into Clarke's office, and I said, "That person wasn't me. If I did you wrong, that person wasn't me." If I had to pay for my actions, I just did by losing my only sibling, and the pain in me was probably more than a person could bear at that time.

It was good to communicate with management and say I was sorry, that wasn't me. I was always the guy you believed in. Alcohol just took me over. I said the same thing to Holmgren, thanking him for believing in me and recognizing the issues I was facing for the past few years. Yet he never put any pressure on me.

Each day I felt more alone, more scared. This was a spot where I had never been in before. There was no locker room, and I grew up in a locker room: born and raised there. That was over as well. The season started, and I read in the newspaper that Comcast SportsNet had hired Primeau to be the pre- and post-game analyst for all Flyers home and away games. I thought to myself, *It would be pretty cool if I had that job.* Yet I didn't deserve that; I didn't deserve anything. I had to kind of rebuild myself, my whole persona. I had a lot of resentment and a lot of apologizing to do. I still wasn't on clear footing.

The 2005–06 hockey season started, and Hitchcock was still the coach at the beginning. The Flyers got off to a terrible start. I recall Primeau doing the first two games, and after the second one, Keith called me. He said that he wasn't going to make it through the whole year and if I wanted to give it a try, just show up the next game in place of me. That's how I started my broadcast career. I just walked in, Keith had quit, and I was the new face of pre- and post- and that's game coverage.

The pressure was immense, and there was no alcohol to fall back on. That's when my smoking habit took off, and that's a story in itself.

SIMILAR TO WHAT I EXPRESSED in Chapter 1: Did I find hockey broadcasting, or did hockey broadcasting find me?

Maybe it was a little bit of both. As mentioned, I watched Primeau perform as a pre- and post-game analyst for the first two games of the 2006–07 season and thought that would be a cool job. Then, just like that, Primeau called me and said he wanted no part of the deal and it was mine if I just show up one night as his replacement.

That's sort of what happened. I didn't know how that would go, and I certainly couldn't have predicted how it would end. My adventure with what was then Comcast SportsNet at the time began. I went into their offices one night, introduced myself in case somebody didn't know who I was, and said Primeau had told me to show up for work. It was almost a laugh. So, I was hired. I did my first game, and it was probably the best I had felt about myself in about three years.

All I was doing was making $250 per game. That was what we got paid, and I was happy to do it. I didn't know what the team was going to look like and didn't really care. I just wanted to get out and watch hockey and get to an area where at least I felt safe with the Philadelphia Flyers and the community around it.

Meanwhile, my recovery from alcoholism was in full swing, thanks to my time in rehab. However, while in the treatment center I picked up a bad habit, or perhaps "renewed" one is a better word to describe it. There were about 60 people smoking in the facility. I was kind of on my own there. When I had been drinking and partying over the years, we would always see the guy with the occasional cigarette in his mouth. I think guys did it more for fun. There was always a stigma about a cigarette smoker, especially if you were an athlete. But I kept my cigarette smoking during my playing days to drinking events. I played with guys who would smoke and thought it was classic. There was the time I saw NHL defenseman Al Iafrate working on his sticks in the hallway light a cigarette with a blowtorch. This was my second game in the league, so I was already wide-eyed to begin with. I thought to myself, *Holy crap, this is unbelievable!* The guy looked like a big Harley dude, lighting a butt with a blowtorch that had about a nine-inch flame on it. Truly an amazing thing to see.

Somehow, I became a regular smoker, perhaps to steady the nerves on top of the medication I was taking. I would go out after each period like a high school kid looking for the boys' room to light up. I would go out after each period or the first break in the first two minutes of a period and grab a puff. This would go on for about five years. It's funny, some days I would never smoke during the day. I think it just went hand-in-hand with the games. I continued the habit even when I went into radio.

Whatever it takes, right? Someone was talking with Holmgren and me one night and he said, "So you quit drinkin' and you start smokin'." I came back with a line about not starting; it was just something I picked up in rehab, and it was something that I wasn't going to do forever. I didn't. I quit for good in 2014, several years after I quit alcohol. It was a stigma phase for me. Back when I was drinking and smoking, the smoking made me feel like I was twice as high or twice as drunk.

During this phase, I would go into the little hallways and the little nooks and crannies, such as the emergency/fire stairwell, to have a smoke, and everyone would kind of just leave me alone. There were times when I even used the compressor room in between the mezzanine level. I also met a rather interesting set of people while smoking. One was Mike ("He beat him like a rented mule") Lange, the long-time announcer for the Pittsburgh

Penguins—just a dynamite guy. There was Dean Brown in Ottawa, and even Billy Clement would smoke with me when he was doing Flyers TV games at the time. He eventually quit, too. So, smoking does occur in the game of hockey in all areas, be it player, broadcaster, manager. We all know the health risks, that it isn't good for you, but a lot of athletes are risk-takers. There are some who might even feel a bit immortal, because they are young and otherwise physically fit. In the end, the majority of them see the light and move on.

I believe smoking has gone down in general throughout society. It doesn't have the aura it once did. Back in my youth, I loved watching the haze of cigarette smoke hanging over the ice surface at the arenas like the old Montreal Forum back in the '70s. All the people with their suits on, and the guys out on the ice playing through this fog. Little did they know that cloud contained some elements detrimental to people's health. Or else they just didn't care.

In the studio I was blessed with two talented, dedicated partners—Michael Barkann and Al Morganti. Barkann is a tremendous talent and person, as is Morganti. Keith Jones also kept me in the business. He was doing pre- and post-game on TV before me. He was a big help to my career. He was a guy who made sure I was in the right place, which showed he cared a lot about me. The feeling was mutual. It's amazing what he's done for a guy who played less than a hundred games here. He found a niche and has managed to survive. Now he's a national celebrity, first on NBC and now on TNT.

Jonesy ran hard with Chief (Berube), too. I was always an admirer of both those guys. That's how that friendship group was formed, along with Tocchet. They were all helpful as the season began and it was a different one to say the least. The Flyers were in transition, and early in the year things already looked bleak. Clarke walked away. Hitchcock was let go. Holmgren took over for Clarke, and John Stevens, who won a Calder Cup with the Phantoms, was named head coach. It was almost like a complete door-opener for many people. I didn't really know Stevens that well. The Stevens regime didn't get off to a good start. The team finished last in the entire NHL and could be classified as the least successful team in Flyers franchise history.

In hindsight, the loss of a number of veterans probably played a role in this grade-A failure. You had young players such as Mike Richards and Jeff Carter but there was not a lot of veteran leadership to steer them in the right direction. They were typecast as the future of the franchise and rightly so. Richards had enjoyed a great history of winning at the junior level and with the Phantoms. I had played one year with them in 2005–06. There seemed to be some promise after that season, but things went south in a hurry. The 2006–07 team won just 10 home games. Think of it. Back in the mid-'70s, one year the Flyers won 36 games in one season at the Spectrum and lost only two!

For a broadcaster, you couldn't have been thrust into a more difficult situation. It actually got more uncomfortable as the season went along because they went through not one, but two 10-game losing streaks. That's hard to do. They were the most pathetic team in the NHL by a long shot. There was no competition. Stevens tried his best, but there was no response.

Here's where things were going behind the scenes: As the Flyers continued to get worse, the amount of criticism going out over the airwaves went up accordingly. How much was too much? This is where the politics of the business came into play. About midway through one of the 10-game losing streaks, one of the bosses upstairs came over to Morganti and me and said, "You two have a green light from the very top to absolutely torch this team." I didn't know if that meant Snider or the higher-ups at Comcast. The impression we got is they wanted the message out that this was an abomination on TV. I was thinking it was totally nuts.

I looked at the guy and said, "With all due respect, I'm making $250 a game, and I'm not here to destroy a team I played a dozen years for and a general manager [Holmgren] I think very highly of both professionally and personally. I'm not doing it." That's the kind of season it was. In some ways, one to remember. In others, one to definitely try to forget.

CHAPTER 24

Radioactive

NOT A GREAT PERCENTAGE of hockey players get to jump right back into the game after they've retired. Sure, there are plenty of jobs open in the junior, college, and minor league ranks but how many wind up behind a microphone working for an NHL team? In that regard, I was blessed because opportunity knocked just months after I hung up the skates. Doing pre- and post-game analysis for the horrendous 2006–07 Flyers was not exactly a puff job, but it allowed me to stay not only connected to the guys I played with, but also share my insights with the great Philadelphia Flyers fans over the airwaves.

I did just about every game with journalist-turned-TV analyst Morganti, a native of Boston and a Boston University graduate who knows his hockey. Having Barkann as my "pilot" helped a lot, too. The Flyers were awful, but it was a good lesson for me. It was a challenge to cover up what was a pathetic product on the ice, covering for the Flyers' brand when I could. I made a commitment when I first started out that I would look at the relationships with a lot of players I had, and I got along with almost everybody. I thought I was very well received by my teammates, and I always figured if I was going to do broadcasting, I still had to be true to myself and to the fans. Just be the person you had always been, whether you liked me or not. There are people who have absolutely no time for my flavor, and certain people have all the time in the world. That's life; that's the way it goes sometimes.

With that in mind, I made the decision that I was going to play the role in broadcasting with the same passion with which I had played the game. That's what made the difference for me. Being honest, being true, but also learning early on how to tap dance out of situations. It was an uncomfortable year and those two losing streaks of 10 games and nine games were simply unprecedented. Those put me in a position to show my loyalty to the team by painting a different picture. I understood that right away. The picture at that time was not about the awful campaign they were having; it was always about what the best parts of the Philadelphia Flyers were, rather than when they got booed. There's nothing worse than hearing and feeling the wrath from the fans of the City of Brotherly Love.

No doubt I heard those boos my last season as a player with the Flyers. I was a mess. I deserved that. I always felt that I had made so many great friends in Philadelphia and had so many great conversations with the sports people about the sports fabric of the city that now I was able to relay that content to the people with a lot of integrity and honesty.

That was something I did right through to my last game with the Flyers. That last game happened to be the final game of the

2019–20 season, which ended in an embarrassing Game 7 loss to the Islanders in the Eastern Conference Semifinals. The team never even showed up and didn't come close to scoring a goal in the lopsided loss. Of all the games I did as a broadcaster, it was probably the most pathetic effort I had seen by any Flyers team ever.

It was hard to find words to describe that abysmal effort; the leadership simply wasn't there. I said if changes weren't made immediately, this team was headed in the wrong direction. Maybe that's why I lost my job. Honestly, I don't have an axe to grind with the people who made that decision. The last two or three years, I don't think I loved the game as much as I once did. The game has changed with virtually no physicality, and buildings are half-empty all around the National Hockey League. It was becoming pretty apparent that NHL fans weren't necessarily in the frame of mind to spend the kind of money the league and the Flyers were trying to get from people.

My next stop was the broadcast booth to succeed Brian Propp as radio analyst. That came about through team president Peter Luukko and Shawn Tilger, two guys who understood Philadelphia. Luukko was an amazing guy to work for. He was a hard ass when he had to be, he understood hockey, but most of all, he understood Philadelphia. So did Tilger. They both understood the fabric of the team, the city, and what people wanted.

I did a year of pre- and post-game and stayed sober. They understood I had kind of turned my life around. Taking over in the booth for Propp was an honor. Unless you start your career at a later stage in life, radio is probably not something you want as a career long-term. Through the year we did every preseason game, regular season game, and postseason game. It was a really big commitment and, at times, a grind.

I was lucky to have a play-by-play man like Saunders. When I first started, I'm not sure he knew who he was getting as a partner. I know he thought he was getting an arrogant guy with a big personality in the locker room who came in at the end of his career. I don't know if Timmy thought I was a big dumb hockey player, but maybe he had established that in his head. We didn't have much of a relationship when I was still a player on the team. In fact, he told me I was the only player who ever told him after a request for a post-game interview to go screw himself. I always thought that was kind of funny. Anyway, to begin a career with Barkann, Morganti, and then Saunders was certainly a blessing. These are the kinds of people who make you look better.

Tim quickly got to know my personality and had no problem with it. I would be watching a football game while the Flyers were in action. I love football almost as much as I love hockey. He would try to get me when I had one eye on the football game and one eye to what was going on down on the ice. But I never missed a beat with what was going down on the rink. It became clear that Tim had a lot of respect for me as a broadcaster, someone who cared even though maybe it looked like I didn't sometimes. We had mutual passion for hockey and that's why you had to love the way he approached the game and the action. He was describing the action for the listeners, not the bosses beyond the crowd. We had a blast. He has an irreverent sense of humor which struck a chord with me. I found I could confide in him, particularly on sensitive subjects. There seemed to always be an understanding; maybe he knew I was in a little bit of pain back then. He said he was there if I needed him. For that, I was really grateful.

We called a lot of great games together. The action down on the ice was memorable, but the laughs we shared in those broadcasts left equally indelible impressions.

It's unbelievable how few people there are at the Wells Fargo Center at the start of hockey games. I think it has a lot to do with corporate. They have bungled up this organization as everyone feared they would. It's critical for me to define the Snider Flyers and contrast that to, in my opinion, what a dumpster fire this organization has turned out to be with the current administration. It's been a disaster, and there isn't a single former player who isn't aware of it. Just about every loyal and honorable employee of the Flyers is gone. That includes me and Flyers legend Joe Watson. A Flyers Hall of Famer, a two-time Stanley Cup winner, and 54-year employee in various capacities was let go mainly for the "sin" of being 77 years old and proudly old-school about doing things the Flyers Way. That's the way the Flyers treat a lot of their alumni nowadays. I am not talking about the Flyers Alumni Association or the Flyers Alumni who still work in the organization. Those guys are absolutely top notch. They are the ones who carry on the identity of Ed Snider's Flyers and all it stood for. I'm talking about the corporation that owns the Flyers in full since Ed Snider's passing.

They don't understand—or care—why the bond between the Flyers and the city was (and the bond between the Alumni Association and the fans STILL is) so strong.

Walk around the Wells Fargo Center complex. Not only is the Kate Smith statue gone (I won't go off on that tangent here, but it still bothers me), tell me where they keep the classic statues of Gary Dornhoefer and basketball legend Julius "Dr. J" Erving. They're not on display anymore, either. Bit by bit, the history that made the fans love the local teams gets chipped away. It's sad, honestly. Very recently, the Flyers organization has begun trying to repair some of the damage that was done to the goodwill of the alumni-at-large and the fan base. I truly hope it's sincere and it continues beyond just some PR-driven gestures. Baby steps have been taken, such as the creation of an Alumni lounge at the arena. The Flyers organization has also stepped up on donations to the Alumni Association's charity drives. It's a start toward healing but there's a long way to go.

AS MY HOCKEY CAREER EVOLVED from player to broadcaster, one thing was for certain: My battle with alcohol was still a day-to-day proposition. Like all afflicted with the disease, I had good days and bad days. People around me who knew who I was often did what they could to help, often with good intentions, but sometimes those gestures were left unappreciated.

Following pre- and post-game analysis in the 2006–07 season, I moved to the radio booth with Saunders. It was a very smooth ride for me. But the hiccups came and sometimes some of the falls off the wagon were painful. They weren't as brutal as they once were, but they were enough to make anyone feel bad about himself.

By 2009, regular drinking had found its way back into my life again. It was a warm, late spring day, and I was sitting in the kitchen. A friend was over, and there was a bottle of wine. Having that bottle was a no-no to begin with. That's why I tell alcoholics that if you have liquor in the house after you've stopped drinking, get rid of it. Get rid of it for at least three years. If you have a spouse who has a glass of wine, it's probably best to get rid of that bottle. The temptation is too great. Because I ended up picking up again from a simple glass of red wine. It took about two months to spiral from there.

I was almost back in the same pea soup I was in before. The best (or worst) part was the Flyers were done for the season. But I was back in the vicious cycle again. It was 3 PM, Diana was outside doing something, and I felt like I was in a place where I could go and try on that drink. I had gotten to almost two years of complete sobriety—22 months to be exact—and then I fell off the wagon. Hard. It was clear to me I had no control when it came to alcohol. It was again in full control. The difference was I wasn't packing a quart bottle of alcohol around with me in the morning. The difference for me this time was the withdrawal pills. I felt like if I had gotten them at Caron, I could surely get them on the street.

That's the main reason why I went out and drank again for two and a half years. Not at the levels from before, because

I was broadcasting. There were nights when I did drink late in the third period when we were getting ready to leave. If anybody knew it didn't matter. Just as long as I did a good job nobody seemed to care. But it's the fact that I knew. It was a level of unprofessionalism that I didn't like living with. Some guys could live with that—live in the moment—but I couldn't. I wasn't being trustworthy to myself and the people who gave me a job. And it wasn't fair to Tim. I was well prepared for the job, but alcoholism is a disease, and that's what happened. That's the pea soup I was in.

During those years there were a few incidents born of weakness. Let me begin about these by saying the actions taken by others were reactions to my questionable behavior. Maybe they had something to do with my reputation. Maybe people were looking out for my best interests, but the conflicts were born out of the way the situations were handled. I felt like my personal demons were my business, and as long as they were not hurting my performance, I believed they were my problems, so live and let live.

Once, we were taking a late afternoon train after a game in Philadelphia and headed for New York, where we were going to play the next day. I was sitting next to Simon Gagné, still playing at the time, on the ride to NYC. I had a full bottle of vodka in my bag and was drinking, and he knew it. No one said a word the whole way. I just sat there, and I was minding my own business. I figured I might as well get started early and head out on the town alone. Go out by myself, not bring anybody along. I didn't want to be a distraction. That's the way I did it, I would go out on my own—didn't want to drag anybody down with me.

Near the end of the ride, my phone had somehow slipped away from me and onto the floor. So as the team bus was waiting outside Penn Station, they did a check to see if everyone was on board. I wasn't, straggling behind because of the missing phone. The team's coach, Stevens, decides to take it upon himself to go find me in Penn Station. I had found my phone and was walking out. I was planning to take a cab to the hotel. The coach asked me what was going on. He asked me if I had been drinking, and I told him I had. We got into it over my behavior on what he considered "company time."

I know he was trying to be a nice guy, offering to ride in the cab with me. But I guess I looked at it as: let people be. I didn't believe it was his responsibility to do that. Other assistant coaches sympathized with my version of the story. Reporting me to Holmgren wasn't going to change anything. I felt like I had always backed up the coach, even when things weren't going well during his first year and I refused radio management's request to be more critical on the air.

That's the way I looked at it, and I knew John was trying to help me, but in my opinion sometimes you have to stay in your own lane. People will say he was right; he was just trying to help me. I just don't believe in this case the actions were sincere.

Ultimately, alcohol did cause a problem, and the coach wasn't the one who brought the alcohol on the train. I did. I was responsible for that. I had to live with that. Holmgren called me

Monday. He asked me how I was. I told him I was fine, but that I messed up. I've messed up a few times. It's not the first time, and I didn't know if it was going to be the last, but I was trying. He understood that, and I think he felt for me. He said, "Just keep working and eventually you're going to get this." From somebody who had a history with alcohol, I was glad to hear that from him. The other coaches knew I wasn't a bad guy; I wasn't trying to do anything harmful to the team. That's not who I was.

Stevens went on to win two Stanley Cups with the Los Angeles Kings, and I'm still waiting for my first, so there's that. That situation in New York is all in the past as far as I'm concerned, and if I saw him on the street today, I would say hello. The problem is mine, not John's.

These are the problems that come with alcohol. I only did radio for seven years and there were several "potholes" along that road. Near the start of the 2010–11 season, I had fallen down drunk getting out of my car one day at about noon and cut my chin and my eye. A complete face-plant. I ended up in Cooper Hospital in Camden for two days, I couldn't drink, and Flyers training camp was scheduled to open about three weeks later. I showed up with a big cut on my chin and a cut under my eye. I lied to people, telling them I fell when I was getting into the pool. Just another thing with alcohol I had to deal with. A complete waste of time.

FENWAY PARK ALWAYS WILL BE KNOWN for baseball but my one visit there was for a hockey game—the 2010 Winter Classic between the Flyers and Bruins—so it will remain a big, open-air rink forever in my memory.

The 2009–10 season was not going well, as the fall from my car attests. Fourteen stitches in my chin, a cut under my eye, and total disgust from Diana. The ambulance came; she probably thought I was dead. These are the problems I caused for her over the years. There was resentment there that she probably still has to this day. It's legendary. But I can't do anything about that. I can't fault her for being angry. The things an alcoholic puts people through are insane. She certainly didn't deserve that, and I didn't mean to hurt or anger her. That's what alcoholics do. They hurt themselves and they hurt the ones they love. They feel guilty yet the cycle gets repeated.

Alcohol has caused a lot of problems for me over the years. I always had to explain myself if I missed something. Sometimes I would go two months without a drink. When I was working, I would pick my spots a lot more carefully. That was hard because I was a raging alcoholic. I was a guy who always needed alcohol. When I put it in me it was like my life juice. I could handle it with the withdrawal pills. Take two of those before bed after drinking and get up in the morning and feel fine. Take another one before an afternoon nap, and I wasn't drinking again. In a sense, it was a catch-22 situation. The pills were supposed to help end the habit but in a roundabout way might have been contributed to keeping it going.

There were people in the Flyers organization that I was trying to help as I was getting sober. They were comfortable coming to me and talking about their own plight while I was still suffering. It was an honor to be able to do that.

But the greatest, or perhaps most infamous, story of all came on New Year's Eve, 2009—the night before the Winter Classic in Boston. I had never been in Fenway before. It was a beautiful snowy day, and I was walking around the rink, taking photographs. It wasn't too cold, but I decided to look for a place to watch practice. Mind you, I had been sober for a couple months, so alcohol was the last thing on my mind.

The lights were on. People were charged up to go out for New Year's. I see a row of luxury suites, and it was a little nippy, plus I wanted to sit down for a second. As I open the suite door, there on the counter are two cases of beer, four bottles of wine, and a bottle of Captain Morgan. My eyes grew wide, and I thought, *Oh my God. Are you kidding me?* Needless to say, the Chris Therien New Year's Eve party was underway.

It went on for two hours, and anyone who knows me is aware that, when it comes to drinking, I have a hollow leg. I gave Flyers public relations director Zack Hill a call and invited him to come join me.

Well, we end up staying until 8:00 PM. Fenway was dark and deserted. When the dust finally settled, the suite was bone dry. We then staggered out of Fenway holding each other up. Zack was headed to a Flyers corporate bash and said I should join him. I said, "No thanks. I can barely stand up." The cab dropped him at the party then headed to the team hotel, but because of the slick roads the driver couldn't make it up the hill adjacent to Boston Commons. So, I got out, and stumbled across the park, weaving in and out of people.

Later, I was thinking, *What a pathetic loser.* Families are out and about, and there I am walking half-sideways. Earlier, Saunders said we would meet at 9:00 AM in the lobby because the game was just after 1:00 PM.

So sure enough, I took the pills and showed up at 8:45 AM, bright eyed and bushy tailed. Tim looks at me and goes, "You okay?"

I said, "Sure." That's the kind of drinking a hardcore alcoholic could do. I could drink until 6:00 AM and be at the running track at 7:00 AM, ready to take on all comers.

The story's epilogue? We did an amazing job, although the Flyers lost in overtime. It wasn't until a couple weeks later that I told Tim how loaded I had been that night.

I am not proud to say it, but that was probably the best night of drinking in my life. For all of the things I would like to have changed in my past, Fenway wasn't one of them. It was innocent, it was funny, it carries a lifelong story with it. I look back with embarrassment sometimes over what I did as an alcoholic, but this wasn't one such case. I remember it with a wink and a chuckle.

CHAPTER 25

Time to Make the Decision

OF ALL THE TIMES I SPENT on the air in my broadcasting career, I would say radio was the most fun. Nothing beats playing the game, especially a playoff game, but when I compare my entire broadcast journey, I realize the radio side was the best of it. The radio side of it was controlled in-house, which was a benefit for me because I knew I could be critical, but I also knew I was working for the team. Plus, there were a lot of good people running the team, like Peter Luuko and Shawn Tilger, who understood the market. They knew that being critical of the team, when merited and within reason, played well with the listeners. They trusted I wouldn't embarrass the organization or throw the coaches or individual players under the bus. Everything was team-focused for good or for bad. Which they also understood my value in the market as a long-time Flyer who had played in the city for most of my career and was part of winning teams. They knew that I cared deeply about the Philadelphia Flyers hockey team as someone who had been there most of my adult life and made my home in the area. I would see Flyers fans out in public and we had a great relationship.

Joe Watson has said, and I agree, that it's not hard at all for athletes in Philadelphia to win over the fans. There are two keys: you have to work hard, and you have to care about the team as deeply in your heart as they did. Do those things, and they'll stick with you through thick and thin. Above all, I thought I was good at what I did, and I think the Flyers' management of the time respected that.

That brings me back to Tim Saunders, who is just a fun guy. We have more in common than I think either of us would have imagined at the beginning.

We worked well as a team. Mark Howe came up to me one time and said that when he was in the press box scouting for Detroit, he would leave after the second period because he absolutely had to listen to us on the radio on the ride home. He said he never heard a duo walk the line the way we did without stepping over. "It's an art, it's unbelievable, and you guys made me laugh," he declared. When I heard a Hall of Famer like Mark Howe say something like that, it meant a lot to me.

Speaking of not quite crossing the line, I almost did during the 2012 Penguins-Flyers playoff series. Sidney Crosby was being a total baby, and I went off. He was kicking guys' gloves, instigating fights. My tirade was epic. It lasted about four minutes and probably belongs in some radio shrine somewhere.

It became an instant legendary classic. It's something people in Philadelphia still talk about to this day and probably always will.

Those were good moments. The reason I was able to do that with Saunders was because I was able to decipher his personality, and he was able to decipher mine. We understood what was funny, what was kind of pushing the envelope a little bit, and what would entertain the fans. If you just talk about hockey, you can overburden the fans with too much. We would sometimes go off on tangents—life in general—between whistles, and I think that's what made the broadcasts interesting.

People would turn their TV sound down and listen to us, especially nationally televised games. We had dynamite ratings. But by 2013, I was feeling like more than one hundred games were too much—from preseason, to regular season, to postseason. It was getting to be a grind.

I went to management and said, "If you ever need someone for TV, I wouldn't mind the change." My kids were getting older; they were playing basketball, and Tim and I did close to 120 games in 2010. It felt like an incredible amount of work. But the radio work was fine. We did some great interviews.

WORKING IN TELEVISION, you always cross paths with some colorful personalities and doing Flyers broadcasts was no exception. Sharing the microphone with Jim Jackson, Keith Jones, and Bill Clement certainly brought out my entertainment instincts. As was the case in the radio booth with Saunders, the idea was to keep both descriptions and analysis concise, informative, and a bit humorous.

Jackson can call a game with the best of them. There were times when he might question penalties a bit much for my liking, but he's always on top of the action and knows the game inside and out. On the light side, Jonesy is one of the best wits in the business, and that's a big reason why he continues to provide commentary on national TV broadcasts.

Bill is a real linguist who sometimes has words straight out of an encyclopedia. One time, Jackson and I shared a good laugh during a game where the Flyers were getting absolutely trashed by the worst Buffalo team you could imagine. Billy starts in on a story about Armenian genocide and how it affected Zach Bogosian, a defenseman then on the Sabres. There was pure silence on the airwaves because Jimmy and I were in total confusion. We didn't know where to go with that one.

There may have been some minor friction among the personalities in this group at times, but ultimately, we all got along. Steve Coates became a good friend and someone I trusted. I always had a good time with him. But we had a producer who was tough to work for. And it wasn't like our broadcasts were all that great. At times they were tired and boring. I tried to bring in another layer, perhaps some behind-the-scenes stuff that people appreciated. I never had one person come up to me and say they didn't like it. I may have heard, "You suck" as a player, but never as a broadcaster. I think the city appreciated the way I handled myself. I was broadcasting for the fans, not at them, and for the ownership of the team. The producer and I just didn't get along. I did the games, I got the information I needed, and that was it.

My dismissal from working "inside the glass" came about a week before the start of the 2018–19 season. I didn't have a contract because that was how the company did business. I walked into an office, they said they were going to make a change, and I was going from inside the glass to inside the studio again for pre- and post-game analysis. That bothered me because I thought some people in the front office had my back, and they didn't. The Flyers picked up half the freight, and NBC took care of the rest.

To backtrack a minute, zip back to the 2018 playoffs where Sean Couturier scored a big goal in the playoff series with Pittsburgh. After the game, I went back to the locker room at PPG Paints Arena. The players were coming off, and the producer said to get Couturier no matter what. The producer didn't care if *Hockey Night in Canada* (*HNIC*) wanted him, didn't care if NBC National wanted him, just as long as I got Couturier first. So, I did what I was told and got Couturier, no problem, no argument.

Nothing was said. I finished up my post-game, doing my job. When I finally got onto the bus, the producer yelled down the aisle, "Hey, Bundy, did you know *HNIC* was supposed to get Couturier first?" I looked at him and just cursed him out. Talk about stabbing someone in the back, this one was performed with a full-blown machete. Now I'm thinking *HNIC* is going to bitch and moan about this to the Flyers, and it's just because he was covering his ass. That said a lot about this character. I went on to do two years of pre- and post-game and then was replaced by Taryn Hatcher, a very nice young woman who's doing a great job.

I can only hope she can handle those people long-term.

I couldn't.

Sometimes those kinds of people win, and in this case they did.

BY 2010, I WAS INTO MY LAST YEAR OF DRINKING. It was getting old for me. I had kids, and they were getting older. I had to be a dad. Even though I was a better dad during the relapse periods, I still wasn't the best version of myself. I didn't want to be that guy. There are alcoholics in every family. I deal with them now. We have an alcoholic in the family that destroys everything she touches. When I see that, it helps allow me to stay sober another day. I understand the destruction alcohol does, and also how it was making me feel. You can't live like that and expect the result where you can say to yourself, *Everything is going to be great* or, *I feel good where I am at,* because that is not really true.

The Flyers had that great run to the Finals in 2010, including the Miracle in Boston comeback from a 0–3 deficit in the conference semifinal. My drinking had become sporadic, maybe once every two or three days. Sometimes the dry spells would last a week or two. I was trying to be a normal social drinker, but that wasn't going to happen. That just wasn't in the cards for me.

In that timeframe was the infamous New York train ride I referred to where Berube gave me a heads-up. I thought it was a joke, but I had to deal with it. Because I was drinking and shouldn't have been. I had anger and resentment toward myself.

Two days after New York, I called Holmgren and said, "I am battling the same demons."

As I mentioned in an earlier chapter, Homer said to me, "You can't fight this yourself; you have to get yourself into Alcoholics Anonymous. You have to do this the right way and make a commitment." He said to me he had my back, that I was a good guy, and I had never caused problems for anybody.

As a matter of fact, I never gave anyone problems because in the infamous words of George Thorogood, "I drink alone."

Quite frankly, it is hard to live like that; I didn't want anyone to think I wanted the life of what was essentially a drunk. That's the degenerate part when you feel helpless at times.

I hated myself for that. I hated myself almost as much as I did the pre-Caron days.

I knew now I had to change for good.

THE 2009–10 SEASON WAS A BANNER ONE for the Flyers and perhaps my most enjoyable year in my broadcast career.

The postseason was one for the hockey books because this team of so-called destiny was about to achieve something that had only been done twice in a century. It all started on the last day of the regular season when my old buddy, Brian Boucher, bested Rangers goalie Henrik Lundqvist in a shootout for the last playoff spot. That was probably the most exciting regular-season game in Flyers history.

After getting past New Jersey in the first round, the Flyers took on Boston next and proceeded to get smacked in the first three games. Meanwhile, my drinking continued. I would go out after games by myself. I didn't want people around me.

The Flyers suddenly turned things around, and the comeback was nothing short of amazing. A lot of things had to happen to pull this off. I watched all seven games with my own eyes. You have to have a ton of luck, including injuries to the other team, and that's what happened after Mike Richards put David Krejčí out of commission. The Bruins' goaltending fell apart, and there was a mental decline. It's not just what you have to do to come back from 0–3; it's what the other team has to do. Nonetheless, that was an amazing sequence of games.

The Montreal series in the Eastern Conference Finals was a bore. The Canadiens were overmatched. But then came the Chicago Blackhawks, a much more talented team than the Flyers, on their way to the first of three Stanley Cups over the next five years. In my opinion, the Flyers were just lucky to be there. Danny Brière had quite the postseason, and Gagné, the hero of the Boston series, was back in the mix, but it wasn't enough. After the Blackhawks won it in Game 6 on that horrible Patrick Kane goal against Michael Leighton, I went on about a 10-day run. I just disappeared and spent most of that time drinking. I guess I just wanted to treat myself. I was thinking, *I deserve this*. It was just an excuse and so pathetic.

Of course, this behavior came with a price. We had rented a house for a weekend near the beach in Ocean City, New Jersey, right after school got out. I ended up going down early on Friday. I started drinking, and Diana showed up later with the kids. We ended up turning around and going home. I had destroyed a summer weekend at the end of the school year with the kids.

I don't blame her for not letting the kids be subjected to that. She made the right call. I remember sitting on the couch, never going outside except to go to the liquor store for two weeks while I watched World Cup soccer on TV. I was alone. Then I realized this was not how I wanted to live. I really found out I couldn't do this anymore. By the time the next season started, I had not been drinking, but I gradually worked my way back into it. By January 2011, I decided the party was officially over. That was January 7. On February 7, I found the vodka in the water bottle, drank it, and that's the last bit of alcohol to touch my lips ever since.

Leading up to that moment, I knew I had to get back to sobriety. My kids were older and were getting into sports. I had to get sober in a way I would never forget ever again. I told Holmgren that if he ever heard I was drinking again, "Fire me!" I realized too many people cared about me. It was time to take the best path forward with my family again. I knew Diana had plenty of resentment toward me and rightly so. I knew it would be quite a mountain to climb to rectify everything in my past. I was a good guy; I was just also an alcoholic.

Two days after speaking with Homer I went to Alcoholics Anonymous. I showed up by myself and then stuck around after, sitting out front smoking cigarettes. I reviewed in my head what I was doing. A month later came the water-vodka bottle incident. That's where my next journey began, being around people who were sober and being a better person.

But it came with a price.

THAT MOMENT IN THE CLOSET with the infamous bottle proved to be a cathartic moment in my life. Something came over me like I was going to finish this but not start a party, not take on the monster again. It was my way of saying goodbye. Maybe it was my way of giving the middle finger to alcohol and all the problems it caused in my life, all the destruction.

Here's the tricky part with an athlete trying to get sober: I had decided long ago that the day I envisioned stopping, all the good in my existence would return that same day. That's just not realistic. I wanted my wife and kids back and all the positive things that come with being a good sober person. The problem is, it's not like anything else. You hear coaches say, "That player doesn't have any money in the bank with me." I understand that; I had no money in the bank with my family. As much as I wanted it at the time and as many days earlier as I wanted to quit because I didn't feel I was getting my way, I didn't. Because I realized for the first time in my life that the bigger picture was to just take care of myself. I couldn't take care of others until I took care of myself.

That was the difference for me. That's why I was finally able to get over the hump, because instead of me trying to do it for everyone else, I had to do it for me so I could do the right thing for everybody else. That's the hardest part of alcohol recovery. I would get up every morning and go to an AA meeting. I did 120 meetings in 90 days—two per day sometimes. That's where I met one of my true friends, Rick Halverson, who is like my little brother. Paul Holmgren sponsors him, and Rick sponsors me. He's younger than me, but he's made a world of difference to me. He has an understanding of family: he's in the program himself. I wouldn't be here without him. I will be forever grateful to him and forever in his debt for saving me when I needed to be saved and more importantly giving me a chance with my kids. I wanted to be a good dad; I never wanted this to happen. But it did.

Rick is someone I view as a godsend in this world journey I am on. Paul is the same way. We're not best friends; we played in different eras, but we have a lot of respect for each other. He deserves all the plaudits, including his recent induction into the Flyers Hall of Fame and the United States Hockey Hall of Fame.

I was going to AA every single day. After three months I brought Rick back to my house, and I was going to do some spring cleaning. At this point I was still doing games on the radio, happy and sober. Finding my way through things a little bit at a time. Yet I still yearned to have my family back and that wasn't happening yet. Rick came over, Diana was at home, and we were still not on good terms. She had hardly spoken to me in three months. I would say I had 30 days sober or even 60 days, and she would say, "Good for you." That attitude kind of bothered me at first but I realized I had left her hanging for however long. So why would she believe me now?

I had to look myself in the mirror and realize the blame was mine. When Rick came over, she wouldn't even come downstairs to meet him. That level of anger she had for me and the fact that she was so done with alcohol that she didn't really care what Rick had to say. Maybe she thought I was having someone over to vouch for me. But at the time I was thinking it didn't matter what she thought, it's what I did. I showed up at meeting after meeting. Because it was making me happy. I was meeting new people and realizing other people with alcohol problems were just like me.

There was a complete difference with what I was in 2006 and what I was now in recovery. There was a lot more emotion, a lot more feeling or thoughts about other people. Again, it has to be for the selfish side of yourself. You can't get sober for someone else, like I did my first try—I felt like I was upside down. But I tried to find that higher power and that higher power was my kids. The second time around the higher power had to be about myself. Because I couldn't do anything else unless I was taken care of.

Over time, as I got more days, weeks, and then months sober, Diana started coming around a little bit. But the damage

I had done was so epic that I don't know if we will ever get back to that original level of trust and respect again. It hurts but I've been 11 years sober, and it's still one day at a time, by the grace of God. I'm still not perfect. But that's where the journey for sobriety started for me.

The one important thing is my kids trust me. I can be a too-strict parent at times, like many others, but at least when I look at my kids, I know they respect me. That is a lot more than they did before when they viewed me as just a waste, a ghost at times. Nobody wants their kids to look at them that way. I changed their view, their future, and I changed my future, too. My oldest, Isabelle, was just 12 then so there was still time. If I had my kids' respect, there was really nothing else I needed in my life.

A lot of the credit goes to AA and the 12-step program. It's the fundamental element of any recovery. It gives you your base of what is important. It's the best program out there. The bottom line is the program works and has for many years.

Yet there were plenty of people who still didn't trust me. I knew that, and it more than bothered me. You can't be like I was and expect people to turn on the friend/trust switch. The only thing I could control each day was getting up and going to an AA meeting. That would keep me on a straight path to doing the right things.

CHAPTER 26

An Honor to Play for Snider, Clarke

WHEN MY HOCKEY CAREER ENDED rather abruptly, I knew I had to try something else. Even leading up to this, being a recovered alcoholic for almost 10 years, I decided I wanted to give back. Being the person I am, always being comfortable around people, I felt like it was something I wanted to do with my life—helping people with addictions, maybe those having difficulty with hockey and mental health. Being a dad and having all different kinds of challenges in the world is how I ended up meeting Dominick Schiavone. Dominick became the president/COO of Limitless Recovery Centers after Paul Kates and I bought the company from a guy named Pat McCloskey. Kates became like a brother to me. Kates lost a brother in the 9/11 attacks on New York City—he's a guy I have great chemistry with and a strong bond as friends. Subsequently, at the end of 2021, Limitless Recovery became Pennsylvania Recovery Center in the Fishtown section of Philadelphia.

I wanted to get involved and to get people into treatment. I wanted to get that drug addict, that alcoholic, look them in the eye and say, "Hey, you're better than this." I've been down that rabbit hole before and I've been through more than my share of bad stories. I would like to help you. I was a drinker but now I'm someone who is in recovery. Someone who now has longevity in terms of sobriety. Every year that went by, I couldn't believe I got another day, another week, another month, another year.

That's where I'm at now. I got to a point where I'm happy. The 12-step program at Alcoholics Anonymous has always been most important. It's really about taking the wisdom you have and helping another alcoholic. That was my goal, to make sure I put the pain that I had into words, follow it up for the betterment of others. That's where the recovery center venture came in. When we bought it, we had two people come through the doors. Four months later we had 20.

At meetings I met a lot of amazing people—firemen, police, military...people who had suffered so badly. One thing I've learned through my journey: addition affects all walks of life. No one is exempt, not doctors, lawyers, what have you. There are alcoholic truck drivers who are out on the highway all day long and unfortunately a lot of them are active drinkers. There are hockey players in the NHL who are alcoholics, and they even have to take a sip to go play. I wanted to reiterate in those stories that it's okay to feel alone; it's okay that you feel that you're at your worst. That was your worst because of alcohol—it's not something someone else did to you. It's what alcohol did.

I guess my message was this: I got to this state of recovery through the help of a lot of people. Diana endured a lot. She kept the family together all those years. I have such gratitude for that. She absolutely gave those kids a chance when I wasn't there. When I finally came around, I think it was a great, great thing for those children knowing they had a father again. I had turned a corner and I said to myself, "I'm never going back." I look in those kids' eyes, I look at their faces when they get up for school and I said, "Never again." So far, I've held true to that promise.

Help came from other people like Holmgren and Clarke, the Hall of Fame player and great general manager. I tried to make amends with Clarke. I never had a chance to do that with team founder and owner Ed Snider. But I thanked him before he died for all the great things he provided me in my life and the opportunities he gave me.

People like Ed are so revered, so respected that they are larger than life. Even Clarke had that same kind of character and that's why they are the two major faces of this franchise. Snider was the Philadelphia Flyers and Clarke was the No. 1 representative. They were legendary men of the city of Philadelphia. I had great relationships with both of them. I think Clarke admired me; he had that twinkle in his eye because I think he knew I had a little bit of the devil in me. Maybe I reminded him a little bit of himself.

Snider was always good to me, always cordial. Clarke was such an honorable GM. One thing I liked about him is he respected his players.

He also understood the team dynamic as well as anyone I have ever met in this game. For one thing, Clarkie understood how important a team's role players are. He always sought out smart, unselfish, team-first hockey players who were quality people. We always had first-rate guys. I'll mention a few here but there are other examples. Omission is not a slight!

Jody Hull was my roommate when John LeClair was on injured reserve. He was a great fourth-line player for a team; defensively reliable, a very good penalty killer. There's a reason why Roger Neilson often brought Jody along wherever he went in the NHL. It was because he was reliable and understood his role. Off the ice, Jody was an awesome guy with a great family. He was also a great roommate: never argued over petty stuff like who controlled the TV. He was laid-back and a trustworthy friend. I could say the same about guys like Paul Ranheim, John Druce or, from slightly earlier in my career, Robby DiMaio.

Clarke understood that there's a hell of lot more to building a team than just finding the guys with the gaudiest stats. And that's why his players respected him. It's hard not to. He's one of the greatest legends the NHL has ever put forth. He was the icon of the entire franchise. The two men were such interesting people, mainly because they were so dedicated to a cause, a dream, an ideal. Of course, Philadelphia hockey fans have picked up on that vibe for generations. Back in 1967, no one ever thought of Philadelphia as a potential hockey town because it didn't have the heritage of a Boston, a Montreal, a Detroit.

But they do now, and it was because of people like Snider and Clarke.

Those two guys were the Philadelphia Flyers and always will be. They understood how to treat people and the right way to represent the franchise. I know this: If I had been just an average player, someone who didn't care that much, I never would have lasted 12 years in a Flyers uniform under the watch of Clarke and Snider. I played the fifth-most games in the history of the franchise, the most by a defenseman, but when you get down to the heart of the matter, my greatest achievement is the greatest leader in pro sports had me here for 12 years as a top pair defenseman.

That's my greatest honor. People ask me what my greatest honor is, and I tell them 12 years in Philly playing for Bob Clarke. How many guys can say that?

Not a lot.

THIS ROAD TO REDEMPTION couldn't have happened without the support of some great people who became best friends of mine along the way.

You could say I was blessed to make acquaintances with Flyers communications boss Zack Hill, who's been with the team for nearly three decades. There's not a better man at his job in the business. He takes his job seriously but not too much himself. He can make you laugh, give you the latest inside information in the hockey world, or list the top 10 all-time Clint Eastwood movies. Not only is he the best PR guy in the league but the most-liked PR guy in the league. Simply put, he's watched out for me. As previously mentioned, we've had some good times. He is so easy to be around, and I believe that's why we've maintained a close relationship.

As for players, LeClair is about as good as it gets. What more can I say about my 10-year roommate? We played together, partied together, and formed a partnership to own businesses. It's a friendship that's bound to last.

I'll tell you another quick Johnny story here. One season, we had a game in Montreal where I was credited with a goal. I didn't get too many over my career, so I tend to remember the ones I did get. When we got back to the bench, Johnny looked at me almost apologetically. "Sorry, Bundy. I think it went in off my shinpad," he said. "The hell it did," I replied. "It didn't touch anything, you goal-suck!" John smiled broadly. Then he broke out laughing. "OK, you got it," he said. "It's yours."

Nowadays, there'd be a big fuss over who got credited with the goal. It'd be reviewed again and possibly changed after the period or the next day. Agents would fuss if their client didn't get credited for a goal he deserved. Back then, it was as simple as Johnny saying "nope" if the ref asked him if the puck deflected off him. I saw him refuse credit for other goals he deserved, including one on New Year's Eve in Vancouver that he made sure Renny got credited for to break a goal slump. That's just the kind of guy John is as a friend and teammate. One of the best.

Craig Berube has played a key role in my recovery. He's someone I've been able to lean on, a source of wisdom and a person who can build your confidence when it starts to come into question. When I played for the Flyers, I became close to equipment manager Derek "Nasty" Settlemyre. He's a great trainer, a good person. The way he was let go from the Flyers bothered me a lot. He's a good person with a lot of honor.

Keith Jones, former Flyer player and now broadcaster, has helped me a lot. He always supported me during my broadcasting career. He would always say I was one of the good ones. He's someone who watched out for me over the years because that's the kind of person he is. I'm truly grateful for his friendship.

My two favorite coaches have to be Craig Ramsay and Roger Neilson. I want to thank them for letting me play my game, even in the playoffs. They never said a word to me, never bothered me, and that's when I played the best hockey I ever had. They understood the game of hockey and how to handle things when they don't go your way. Roger was a true innovator and knew exactly the value of reviewing plays to correct mistakes, hence the nickname "Captain Video." He may have been quirky, but he knew his stuff. It wasn't by accident Ramsay got us to within one win of the Stanley Cup Finals in 2000, despite all the mess with a certain captain on the team (initials E.L.). In terms of coaches who served as teachers and mentors, I also owe Terry Murray a thank you for teaching me and quietly but bluntly pushing me to improve.

Now for another list, namely the five best players who seemed to give me the most trouble.

Hall of Famer Joe Sakic rates right up there among the guys who must have enjoyed playing against me the most. The Quebec Nordique/Colorado Avalanche star might have been small in stature but he was large in talent. Water bugs like him just seemed extra elusive. You couldn't take your eye off him, or he would be past you.

Paul Kariya, one of the best players to ever suit up for the Anaheim Ducks, also came from that mold. Then there was Saku Koivu, who did some of his best work for the Montreal Canadiens. And last, but certainly not least, Martin St. Louis, another Hall of Famer who helped deliver a Stanley Cup to Tampa Bay in 2004, just before I got shipped to Dallas. Man did this guy have a high motor. He and the rest of those guys turned me inside-out more than a few times. You don't like getting turned inside-out in front of 20,000 people. But it's happened to every defenseman in the league, and I'm no exception.

Finally, this book would not be complete from a hockey standpoint without mentioning superstar Jágr, who will go down as one of the greatest ever to play the game...if he ever retires! The man is pushing 50 and still truckin' in Europe. Desjardins and I developed a reputation for giving Jágr a hard time. I seemed to always bring my "A" game against him. For some reason, Jágr would always seem to try to go wide on me, which wasn't going to work. He wasn't going to get past me with my long reach and good backward skating speed. In fact, I bet I was just as fast a skater as he was. I would pop him into the glass, and the Flyers fans would go crazy. Of course, there was plenty of help in the form of good backcheckers like Primeau.

The way it played out, I had trouble with the smaller guys and success against the bigger ones, like Forsberg. When he was in Colorado, I had very good nights against him. It was just part of my ability to square off with the bigger bodies in the league, and I finished with more than my share of wins.

TO SAY I WAS BLESSED with some amazing teammates over the course of my career would be a gigantic understatement. They say the true marker of a hockey friendship can be summed up in one word: trust. It goes back to that old line about who would you want with you in a foxhole when the bullets started flying. In my case, almost all the guys I knew. You would need a trench to hold all the players who had my back.

LeClair ranks right at the top of the list, and we've already reviewed many of the stories about us that made our relationship special. If I had a vote for the Hockey Hall of Fame, he would have mine.

There were many other characters in that decade or so during my time with the National Hockey League and a lot of them are still my friends today. Speaking of characters, was there anyone more flamboyant than Jeremy Roenick, also known as J.R.? Actually, his nickname was "Styles," because he certainly was "stylin'" during his time in Philadelphia. He came in with a very easygoing approach. Fun, likable, and a guy that

I really trusted on the ice. I've stayed friends with him to this day; we broadcasted together and always kept in touch with one another. He's a guy I really think the world of. He's a character, and there aren't enough of them in the National Hockey League. If there's anybody who should be in the Hall of Fame, it's Jeremy Roenick. For the person he is, for the character he is, and for the hockey player.

One of the guys I have a great deal of respect for is Primeau. When Lindros was pushed to the outside, Primeau kind of filled that void. He was not in the same class as Eric talent-wise by any stretch, but he was a big, strong center that could play both ways. He was a good leader and a guy who really elevated his game. Even though I wasn't in Philadelphia for the conclusion of the 2003–04 season, it was Keith who carried the team when it went on that run to the Eastern Conference Finals. That was something else to watch. It wasn't like he stepped out of some kind of shell; he had already proven himself going all the way back to that winning goal in the 2000 five-overtime classic in Pittsburgh. With Lindros gone, it was an opportunity to become that big first-line center and he didn't disappoint. There was one incident that created a bit of friction, and it was about my drinking. As captain, he might have felt it was his duty to pull me into Clarke's office, and as it turned out, Clarke told him to get out because he didn't want to hear that about another guy or certainly another player bringing him in. I know Primeau had good intentions. But it was really bad timing and ironically, after that meeting, the Flyers had kind of lost me. I knew that would be my last year in Philly.

When Tocchet came back for his second tour of duty with the Flyers, it was a revelation. He started with the Flyers, made a name for himself, went to Pittsburgh, and won a Cup with Mario Lemieux. Now he was bringing all that experience back to the city where it all began. He was on that 2000 team that came up just short in Game 7 of the Eastern Conference Finals and still, in his mid-30s, continued to be a factor on offense. Now, in 2022, when I hear he and Holmgren are going into the Flyers' Hall of Fame, it makes such great sense. "Toc" was a warrior; I would watch him when I was a young kid, and I had a lot of respect for him. He was a fiery leader and what a character. Just a great guy. Like me, he went on to broadcasting and also proved himself to be a legitimate coach with Tampa and Arizona. We remain good friends to this day.

When I first got to the Flyers in the mid-'90s, Recchi was one of the stars of the team. After the trade to Montreal for LeClair and Desjardins, he continued to excel with the Canadiens, and we were excited to get him back in another trade a few years later. I loved him when he returned and still do to this day. We talk and text a lot. When we see each other, we give each other a big hug. I just know it's going to be positive at all times.

Another guy who I admire is MacTavish, known for his strong defensive work with Edmonton's '80s dynasty. I don't know if he was a good force for Lindros. Craig was at the end of his career when he got here. He had won multiple Stanley Cups and that didn't exactly resonate with Lindros. I never felt that was a productive relationship. MacT was coming in here to try to help Eric hone that and keep him focused, but I don't think he was the kind of leader that Eric should have had at that point in his career. I was friends with MacT, but I would have loved him at that point in his career for all the wrong reasons. Lindros needed someone to show him the ropes in the NHL and get him away from the "mommy's boy" attitude he lived in all his life, and Craig probably wasn't that guy.

Maybe that's why the Flyers went and got Dale Hawerchuk the following year. It was a strange trade to see happen. But I really thought highly of MacTavish, he is an unbelievable guy. Likewise, Lamb. Two guys with great pedigrees. Then there was Otto, who had that championship ring and was also someone I followed closely on television, a big strong leader with a quiet demeanor. Svoboda was also a favorite of mine during his tenure here.

Mikael Renberg is one hell of a nice guy. Modest to a fault. Great teammate. It's a shame he had all the injuries in his career that took his abilities down a notch from when he was a fast-rising star early in his career. But as a human being, he was always the same great guy. As for Eric Lindros, the truth is that he never really knew how to be one of the guys. He was always guarded, always suspicious that someone was trying to get something over on him. I don't say it with malice. It's just how it was.

One time a bunch of players were over at Svoboda's house, sittin' around and shooting it. Lindros was outside in the back;

he'd had a few drinks, and this was when the team was in a bit of a rut at the time. I turned to him and said, "You know what, E? Everybody's just waiting for you to lead. You're the best player in the league, people want you to lead. Just lead the team, man, just let it happen." Lindros leaned over and sucker-punched me right in the face, as hard as he could. Otto and Svoboda just shook their heads in disgust. Who does that kind of thing? I was thinking to myself, *No wonder nobody on this team likes you.* Teammates just don't do that to each other. He did it simply because he didn't want to hear the truth. We all put up with a lot regarding Eric, we had heard about the phone calls to the GM and coaches making demands about who Eric should and should not be playing with. Why he would be better off playing with this guy or that guy. That wasn't Eric himself doing it. It was his "representation," but he needed to tell them to back off and just let him be hockey player and teammate. He never did that, as far as I know. I think everybody kind of laughed at that. It's incredible that someone would say and do things like that and moreover that it actually happened at the National Hockey League level. When you traded for Eric, you didn't get just Eric, you got the whole Lindros package—his parents, Bonnie and Carl, his brother, his sister, the dog, the cat, everybody. That's a lot of baggage. Again, I'm not trying to pile on here. Just being real about what it was like.

On the flip side, another guy who falls into the category of heart-and-soul player was Shawn Antoski. He was known for his physical tactics, but he always worked on his overall game. He was a big, tough guy as a former first-round pick by Vancouver who thought he was more than just a fighter. Hockey teams need a few personalities like that to keep other teams "honest," especially when your star players were on the ice.

"Anton," as we called him, was a free spirit away from the rink. And he could skate like the wind. One time, he and assistant coach Keith "Woody" Acton challenged each other to a skating race after practice. Now, Woody had been one of the NHL's fastest skaters in his playing days and he could still really jet around the rink. The Flyers players anticipated the day of the big race, and we laid down some wagers on who would win. The consensus was that Woody, despite no longer being an active NHL player, would win the race. Instead, Anton won it. He earned the bragging rights and enjoyed the hell of reminding Woody and the rest of us. It was fun. On the ice, Anton won most of his fights. I remember him getting the better of Luke Richardson, for example, who was no slouch in the fisticuffs department. He held his own with Mick Vukota; another tough customer. The one big loss I remember was when Tony Twist tuned up Anton one afternoon in St. Louis.

Clarke loved to bring in the big-name players such as Hawerchuk and Coffey because they were proven winners, and the hope was some of that magic would rub off on the Flyers' players. Hawerchuk was the first honest-to-goodness rock 'n roll superstar player I ever suited up with. He was a first overall draft pick, 100-point scorer, who was basically stuck in Winnipeg and never won anything. If not for Gretzky and the Edmonton

juggernaut in the '80s, Hawerchuk might have gotten more recognition. I always thought that playing with him was so cool.
Then there was Coffey, one of the coolest teammates I ever had.
The day he came, he was putting pucks between my skates, and
he looked at me and called me "Meat" from the "Nuke" LaLoosh
character in the *Bull Durham* movie. He said, "Hey, Meat, why
don't you get some of your buddies over there and see if you
come get the puck from me?" Laughter all around. Coff was an
unbelievable guy and someone I was so honored to play with.

Those were some great teammates. Coffey, Hawerchuk,
and in with that group I'll put Adam Oates, an uncanny passer
who could thread it through traffic with the best of them. He's
eighth all-time both in total assists (1,079) and assists per game
(0.87). LeClair and I would talk about that from time to time, the
topic being, "Just think of all the legendary players that we had a
chance to play with." Later, Sean Burke and Esche came along, a
couple of guitar-playing goalies who brought some real personality to the room. Then there was Richardson and Dan McGillis,
my two brothers from different mothers. Think of it: out of the
starting six on a roster that was going deep in the playoffs, we
were three defensemen on one team all from the same town,
Ottawa. They were a big part of my story line, kindred spirits
who were my running mates off the rink. We would tip a few,
head out to watch sporting events, and do a lot of guy things
together.

Brian Boucher lived right next door to me, so I had the inside
track with what was going on with the goaltending situation.

Now he's a big-time TV analyst but still a very down-to-earth guy. Boosh actually bought his place from Adam Burt, who was a born-again Christian. We had been neighbors. When Burt first got the place (in 1998) and unpacked his stuff next door, Clarke couldn't help himself. He cracked, "Holy geez, talk about Jesus moving in next to the Devil!" You can figure out the implication there.

We've saved the best for last. My defense partner for much of my time in the league was Desjardins, someone we've discussed as far as hockey skills go. He was the best. He was my defense version of Gretzky. The one thing that people say is, "You were lucky to play with Desjardins." You know what I tell them? "Go ask Desjardins what he thinks of me." Because he really enjoyed playing with me; it gave him a lot of freedom. I really understood his game, and he understood mine. In turn, we understood what we were allowed to do within those parameters. In Clarke's own words, we were one of the best defensive pairs in hockey for 10 years in this league. That was a special feeling. It's one of those feelings when you believe in something, and you have the luxury of having it last for a long time. That's what my partnership with Desjardins meant to me and how important it was. It was an honor to have one of the game's great gentlemen as my partner.

There were also guys who I had great kidding relationships with, much like Karl Dykhuis and the "sound system from outer space" story. Andy Delmore was a talented defenseman who once somehow scored a hat trick in a playoff game. Also, Daymond Langkow. We would tease each other all the time. To avenge a prank he pulled on me, I once got his sports jacket in Chicago and cut the sleeves off. Then I had trainer Jim "Turk" Evers put one thread in each sleeve (to keep the sleeves temporarily on). When Langkow put the jacket on, the sleeves fell off, and he nearly started crying. People were howling with laughter. Payback is a bitch.

CHAPTER 27

A Life in the Balance

ONE OF THE INCIDENTS that happened to me in my NHL career may or may not have been a contributing factor to my alcoholism, and when I think about how it affected me emotionally, I'm fairly certain it at least played a part in my going off the rails.

It was a Saturday afternoon game at Montreal on January 29, 2000, and as always, the excitement level was high. This was a *Hockey Night in Canada* game even though it was being played with the sun still out. I stepped into a shot that I knew was going to be an absolute rocket. Little did I know it was never going to reach the net because a Montreal player, Trent McCleary, dove in front of me. For whatever reason, McCleary slid and led with his face.

The shot was really hammered. The puck hit McCleary in the throat, and immediately I heard a crushing sound and gurgling noise coming from his direction. In a split second I looked over to the Montreal bench and gestured almost frantically to get the hell over here. It was, "Hurry up, this is bad!"

There was a range of emotions. On one hand I'm thinking this guy is in serious trouble, on the other I'm marveling about what a courageous play that was. I was also thinking, *What the hell kind of a block was that?* As they wheeled him off, I skated over to our bench and was still thinking, *This is a nightmare.* I ended up playing the rest of the game. Later, I was out back of what was then the Molson Centre by the TV trucks. There were reports about McCleary, speculation about whether he was going to live. He had a fractured larynx, and as they performed an emergency tracheotomy, his lung had collapsed.

The newscasts mentioned I was the one who took the shot, and it was, of course, a complete accident. I was devastated when I heard that. The first emotion that went through me was, *This guy is the same as me, just a guy who is trying to play in the NHL.* A guy just trying to make it through, trying to make his parents proud. And now his life is hanging in the balance, let alone his career. It was a tough feeling. We got on the plane for a game at Washington. I was sitting there, sort of staring into space, and a couple guys could see I wasn't myself. Desjardins and LeClair came over to ask about me. Then one of the trainers came up to me and said Clarke wanted to see me at the front of the plane.

It's safe to say Clarke is not the world's most empathetic man, at least not outwardly or in public. But that day he told me he knew this was a tough situation, that I didn't mean to do it. It was a total accident, so just let it go and move on the best you can. Stuff like this happens, guys get hurt. Don't beat yourself up over what happened.

I went back to sit down, thinking I really didn't sign up for this to try to kill somebody. Clarke had said the right things. Just enough compassion to make me feel he knew what I was going through and could appreciate the process of coping with it. It was about all he could realistically muster up at that time.

What was interesting came about when we were in Washington. This was before the Internet. Well, we finally heard a report that night that McCleary was going to be okay. I heard that and was relieved, but the X factor was whether he could resurrect his playing career. Although McCleary's life was out of danger, I still had trouble getting to sleep that night.

The next day we played the Caps, and I did my usual pre-game stretch at the red line. I was down on the ice on one knee and felt a tapping on my shoulder, then another. Pretty soon almost every Capital player came over to give me a pat on the pads. I thought that was pretty cool. It was a sign of the brotherhood of NHL players and how they stick together in times of need. We might be professional athletes, but everyone has feelings. I appreciated that from the Capitals players. Even ex-Flyer Chris Simon, one of the game's tough guys and a guy I was drafted with back in 1990, came over. The message was, *We don't play the game for something like that to happen.* We are men, we play hard, we have fun, but sometimes things get crazy by fighting or whatever it might be. Nobody wants to see anything like that happen to anybody.

McCleary had to undergo a pair of operations at Montreal General Hospital. We didn't know it for sure at the time, but his professional hockey career was essentially over. It would be too risky to allow him to play again and risk a serious re-injury.

I don't know for certain how the whole thing affected me long-term. I do know I reached out to McCleary two days later. I didn't hear back from him, at least for the next 18 years. The initial snub was disappointing in a lot of ways. All I wanted to know was if he was okay, or at least have his wife say something to me. I didn't get an answer back.

At the time I was thinking that I really didn't know what his feelings toward me were. Maybe Trent hated me. I didn't know. Suddenly, in 2018, I got an email from him. His wife had actually watched a show on TV where I discussed what happened and how it had affected me.

Privately, I wasn't sure how much the whole thing contributed to my alcoholism. One could point to that date as the time when my game began to slip ever so slightly. Hockey can be a violent sport, and when your will to participate in the physical side of the game begins to diminish ever so slightly, the meter is running on your impending retirement from pucks and sticks.

Three years or so ago, I received this email from Trent and his wife. They said they had no animosity toward me. They added they just never knew the emotional pain that the incident had caused me, what impact it had on me. It's never too late to reach back out to a person. One of the media outlets in Canada called it one of the worst injuries ever in professional sports. It was that dire. It's one of the most difficult times I've ever gone through in professional sports. I don't know what lingering effect it may have had on me. But I'm sure there was some connection to my alcoholism.

It's hard to just put out of your mind that your actions, albeit accidental, took away someone else's livelihood. It lingers and haunts you. My way of coping, increasingly and for many different emotions, was to drink that much more. Being numb was better than feeling lousy about something you couldn't change.

I don't know about the mental side of it either, from a hockey playing standpoint, but I do know that during the playoffs that year I wasn't myself. I didn't feel the same way in the final five or six years after the playoffs as I did during the first five years of my career. The whole thing let me know this is a rough, physical game. At the end of the day, we care a lot about people. Most hockey players come from humble beginnings, and we all get it.

LOYALTY IN THE NHL can be a two-way street and from a player's perspective, you're really only as good as your last game or season, depending upon the mileage on your skates. After 10 years with the Flyers, I went to training camp, did okay, and then found myself placed on waivers.

In my last preseason game at Washington, I played very well. But my agent got ahold of a report that said I was going to get waived. If you looked at the waiver wire list, my name was probably the most prominent. Before the regular season started, we played the Phantoms in an exhibition game at the old Spectrum.

The game was played during the waiver period, and that's where the story gets dicey. The waiver deadline was supposed to be 4:00 PM. I thought I was getting picked up and Clarke thought the same way. Anyway, we were told to play the game as if it were a regular competition. However, I ended up going with some of my teammates to a restaurant in Voorhees where the practice rink is. A lot of the guys were acting like they were saying goodbye to me, like I was headed to another NHL team, like this was my last hurrah in Philadelphia.

In a rather misguided stroke of wisdom, I decided to purchase two bottles of red wine. I opened one, which I had never done at a pre-game luncheon before. I proceeded to drink that. When the waiver wire came in at 4:00 PM, I realized I did not get picked up. It was hard to believe. I was thinking: *What the hell is going to happen now?* Was I still on the team? Were they going to send me to the minors? I didn't really care; I was still getting paid my NHL salary. I don't know why I was left to dangle like that because, honestly, I felt like I still had a lot of fuel left in the tank.

We played the Phantoms that night, and I walked into the Spectrum loaded. I had gotten a ride over from a neighbor because I didn't like to drink and drive. In fact, I thought the people who drank and drove were complete morons. Me included.

I showed up at the Spectrum, and Hitchcock found out I was there. Someone shouted, "Hey, Bundy's here, what do we do with him?"

Hitchcock responded with something like, "Well, get him ready to play! He's still on the Flyers." Well, I was blasted, and meanwhile the baseball playoffs were going on. We had guys throwing money around the locker room like it's their last night in Vegas. It was practically complete chaos. Our de facto coach, journalist/broadcaster Morganti, was having forwards going up to him and asking if they can play defense and defensemen asking if they can play forward.

We ended up losing 8–3? Or 10–6 to the Phantoms: we got completely smoked. I looked like a turnstile out there. No one knew (or maybe they did) that I was probably at a .20 or .25 alcohol level. It was a joke. Brashear, a forward, was trying to get the pads from the goalie at the first intermission to try his hand at netminding. Everyone was betting on the Series. Nobody gave a crap about the hockey game. That was the problem. Our minor league guys took it much more seriously. Our NHL guys treated it like a big joke. Well, the joke was on us. At one point, LeClair went up to Morganti and yelled, "Get Bundy off the ice before he or someone else gets hurt out here!"

The Phantoms were playing for their Stanley Cup. Jones' two assistants, hockey writers Ed Moran and Wayne Fish, were standing behind the Phantoms bench laughing at us. It was weird for me. For the first time in my NHL career, I felt like I was on the outside looking in.

If they were judging me off that game, it made sense I didn't get into the top six defensemen when the season began. I really didn't know why Clarke was trying to get rid of me, because I ended up playing pretty well that season. Eventually he would trade me to Dallas. But the underlying theme was that the players weren't taking the preseason too seriously.

The regular season began, we got to the West Coast, and LeClair and I had a good old time. I wasn't playing so I was letting it all hang out. When we got back from the West Coast, I was skating after practice one day, and I saw some assistant coaches watching me through the glass. I knew I was going back in. I got called up to Clarke's office, and he told me I was a better player than an American League player and that they needed me to start playing like I was there.

So, I asked Clarke, "Well, why did you waive me?" He said he wasn't really sure. I almost laughed. I think it was his way of saying the coach didn't like me, and he was just trying to eliminate a problem in the room early in the season.

Ultimately, I got scratched all those games with the Flyers, and then they were having second thoughts. After the two-game trip with the Phantoms, we got back and the Flyers were scheduled to play a Monday night game against the Montreal Canadiens. So, who was the number one defense pairing that night? Chris Therien and Éric Desjardins. The top pair reunited, just like an old homecoming. And it stayed that way for the rest of the year. I mean, come on, what was everyone thinking? Did they suddenly believe I forgot how to play hockey overnight? Why put a guy through the wringer and then expect him to come back and play top D minutes after running him around like that?

In the Montreal game I did commit one horrible turnover. I tried to throw a pass up the middle, and Brian Savage picked it off, walked right in. Esche had to make a sensational save. Esche, a real good guy to begin with, told the media everybody makes mistakes. He said, "Bundy made that one mistake, but he's been a rock for us. I trust him every time he's on the ice." Now that was a great vote of confidence. On top of that, I think the players enjoyed having me back.

Those days were insane but somehow funny at the same time.

MOST GUYS IN PROFESSIONAL SPORTS end up with nicknames. Some are clever, some are plays off someone's first or last name, and some are just downright silly. You have the obvious, like calling a heavy guy "Slim" or Bernie "Boom Boom" Geoffrion for his wicked slap shot. Others can be a single letter, like "G" for Claude Giroux, or the shortening of a name, like "Coots" for Sean Couturier.

Me? I ended up with "Bundy," thanks to the dry wit of former teammate MacTavish. Of course, the name Bundy comes from the title character Al Bundy on the old TV series *Married with Children*. Bundy was sort of this semi-tragic/comedic figure who constantly found himself in one little family challenge after another. His wife, Peg (played by actress Katey Sagal), had a great sense of humor and was perfect for the part.

It's interesting, when you think of my full name, Chris Therien, there wasn't a whole lot of nickname material there. My friends back home would call me "Ter," which wasn't all that original. Most of the time you take a guy's name and do a play on words with it. Actually, I was very good at giving out nicknames over the years. But I never thought I would end up with one myself that would stick forever.

This whole thing started the opening day of my first training camp back in 1994. I walked into the locker room at the Coliseum (the practice facility used before the current one on the other side of Voorhees, New Jersey), and I really didn't know anybody. I would pass the time by watching the reruns of *Married with Children*. In walked MacTavish, who won a few Stanley Cups with Edmonton, and I was sitting there most likely scratching my private area like any player does before practice. He started watching with me and everyone knew who Al Bundy was by 1994. MacTavish turned to me and said that I kind of reminded him of Al. I started laughing a little and that was probably a mistake. I responded with an, "I guess so." He said he had a teammate up in Edmonton, Brian Glynn, who already had that nickname. I guess he felt there was a correlation between him and me. It could have been a certain look or a style of play.

Actually, I think it had more to do with my personality, my sense of humor. It could be dry, it could be diabolical at times, like the whole prankster trick involving Karl Dykhuis and his mysterious sound system. But boy did it ever stick. It reached the point where I could be walking down the street and if someone yelled, "Hey, Chris," I probably wouldn't even turn around. They would have had better luck shouting, "Hey, Bundy!"

That became my household nickname. My kids don't dare call me that; they just laugh because they think it's funny. I really don't believe they knew that's what people called me even way back in the day. It's fine. I like nicknames. Maybe this even shaped my behavior. I don't know about that, but Bundy seemed to go along with my fun-loving, big personality—someone who loves life but wasn't always perfect. For me, it sort of ended up describing who I was.

Naturally some stories were spawned out of the whole phenomenon. At one point, journeyman player Daniel Lacroix was on the Flyers. Daniel is a great artist. He would do some great caricatures, especially when I put a few pounds on. He would always put sketches up on the bulletin board, and Bundy was the target of more than a few of them.

I was "wall fodder," but I liked it. Know why? Because that helped me become a bigger voice in the locker room. The name stuck. It got crazy. Guys on other teams would call me Bundy. Even now, younger people know that was my nickname.

One night we're playing the Pittsburgh Penguins on a Sunday afternoon during the NFL season. Two minutes into the game, Jágr, a guy Desjardins and I used to dominate, lined up alongside me for a faceoff and said, "Hey, Bundy, who do you like today?" Big grin on his face.

I said, "Shut the hell up, we're going to murder you today!" And we did. In the final analysis, J.J. was trying to endear himself to me so I might go a little easier on him but that was not happening. Every time they came to Philly, we unloaded on them. We used to abuse Jágr. When it wasn't our pairing, McGillis would go after him. Coincidentally, McGillis clobbered Jágr that day, and he immediately went to the locker room, never to return to that game.

It's pretty funny when your teammates call you that nickname but it's even funnier when guys on the other team over time start calling you that. You accidentally shoot a puck over the glass for a delay of game penalty, and you're bound to hear, "Hey, nice play Bundy!" I'm thinking, *How the hell do they know that nickname?* I guess they overheard it from our guys on the bench or on the ice. Word travels fast in the NHL. Even coaches started calling me that.

Even when I went into broadcasting, it was still Bundy. Writers, PR guys, the works. If someone calls me Chris, they probably don't know me very well. Saunders called me Bundy a lot on the air and still does to this day. He would ask me if it was okay, and I said sure.

Strangely enough, when I moved from radio to television, they tried to rebrand me as Chris Therien. I felt that was kind of stupid. Why change a good thing? They should have just left me as Bundy, that's who I am. It seems to me it would have been easier if they just called me Bundy. But you know how it is with corporate America—every shirt has to be starched and buttoned to the top. Heaven forbid we get a little folksy with a nickname.

It's a name that has stuck in all places and instances. I show up for a celebrity golf tournament or alumni game and the nickname Bundy is still very much at the forefront. It's a name that stuck, and I like it. I know exactly who I am when they say it. It's a better nickname than being called a particular lower body part.

CHAPTER 28

Sex and the Road City

TAKE A 20-SOMETHING-YEAR-OLD PROFESSIONAL hockey player, give him a few million bucks a year, put him up in a five-star hotel, dress him up in thousand-dollar suits, and send him out on the town after road games.

What could possibly go wrong?

Well, it might start with looking for "love" in all the wrong places. Perhaps love isn't quite the right word, but "fun" might better describe what goes on once the rink lights go dark and the nightclub lights go bright.

The chase for a few thrills most likely has been going on since before the invention of the hockey puck. When it comes to top-notch players and their behavior on the road, everybody wants to hear stories involving extramarital affairs and all those scintillating things. Regardless of any player's emotional fortitude, there probably hasn't been anyone who hasn't thought about some sort of tryst once he's away from his family. Especially when said player is young.

One of the great stories of all time involving a Flyers player took place during my first year in the NHL. In January 1995, we were in Montreal to play an early afternoon game on Super Bowl Sunday. After the game, some of the veteran players asked our travel secretary to hire a few strippers for the halftime entertainment at the Queen Elizabeth Hotel, where we were staying.

There was only one problem: Something got lost in the translation, and the travel guy brought in a couple hookers. Long story short, at halftime two girls showed up and one of them promptly selects a player to receive some pleasure of the oral variety—in plain view of everybody watching the game. Maybe because other people were observing, it took the player the better part of an hour to consummate the relationship.

Now here's the kicker. When things had finally settled down, a bunch of players went to the doorway and yelled down the hall: "Hey, we wanted strippers, not HOOKERS!" I was a raw rookie, so I was sitting there with a big grin on my face thinking, *If this is the NHL, what a start this is!* To be honest, I never saw anything quite like that again in my many years after that Super Bowl Sunday.

There were times when guys would go out on the town with the full intention of getting lucky. Sometimes there were commotions late night in hotels. It was mostly the younger guys. The veterans would kind of laugh it off. And it raises a good point. The Flyers talked to my agent, and they said they appreciated that I was one of the guys who didn't chase after sex. I wondered how they could judge a player's character by that. The team official said he didn't mind players going out for a beer or two after a game, but if too many guys are out there looking for trouble, then your team is going to struggle through the course of the year. He figured guys would be out all hours on the chase.

When I heard that, it gave me pause for thought. But as I got older, I realized there was some truth to that. If you're running around all night on the hunt for some bedroom action, it's more taxing than having three or four beers and hitting the pillow by 1:00 AM. Going out to bars on the chase was never my thing. I'm not a dance card guy. I was more into going out with the guys, having some laughs, and watching some games on television.

One of the weirdest stories took place back in 2007 just after I retired. I had a former teammate playing on another team that was in the playoffs and I noticed he had a really terrible playoffs that year. I thought that wasn't like him. Anyway, I was down in South Jersey for lunch one day at a place where I knew the manager. He said he knew someone who was dating that player over in Pennsylvania. The topper was, she had a baby with this guy, who already had a family with three or four kids.

At first, I kind of dismissed it as just a rumor but my curiosity was killing me. I decided the best thing to do to put this story to rest would be to call my friend and just flat out ask him.

I picked up the phone and dialed, and he answered. Without any small talk, I said, "Just one thing, there's a rumor..."

And before I could say another word, he replied, "It's true. All of it is true. Yes, my wife had a baby one week, and my girlfriend had a baby a week later...."

That's about as crazy as it gets. It destroyed his family. But he moved on and he's still with the woman who had his child out of wedlock.

Sadly, a lot of these stories end this way, with separation and divorce the ultimate result. Years of travel can lead to problems when a player retires because the husband and wife suddenly have a lot more time together. They fail to realize that being in that routine, and then having it end, is when the trouble can start. That said, there are still a lot of guys who are still together with their wives despite all the stresses through the year. That says something about the strength of their marriages.

HOCKEY IS A VIOLENT GAME, pure and simple, and with those physical confrontations come bodily harm as well as mental stress. Some players deal with it better than others. Yet when all is said and done, we've all taken an aspirin tablet to deal with a headache. In the sport of pucks, sticks, and razor-sharp blades, it's just a matter of each individual's pain threshold. If the discomfort is 10 times worse than your average headache, eventually some will cope by reaching for whatever they can get their hands on. Painkillers come in all strengths and sizes, and when it comes to the NHL, these are not medications found in Aisle 6 of your local CVS.

The pharmacy side of the sport doesn't end there, of course. There's the whole can of worms involving performance-enhancing substances, such as steroids and stimulants. Maybe hockey doesn't have quite the problem with this stuff that other sports do, but when you're talking about salaries in the millions of dollars, level-headed reasoning and concerns for long-term health go right out the window.

My entire time in college, starting at age 18, then the Olympic team, then pro, I can say right now with complete certainty that aside from a cough medication like Sudafed or a caffeine pill, I never took drugs. Personally, there never was a need to take a steroid or a painkiller and as far as addictions go, alcohol was first, foremost, and the only poor-choice substance I placed in my body.

Doing a review of guys who had more outgoing personalities, partied more, womanized indiscreetly, and in general fit into the stereotyped perception of hockey players, they were in direct contrast to guys who you didn't hear much about. Whether one group was more prone to looking for "something" remains to be seen. What I did find interesting was that while I would go home to drink, I never realized the number of players who went home and smoked pot. That was a foreign culture to me in my playing days; something no one really discussed.

I guess that would have been a better alternative because I am an advocate of marijuana. I believe it is a better source for healing than prescription painkillers that "big pharma" basically made the entire country dependent upon, along with the inevitable deaths which followed. Also, there's a difference between taking drugs to counteract pain versus just getting buzzed to have some good times.

That scene was never part of my hockey career. You can go all the way back to the '80s before my time when there were rumors of cocaine use throughout the sport, almost entirely for recreational purposes. That said, throughout my career I never saw a player do a line of cocaine. Not once. Coke re-entered the hockey scene later, at least much more prominently. On the flip side, painkillers were a different story. Over the years I've seen guys take them. There was a time when teams handed out painkillers and sleeping pills, such as Ambien. That was prevalent. You didn't need a prescription from the doctor. It was usually distributed through the trainers. But let me be clear, this is not a shot at any NHL trainer in today's game. However, back in the day, if your body was beat up and your charter plane was landing someplace like Winnipeg where it was really cold at 1:30 AM, you probably knew you weren't going to get a good night's sleep.

Players who had a problem with this would get into a sleep pattern, and they would start to use the Ambien. If you were already on painkillers for something like a sore shoulder or back, that's going to gum you up for the night. How prevalent this was, I don't know. I have heard all the stories, going back to the days of baseball's Mark McGwire, Sammy Sosa, Barry

Bonds; those guys looked like specimens. They looked like they were on steroids. Think of wrestling's Hulk Hogan. The goal was sheer entertainment. What they did to their minds and bodies through those journeys probably caused extreme damage.

Do I think players in hockey were using performance-enhancing drugs? My answer is a definitive yes. They had to. There's no way they could not have. Whether they were using the same stuff baseball players were taking, like what steroid cheat Alex Rodriguez admitted to including in his regimen, it probably was more along the lines of blood doping, which is harder to uncover in testing.

In my sphere, I considered myself tough. For older guys like me from another generation, hockey was a sport where you play the game, then go out for beers with buddies afterward. That's why I didn't go near that drug scene, because as I've mentioned, I believe I was brought up the right way. I was scared of doing a drug, something that would get me in trouble while at the same time might do me physical harm. Although for me there was nothing more destructive than alcohol, there remained the fact it was legal.

I've seen guys come to training camp over the years: some guys looked far bigger, really built from what they did over the course of the summer. Their bodies had changed. They may have done more cardiovascular training, but they were also into physique training, more bench work, more lifting. At the end of the day, I really believe there was a performance-enhancer and pain-killer era in hockey. But having been in a great number of locker rooms, I did not see a lot of it.

Still, you hear the stories, and it's not just hockey. In the NFL, a friend of mine who played for the Denver Broncos confirmed there were performance-enhancing steroids lying around on the tables. Need proof? Just read the biography of former Denver player Lyle Alzado. Before his death at age 43, Alzado confirmed he was an active taker of anabolic steroids. Here's a terrifying statement from him: "Ninety percent of the athletes I know are on the stuff. I did things only crazy people do." Performance-enhancers are still prevalent in sports today.

The culture in hockey is different, probably because bigger doesn't necessarily mean better. You think Hall of Fame players could skate at close to 30 miles per hour if they were carrying an extra 30, 40, 50 pounds of steroid-created muscle? Not happening.

I can tell you this: The last year I played, 2005–06 on the Flyers, when I was as big a drunk as I could have been, I know there were two players on that team who were completely hooked on painkillers. One guy was playing with painkillers in his body every single night. He was probably fully addicted to them. One player put in an order for 200 pucks. Right away I knew that was code for pills. That was where I saw an uptick in painkillers.

Cocaine had seamlessly made a comeback, not that it ever really left. I've been to some of the biggest parties you can imagine, in Los Angeles and notorious hot spots in Chicago, but I haven't seen it. All that considered, insiders have made it known the NHL has had issues with cocaine. There have been players who have been picked up; it's been discussed over the past few years. The reason guys use cocaine now is because it leaves your system in about 24 hours.

Drugs of any sort in any sport will never go away. It's the nature of the beast.

ONE OF THE BIGGEST DRAWBACKS to alcoholism involves how it clouds your judgment. In the case of a betrayal by one of my closest friends, I never saw the dark cloud forming but should have. The old saying about not letting money get in the middle of a good relationship applied here, but I was in no shape to figure out what was going on.

A friend of mine was an intimate part of my life dating all the way back to our high school years at Northwood. He hailed from Saratoga Springs, New York, and I was from another country, so we were both outsiders. Even though he was not in my league as a player, we clicked. We ended up getting along, becoming friends to the point where he even came up to my family's home in Ottawa to visit.

As we got older, he became a big supporter of my hockey career. He was the best man at my wedding and the godfather to my daughter. And he stole a truckload of money from me as my financial advisor.

The amount, more than half a million bucks, was significant but not the painful point here. It was the betrayal by someone I thought was a close friend that really got to me. He misled me, put me in a situation where I lost that money with him at the steering wheel. The rubber hit the road in 2008 when I was back into serious drinking again. He was misallocating funds behind my back, churning my accounts so he would make profits on them.

Ultimately, the brokerage house that employed him had to pick up for his malfeasance, and I won a small payback out of it. What I've learned from that experience is when I trust somebody as much as I trusted him and then find out he misled me, it became one of the more painful things I had to deal with in my life. We shared a lot of time together. I became the godfather to his child. It's amazing when you think you know someone, and then money gets in the picture and changes things. I don't know if people feel they have some sort of entitlement when they are dealing with people in pro sports, but it turned out this was one of the worst things that ever happened to me. It's about as disappointed as you can get with another human being.

We knew each other at Northwood, drifted apart a bit, and then reconnected when I made it to the NHL. That should tell you something. One thing that did happen through this: I was finally able to open my eyes. I realized it was on me. A lot of the things that happened to me were because I didn't take good care of myself. I finally stopped blaming myself. Someone took advantage of me because of who I was at the time.

And I realized as my final days of drinking were coming to an end and hopes of sobriety were on the horizon that this experience was something that could serve as motivation. You say to yourself, "You know what, you're never going to put yourself in a position of weakness again where you're going to let someone take advantage of you."

The whole thing was eye-opening to say the least. It resonated with me as an individual. Not only did I lose a friend—a person I've never spoken to since—but I lost a sense of my own being because I felt vulnerable, having allowed someone to take advantage of me. Everybody who knows both of us knows the truth. It's sad. The price he had to pay for the so-called "30 pieces of silver." I've tried to have him removed as the godfather of my daughter but essentially there's too much red tape with the church to even bother. Deep down, I'm sure he knows there is no longer a spiritual connection. There's nothing on a piece of paper that's going to change the way I feel.

The whole thing kicked me to the curb, but in a way I'm probably better for the experience. I came out the other side because that's what I do and will keep doing.

CHAPTER 29

Doing Right by My Loved Ones

THROUGHOUT OUR LIVES, probably all of us try to make ourselves better for the sake of those loved ones around us. As adults, we strive to provide the best of everything to family members near and dear to us. When hockey players sign contracts, big or modest, they're thinking about how they can put themselves in position to one day pay for their kids' college tuition or take them on dreamy vacations. Yes, in the short term there might be new cars or fancy townhouses but in the long run it's all about family.

There's nothing in this world that was more ever more important to me or that I cared more about than being a loving and caring father my children would have the utmost pride in. Playing in the NHL, having a bit of notoriety, and having been around the Philadelphia sports scene for many years doesn't make you a great dad. It just gives you a name. No matter who I was, my goal as a professional athlete first and foremost was to be a great person. And also, to be a great father.

During my time of active alcoholism, I never lost sight of the fact that this is a disease that had taken control of me. I was saddened by that. I was disappointed in myself, disappointed I could feel like that. I believe I let myself down in a lot of ways. I had seen signs of this coming on earlier. People ask me about it and the biggest question is, "Why?" Why did I drink? Why did it go past the normal acceptable level? Why did I do those things to myself?

There are probably a lot of reasons. Maybe it was being bullied, from the time I was a 10- to 15-year-old kid. I do know there was a private celebration when I made it as a player—it ripped down a lot of barriers for myself. I was determined to be better than any player I had ever played minor hockey with or ever came up with to get to the NHL.

When I got to the NHL, I knew I was one of many. I wanted to plow through the negativity. So that everything I had going on in my life, people would look at with respect. That was the journey that hockey had given me. When I go back to Ottawa and see people I've connected with on Facebook, I know what I've done. I knew the journey I had taken to do that, and it was difficult. I'm proud that every single roadblock I faced, I somehow pushed through, I never went around anything: I always went through it. I wish I had the opportunity to go around things, but when you go through things in life, you get more of a reality check. You find out who you are as a person, and you find out pretty much who you're going to be for the rest of your life.

I guess I consider myself a survivor. I considered myself a good player; you can't go in there and just play on a first defense pairing if you're not. I know the jokes sometimes about, "Oh, you just played with Desjardins." It took me a while to self-analyze that until I reached the conclusion that I was a good player and had earned the right to be a top pair guy for 10 years. Was I a complementary player to a great player? Yes. Was I a GOOD complementary player? Yes.

In 1995, I started dating my wife-to-be, Diana. We were married in 1997 and knew we wanted to have a family. Our first daughter, Isabella, was born in November 1998, and almost instantly she became one of the great loves of my life. In many ways, she's my best friend and someone I trust, someone that I spend so much time with. I had almost forgotten what it was like to love someone so much. We brought her home from the hospital and two days later, when the Flyers were playing the Toronto Maple Leafs, I had the first assist on Brind'Amour's game-tying goal in a game we went on to win. Those are proud moments that I have fond memories of. Our second daughter, Ava, arrived in January 2001. She was followed by Alexa in July 2003, and finally our son, Christopher, was born in November 2006.

The birth of our son came right around the time of my worst drinking, just after my trade to Dallas and followed by a lost season due to the lockout. Things really got bad in 2005–06. I hated who I was: a drunk, a weekend warrior. I despised what I had become.

I had become a full-fledged alcoholic and knew that was not conducive to being a good parent. I had read, seen, and heard all the stories about parents who were less than they could be and somehow their children always ended up on the wrong path. One thing our kids always had was the structure of sports behind them and one incredible mother. I'm so lucky to have her for those four children.

It's my belief that everything happens for a reason in this world. And I believe things happen for a reason because God has a plan for us. I don't know if I've had a stronger belief in God than these past couple years because I think everyone has changed their view of the world, what's important and what isn't.

When I got out of rehab in 2006 after the death of my sister, the only focus I had at that time was my kids. With my alcoholism past, I was just trying to get through one day at a time. I still wasn't the best version of myself. It was a godsend that Diana was there for the kids. She did such an amazing job—she was there for those kids when they needed her. I'll never be more thankful for that because I let an addiction take control of me. That can just never, ever happen again.

Alcohol beat me and it will always beat me. If I were ever to go back down that path again, it would surely beat me. I know that now. If I climbed back into that ring, it would knock me out by the fifth round. The only problem this time would be I might not be able to get back up off the canvas.

That's the part about my alcoholism that I've come to understand: I'm scared by it, and I'm scared of what I might do to the world. That's what I hate the most about this "drug."

When people talk about recovery and what they did it for, I can truly say at the time I wanted to do it for my family, specifically my kids. They deserved so much. Finally, on February 7, 2011, alcohol and I parted ways. I told the kids that was it, no more drinking. For about six months after that declaration, Diana still didn't seem convinced. She had kind of had it with me. It was frustrating because I thought things were really changing. But I guess when you tell someone so many times that you're going to change and then don't, you disappoint them. It's hard to sell someone on the "new you." That's what I tried to do. But in all fairness, I could not expect her to listen.

THE DECISION TO RETURN TO ALCOHOLICS ANONYMOUS came on a frigid morning. It was fitting because I was faced with one cold, hard truth: I couldn't do the transformation to alcohol-free without help. This time I was going to stick with it, whether I liked it or not. I had done it my way 50 times, and it never worked. In some ways I was becoming a laughingstock—no one was taking me seriously. Even my oldest daughter, Isabella, was taking notice now. She knew when I drank; she said the eyes gave it away.

At age 34, I knew I had to stop. There was no way to continue the way I was going. It didn't matter about Diana's seeming lack of concern, because I knew the only thing I could dictate was my actions and those would be a daily abstention from drinking. And doing it in a way that was meaningful. Going to more meetings than were prescribed. Getting to know my sponsor, Rick Halverson, who was as close to being a brother as I would ever have.

Rick knew I wanted to make a serious change, and he's been a very spiritual, inspirational person for me. I wouldn't be here today without him. From the AA meetings I built a base. This went on for two years. I believe that pace slowed down a bit when I regained the trust of my kids. At that point I was doing radio, TV, and sometimes I wouldn't get home until 2:00 or 3:00 AM. There were days when my AA meeting was at 8:00 AM, so that made it a little harder, but my life was changing.

I was building a foundation I never had before. This afforded me the opportunity to be around sober people, around the program, to be honest with myself and not care as much about what people thought. Diana played a part in this aspect of my recovery. She never told the kids I was a loser; she just told them I was sick and was trying to get right. That was the truth. I had a disease. For her to tell the kids that and allow me to be a dad, I will be forever grateful.

Simply put, what I did earlier in my life just wasn't me. A part of me will always be sorry for that. After 11 years of sobriety, I can take stock in my life. First, why did I stop? I did it for my kids. People would tell me it had to do with a higher power. I wondered what a higher power was. It was something I struggled with for a long time when I went to Alcoholics Anonymous. Who was I talking to? What was God? What was God going to do for me? All I knew was if I didn't drink every day, I would be doing something for myself. Without getting too religious, it's been my experience that if you ask God for help, for guidance, he will be there for you. Having said that, I'm not really a spiritual person. But you have to face your values, have to believe in something. I've been on my ass so many times, I can't believe there isn't someone watching over me, hoping that the day gets better, my life gets better, and I can continue on my journey.

Here's a sampling of why I needed to get better: When Isabella was 11 years old, she picked up a basketball and went to play in a girls' basketball game in Marlton, New Jersey. Her mom was there, always keeping the kids focused on sports. I tried, and even though I was your run-of-the-mill alcoholic, I always had their best interests in mind. Isabella became a basketball phenom. This was a girl who played softball, soccer, and basketball at Cherokee High School. First team All-South Jersey as a sophomore. Great physical skills and a killer attitude to win.

She's now 23 years old and I'm just filled with pride over what she's accomplished. She's one of the best players ever to compete in South Jersey. After graduating from Loyola University in Maryland she's gone to work for Goldman Sachs and has started her own construction business with her boyfriend, Will Fries, of the Indianapolis Colts. Every single year I get a card from her saying how proud she is of me. That's the best feeling you can have—your kid acknowledging what you've done.

Ava followed her sister to Loyola and is a junior there now. She might not be the most outgoing person, but don't underestimate her. She figures stuff out quickly and she is filled with unconditional love. She has a kind and sweet heart and comes across as very delicate. As I said, though, don't underestimate her. She is a strong young lady and an amazing human being. Ava has by far the driest sense of humor of my children; her sense of humor is much like my own. Ava is nearly six feet tall and is the best natural athlete in the family. On the court, she's lightning quick and what makes that even more impressive is she survived a catastrophic ankle injury when she was in the seventh grade. It was almost a compound fracture. The fact she came back with that kind of speed after having screws inserted in her foot is nothing short of miraculous. She doesn't get her speed from me, and I don't believe she gets it from her mother, either. Sometimes things like those just remain a mystery and good ones at that.

THERE'S A LOT OF ME IN ALEXA, and by that, I mean we don't necessarily back down when a confrontation arises. Some might use a word like "abrasive" to describe this characteristic, but to me it just means sticking to your beliefs and not worrying too much about what other people might think.

She has little pieces, small emotional parts of everyone in the house. At 6'2", she followed in Isabella's footsteps and became a South Jersey player of the year. Like her older sister, she is a go-to player because of her size and the other attributes she brings.

Perhaps the only difference is Isabella brings a better long-range shot to the table.

Alexa will say what's on her mind. For example, she did not want to go to Loyola at first because she didn't want to just follow Isabella's lead. She originally committed to Boston University which I thought was a great choice. When the pandemic started, both Loyola's and Boston University's programs were in transition, each firing coaches and hiring successors. As it turned out, the new BU coach got on a Zoom call with all the incoming recruits, including Alexa, and told them that he was the new coach and that he didn't have to honor any of their scholarships although he planned to.

What does Alexa do? She said, "Good luck with that."

She called up the Loyola coach, who also was brand new, and said, "I'm Alexa Therien. My sister is Isabella Therien, and she's not going back next year even though she has a year of eligibility left [due to previous injuries]. I would like to come play for you." The coach did a quick background check, and the deal was done.

Alexa called the BU coach back and told him, "Thanks, I'll be seeing you eight times in the next four years." That's pretty much Alexa in a nutshell. That's the kind of kid she is; the kind of confidence she exudes. A chip off the old block.

All three girls care a lot and like to bring people together. Oh, and they love their dad. Girls are different than boys. When you're a dad and you have girls, there's a certain standard you want to set for them. If you look back at my history and the good things that have happened to me, I know I'm truly lucky to be the dad of these three girls. They respect me now. It's not perfect, just as it isn't for most people. They now know they're talking to a real dad, not some alcoholic father.

Last but certainly not least, my son Christopher Jr. just turned 15, and he's already grown past 6'4". Fortunately, he's too young to remember my drinking days. There's a strong connection with Halverson, someone he's known since he was three years old. As far as hockey "genetics" go, not only is he a Therien, but we believe he was conceived during a visit to Montreal. How much more of a hockey bloodline can you get?

He was born around the time my sister Sarah passed. Up until then, my parents had only their three granddaughters and now they had a grandson. Being a former player, my father was looking forward to having a grandchild to talk hockey with in the years to come. It certainly eased the pain of losing Sarah.

Later, I coached Christopher's youth hockey team for three years, but I finally had to just get out of it. There was at least one coach on the staff who thought he knew more about hockey than I did. For some reason South Jersey hockey parents somehow believe they invented hockey. The mystery for me is their sense of entitlement. As a former professional player, I'm almost embarrassed by this attitude. They still think they have all the answers rather than simply telling their kids to play to the best of their ability.

By the time Christopher got into his teens, he was already being held up to the standard set by his three sisters. Some kids might have folded the tent and called it a day but not him. I look at him sometimes and see so much of myself in him—some of the innocence, some of the want. The one thing I tell him is to allow himself to dream. If I hadn't dreamed big things for my life, I never would have had them.

Upon reaching his freshman year at Cherokee High School, he played hockey and also basketball. I don't know what his future is in that sport, but if he ends up being 6'11", 270 pounds, who knows? That height and some hand-eye coordination are pretty much all you need. He could ultimately wind up playing football as his primary sport, because that's probably his best sport.

As for hockey, it's not always a healthy environment at high school varsity/JV levels. Hockey parents are so stupid that they think putting their kid on the ice five times a day is helping their kid, when I know actually it's not. It's stupid, ignorant, and arrogant. When their kid doesn't make it, don't come up to me and ask, "Why?" Or, "What could we have done differently?"

What I love most about my kids is who they are. They are amazing people and a lot of that came from their great mom. She gave them the grace that they have. I had a voice too, telling them to be strong people and do things without fear. Deal with adversity head on. Love with everything you have. Try to get better each and every day. Be the real version of yourself even if it ends up hurting you some day. We can fall down in a ditch, but pulling yourself back up with honor and doing it in a way that's going to make your future that much better is very important.

Seeing our daughters play at a mid-major school has been rewarding in so many ways. Some of the best times we've had as a family over recent years have been traveling for basketball, whether it was Chicago, Louisville, Atlanta, Harrisburg, or Baltimore. For this all to happen while I was sober was indeed a blessing, a shining moment. To be able to share those times meant a lot. I was not one of those fathers who went crazy in the stands like some parents do. I often wondered why they did that, probably because they had an unathletic kid for whom they somehow had visions of grandeur.

When Christopher was playing youth hockey, I had a chance to witness parent behavior up close, and I've never seen such misguided actions in my life. Their lack of hockey intelligence was staggering. I was an assistant coach for three years, but I realized pretty quickly it was an embarrassment. Chris eventually told me he was more drawn to football, and I was kind of happy to hear that. I thought I would regrow some brain cells being around football parents after wasting my time around hockey parents.

My experience watching Isabella's games before college took place in a much more respectful atmosphere than the one in hockey. Go to games, cheer like a respectful parent, don't yell at kids, and don't disrespect the agenda of the sport. Let your child have fun. If he or she has come this far to play on a team of that caliber, enjoy it. I sure did. I also understood that a kid's body would grow, kids' attitudes would change. Plus, there would be a social aspect, which could involve new girlfriends or boyfriends.

In basketball, my daughters have been social butterflies, but they're also the most committed athletes you can find. They've found a way to reach a happy balance. They've never lost sight of the importance of friendships and family along with the commitment to play with a sense of integrity.

I never realized how much my kids meant to me until I got clean and sober. When I put my energy toward something so meaningful as my children and get to reap the rewards from that, it makes it the most rewarding 10-year segment of my life. It's because I've been the one making the decisions, both wholeheartedly and with a clear mind. It's allowed my kids to say, "That's my dad. Is he perfect? No. But he doesn't drink, he doesn't use drugs."

They could say, "He may be a little crazy," because I am at times. I'm a retired hockey player and at times I have assorted nerves and anxieties that probably still flow through me.

But because I don't have a dependency on alcohol anymore, I can—with a clear mind—make decisions that are in the best interest of my kids. Even if the decision isn't always the right one, the process of making it is. That's what the gift of abstaining from alcohol has given me. It's given me purpose, given me a will to live. It's given me my children back and a say in the direction of their lives.

When we engage in an adult conversation now, I know I'm fully engaged because I can see clearly, and I can understand it. At the end of the day, for as much as I joke around and needle and grouse about this or that, I feel more grounded and happier than I ever did before in my life. My family is everything to me.

CHAPTER 30

Transition Time

IN ONE WAY OR ANOTHER, the pandemic changed everybody's lives and most of it not for the good. I can attest to that because my career in broadcasting came to a screeching halt. However, there are times when I wonder when the health/safety crisis was just used as an excuse to make personnel changes.

For years I was the top Flyers analyst for NBC Sports Philadelphia. The National Hockey League shut down in March 2020 and picked up again mid-summer. Things changed quickly. I was let go by both the Flyers and NBC Sports Philadelphia for reasons unknown. They just said they were eliminating the position.

I'm not a guy to sit around. That's why me and a couple people I know got involved in Limitless Recovery Centers. It was a company that helped people with a problem like the one I once had. I needed a job, or perhaps given my secure financial standing, I wanted a job. Again, I felt that helping people, and at least allowing my voice to be part of that process, was going to be a gratifying calling moving forward.

Kates and I shared a similar vision. I knew Paul as an Eagles season ticketholder sitting next to me at games. We became good friends. I told him about my vision for the company and asked if he wanted to come on board. He stepped right up to the plate with a financial investment. Like you would expect from your typical Eagles fan, he's a dynamite guy. Together we purchased the company.

We brought two other partners, including one of my in-laws, on board but eventually there was a falling out over some rather questionable dealings on their part. It's funny, when you trust people and you have a good heart about things, it's incredible how someone who has problems—maybe living in their own skin—would come into the venture with bad intentions. Again, I don't know when people will stop learning the hard lessons that have been thrown in front of me, but if I had a choice to go back to the beginning of this, I would have done this with just Paul. I would never have involved family in a venture like this.

Getting involved in the project is all about believing in doing some good for this world. People know me better now because my story has been made public. It was important for me to let people know it's okay to have a problem. It's okay to be an alcoholic. These things happen. They don't happen to everybody, but if they have found you it's not the end of the world.

That's the voice I need to carry. I feel like my voice reaching the masses is the best avenue for me. To continually have this discussion on the table so people know that you can be kicked by this, and it can be debilitating, but you can also fix it. That's the part of addiction and recovery that's in my message: Don't ever give up. Don't ever think there's not a way out.

I checked into Caron Recovery Center with a .63 blood alcohol level, and I didn't give up. It took me a while, but I never gave up. I always wanted something better and was never willing to sell my soul to find that betterment. My sole goal now is to help people by sharing my message.

JUST ABOUT ANY BUSINESS VENTURE has its ups and downs, but the ones that help people better their lives hopefully succeed because they serve a higher purpose than just making money.

That's the intent of what's now called Pennsylvania Recovery Center (formerly Limitless Recovery Centers). They help those who are caught in the fishnet of addiction and can't find a way out on their own. I should know. I was one of those folks for many years. As someone who is invested in one of these projects both financially and emotionally, it's one of the most worthwhile and gratifying projects I have ever undertaken.

There have been some complications with our business in recent times, but the goal has always been to help people, and we are doing that, even through some dysfunction. Hopefully bigger and better things will come along in the recovery industry for me. When I talk about Pennsylvania Recovery Center, I have to mention how valuable these places are.

Rehab is broken down into different categories. The first one is detoxification. You have to get people into detox before you can get them into recovery. The biggest problem is getting them the proper medication so they can ease off whatever drug or form of alcohol they're on. The idea is to get them as clear-headed as possible. Then the patient is placed in a 30-day, 60-day, 90-day, or extended care rehab center where the person learns about the addiction, how to handle it—because addiction is always knocking on your door, always tapping on your shoulder, trying to manipulate you.

The biggest component to a successful recovery is to be able to make good decisions, making clear-cut decisions in your life. The biggest challenge with any sort of recovery institution is getting someone to the point where they can be clean and clear of the drug. Extended care places are great, but not a lot of people can follow that model because they have to work. They have to commit a lot of their time to their kids and families. Those with addictions come from all walks of life. It affects everybody from blue collar to white collar. The stereotypical perception might be that most people with this problem might be down on their luck or not from a particularly high social stratum. But it can happen to anybody. Lawyers, doctors, teachers, hockey players, or judges—it doesn't pick and choose.

With Pennsylvania Recovery Center, I've been working with people once they get out of rehab. The best part of treatment is when you're there behind those walls for an extended period of time: You're safe. You're with everyone else trying to get sober. Your goal and your mission are the same—to get back on your high horse and feel like you could conquer the world again.

There are no guarantees. There are situations like where the father of a guy I knew spent $90,000 to send him to a place in California, one of the best rehab centers in the country. The young man, about 30 years old, was scheduled to fly home from Los Angeles to Philadelphia after getting out of rehab, and the father was scheduled to pick him up at the airport. When the man got off the plane he was practically falling-down drunk.

It's one thing to be in a rehab center. It's totally another thing to live life afterward. Those liquor stores that alcoholics frequent are still going to be there on the corner. The drug dealer you met in Camden or North Philadelphia is still going to be waiting for you in a back alley. As a new person, you have to learn to live in the moment, to learn to live with all these flying objects coming at you all the time.

That's where a place like the Center comes in. It's an after-care facility, a maintenance program. When people couldn't get to Alcoholics Anonymous, they would come to us for essentially 10 hours per week—nine hours of clinical work in a group and then they spend an hour with a clinician to talk about a lot of the matters and issues going on in their lives. What is it really all about? It's about learning to handle the situations, big or small, that are going to come about.

You're going to stare down alcohol again. Hopefully you get to a point where it doesn't bother you. While you're back out, unfortunately, you can't get away from all these things. You don't want to relapse. That was my biggest problem, and when I overcame it, that was my biggest achievement. You know, alcoholics want everything, and they want everything right away. When I first went into rehab, I wanted to be 10 years clean and sober the very next day. But the problem is, an alcoholic can only have one day at a time. That's just the way it works. Like almost anything else in life, patience is a virtue.

That's the key. Alcoholics Anonymous is the greatest gift ever to people struggling with addiction. It's all based on the 12-step format, and I think it's necessary for people to go through the steps. A lot of people become spiritual and many of them delve into the question of, "What is a higher power?" I struggled with this mightily when I first started participating in AA. I didn't know or understand the concept of a higher power. I was kind of thinking God was going to descend out of the sky, sprinkle my head with stardust, and cure me of alcoholism.

Well, obviously, it doesn't work that way. For higher power, the definition could be anything—it could be your kids or the group of Alcoholics Anonymous people around you. It's just something bigger than yourself. It could be a player on a professional team, and the fact is, the team is always bigger than just one player. Getting to that point and understanding it is something I believe is very important but not necessarily critical. You can really dismiss the higher power part of recovery and basically overthink it. And I actually did that my first time through the program. I kept wondering what they meant by higher power. I just couldn't grasp the concept. It was a little deep for me, and I ended up relapsing.

What I did the next time, successfully, was integrating myself into AA when I got my sponsor, Halverson. My life completely changed for the better. I started hanging around people who were sober and didn't use alcohol as a crutch. I started listening, rather than talking. I shut my mouth and sat in the back of the room. I listened. Then I hung around, speaking and searching for wisdom from others. I also searched my own feelings.

One thing I did each morning when I woke up was say a prayer. I was asking for another day of sobriety, another reprieve from alcohol, one day at a time. That routine has lasted for years, and I still do it every day. I ask for help to get through the day. That's made all the difference for me. Pennsylvania Recovery Center is a place where you can come in, feel safe, and feel cared for. We have an amazing clinician and counselors. We tell people, "If you want to have a chance, if you want to get back to work, to being a loving parent, brother, sister, then put the work in."

In the past, we used to go drinking for eight to ten hours. So it shouldn't be that hard to put one hour into your sobriety through the course of a day. Or to reflect on it throughout the day. Those are things that have made a gigantic difference in my life. I think maintaining a meeting structure is super important, especially the first three years. After three years, you start to feel good about yourself. You want to make sure you're with a group of like-minded people who are also trying to get to that special place of one day at a time. It's the foundation of building a long-term sobriety.

Very rarely will it happen with you and you alone doing it. Imagine standing in a crowd with 20 people surrounding you. You try to fall backward or sideways. You never can really fall because there's always someone there holding you up.

The first and 12th steps of the AA program are perhaps the most significant ones. The first states, *I'm powerless over alcohol, that my life had become unmanageable.* And number 12: *Never forget to give back.* I rely on the pain and suffering I went through as a reference point, but I also rely on the joy and the hope of recovery and what that has meant to me and what it's meant to my family.

Stay in the fight. It's worth it.

CHAPTER 31

The Road to Redeeming Myself

THE BIGGEST AND CERTAINLY THE MOST MEANINGFUL decision I've ever made in my life was to part ways with alcohol. I don't believe it's an exaggeration to say this was a matter of life and death. If I hadn't driven off a highway somewhere, I probably would have died of liver disease before the end of middle age.

It wasn't really a relationship, it was more like a nasty, angry couple who just couldn't get along. The only way to get better was to remove it from my life. Since I've done that it's made a gigantic difference in the way I've been perceived and the way I've perceived myself. More importantly, it's changed how the people in my world perceive me. That includes former teammates. Before, when I'd go to a golf tournament or an alumni game, I'd be approached by many who know my story, because I was a funny guy, a guy who liked to party. I was someone who kept the mood light but at the same time was serious about drinking.

Now, the guys see me sober and, I hope, see someone who was a good guy. Unlike some people, I learned that the best route for me would be without alcohol. Now I get up every morning and pray to God that he will give me an opportunity to not drink. And fortunately for the past 11 years that's been the case. Even as a lot of time has passed, I can never forget who I once was. I know I can never go back again. There's no doubt in my mind: if I had one drink, I would be a full-bore drunk in seven days. All the trust I had built over the last 11 years would be tossed by the wayside.

That brings me to what has taken place with my marriage. I've known Diana for 26 years, and she's been the greatest person to ever enter my life. She's had compassion to put up with what I put her through. She understood how hard the drinking was on me. It was about regaining that trust, while at the same time I was learning to love myself again. That's the biggest part of recovery, learning to love yourself again. Yeah, I hated myself, even in the good times. A lot of people are out there suffering from things like mental illness, from anxiety, depression.

I don't think it's enough for an individual to get through all the clutter that you have during the course of a day. Ask for help. Ask for love. It's one thing to want to be loved and be cared for. It's another thing to be able to care and be loved at the same time. When you've been broken down over time and built up one way, it's best to shed that skin like a snake and be happy with the one you're in.

Life's a long journey, but it's a marathon, not a sprint. You're going to meet a lot of characters in your life. You're going to meet a lot who love you and people that hate you. You're going to meet people who promote positive thought in you and people that won't. And those are the ones you kind of have to let go.

That was not always easy for me to do. I still carry a lot of resentment, which is not a good thing to have. But it's not enough to make me take a drink because I've seen the destruction it wreaks with my mind, health, and the people around me. I want everyone to know that just because I stopped drinking doesn't mean that the journey ends. Because nothing ended. I have to remember every single day who I am.

I have to be proud of that, to live with that. Social media can be a crutch at times with society. We have to be careful with that, too, as to how we expose ourselves. But I have no doubt about sharing my story concerning alcoholism. Since I was a kid, for more than 25 years, I've lived in the eyes of Philadelphia as a player and broadcaster. When people get to know you, they form an opinion. They form an opinion of how and what you've seen. The one thing I believe through it all is that I've remained true to myself and how I treat people. It doesn't mean I've always been great to everybody. I'm sure there are people out there who have not been impressed with me over the years. But I think if you walked up to me and said hello, you would be on the right side of history with me for the most part.

I love people, be it from my hometown of Ottawa or my adopted home, Philadelphia. The people in this Pennsylvania town have made my life so incredible. God gave me the strength and the fortitude to make it to the best hockey league on the planet and to be a force in that sport for some time as a top-end player. The rest of my life, I was put through a wringer, tested at every turn. Somehow, I don't think I ever lost sight of who I was meant to be.

Taking stock, I'm proud of the fact I was able to pull through and also of the people in my life who helped me get to places along the way. Sometimes those conversations weren't easy. Now I'm happy to be Chris Therien. God has given me the strength to share my story, to put myself front and center, so perhaps I can make someone else's life an easier journey.

What I want people to know at the end of the day is, it's okay to ask for help, never be afraid to ask for help, trust in the people who believe in you, and never lose confidence in your ability to persevere.